T0333409

BONJOUR, MADEMOISELLE!

Bonjour, Mademoiselle!

April Ashley and the pursuit of a lovely life

JACQUELINE KENT
and TOM ROBERTS

SCRIBE

Melbourne | London | Minneapolis

Scribe Publications
18–20 Edward St, Brunswick, Victoria 3056, Australia
2 John St, Clerkenwell, London, WC1N 2ES, United Kingdom
3754 Pleasant Ave, Suite 100, Minneapolis, Minnesota 55409, USA

Published by Scribe 2024

Typeset in Garamond by the publishers

Printed and bound in the UK by CPI Group (UK) Ltd,
Croydon CR0 4YY

Scribe is committed to the sustainable use of natural resources and
the use of paper products made responsibly from those resources.

978 1 761380 31 0 (Australian edition)
978 1 915590 32 9 (UK edition)
978 1 761385 82 7(ebook)

Catalogue records for this book are available from the
National Library of Australia and the British Library.

scribepublications.com.au
scribepublications.co.uk
scribepublications.com

CONTENTS

PART FOUR

The Unsinkable April Ashley

List of illustrations

Authors' note

When describing her early life, April Ashley spoke of 'George Jamieson'. She chose to use 'he' and 'him', switching to 'she' and 'her' only from the point at which she decided to live as a woman, three years before gender-affirming surgery.

'I started out as a boy,' April told her first biographer, Duncan Fallowell. 'As I grew up I turned into a feminine-looking boy. Perhaps I should have accepted my androgynous nature — most feminine-looking boys do, both heterosexual and homosexual ones. But I couldn't accept it because I felt myself to be essentially female.'

Every night, April prayed to God, *Please may I wake up as a girl.*

And yet young George really tried to fit into his working-class background, with its heavily masculine orientation. The results — constant bullying at home, school and elsewhere; an unhappy stint in the merchant navy; two attempts to end that painful life — were disastrous.

In none of the innumerable television, newspaper, and magazine interviews April Ashley gave, nor in her as-told-to autobiographies, did she deny the pain and humiliation she endured while identified as a boy. The trajectory of Ashley's story is one of despair in being trapped in one gender, of gradually understanding that this was not inevitable, and of a triumphant transformation, even with all the problems and difficulties that followed.

Throughout this book, we honour April's own gender identities and the language with which she described her experience. We aim to present to the reader as authentically as possible the searing events and tensions in April's youth, and her reactions to them — events and tensions that made her the tough, pragmatic, and empathic person she was, and which enabled her to become an advocate for the transgender community.

April always insisted that hearing her surgeon greet her, 'Bonjour, mademoiselle', was the happiest moment of her life. In telling her story, we wish to honour and emphasise the sheer courage and tenacity April demonstrated in defying her alleged biological destiny — rare qualities known to anyone who has successfully made the same decision.

INTRODUCTION

'I was my own Pygmalion'

On 28 April 2015, a very tall, stately woman walked, slowly and supported by a cane, into the Catholic church of St Teresa of the Child Jesus in Liverpool. She wore an elegant maroon velvet trouser suit; her white hair was immaculately coiffed; she wore stylish glasses and the kind of makeup that spoke of practised attention to her appearance. She was accompanied by a beaming, solicitous priest and — not incidentally — by a television camera crew. 'I was terribly religious,' she told the priest in the modulated upper-class tones that owed nothing to her birthplace. 'And I would pray to God that I would wake up the next morning as a girl.'

April Ashley, born in Liverpool in 1935 and named George Jamieson, was walking through her childhood memories on the day before her 80th birthday. Over the years she had spoken of her early life many times, on radio and television and in interviews. In 1977, she had told television journalist Mavis Nicholson, 'There was this problem of being terribly feminine and having to behave as a boy. There wasn't a day when I wasn't beaten up. They jumped on my legs and I was crippled for four months. But I think that gave me the strength to carry on, regardless of what people think of me.'[1] The disconnect

1

— the incongruity between the assurance of April Ashley's glamorous appearance and the early life she described — was always jarring. For her, that was the point.

On that April day, Ashley stopped outside the gate leading to a neat row of terraced houses, part of the Norris Green housing estate. 'This is where I slept as a child,' she said, indicating a small window on the first floor. 'The boxroom. You could touch both walls with your arms outstretched. And this' — she nodded towards a bay window next to it — 'this was where [my brothers and sisters] slept.'

April didn't say why her room was separated from theirs, but she told Mavis Nicholson: 'I was called pansy, cissy, you name it, and my brothers and sisters never wanted to be seen with me. And my mother was ashamed of me.' Her tone, as always, was matter-of-fact, untrammelled by sentimentality or nostalgia.

She was turning to leave, when a local boy, who had clearly never seen anyone as exquisitely turned out, asked her in an awed and curious voice: 'D'you live in a mansion?'

'Noooo!' said April, grandly amused.

Perhaps in this moment she remembered the small boy George had been so long ago: the unhappy child desperate to escape the grinding poverty of post-war Liverpool and to find a way of becoming rich — of having the 'lovely life' he wanted and, indeed, living in a magnificent house.

The next day — 29 April 2015, her 80th birthday — April Ashley was named Liverpool's Citizen of Honour. It was a warm, heartfelt ceremony, during which a group of earnest young girls wearing the uniform of St Teresa of Lisieux, Ashley's primary school, led a small group of civic dignitaries in singing 'Happy Birthday'.

The speeches were brief and sincere. 'She truly has been an inspiration, not just to the LGBT community,' said one councillor. 'She means a lot to us.'

The mayor, Erica Kemp, said to April, 'We hope by making you a

Citizen of Honour we can highlight the inequalities that individuals suffer today.' For the audience's benefit, she added: 'We still need people like April to be an example and an inspiration to us all ... I will always look at her and think she was the first to take that leap on behalf of thousands of people.'[2]

April Ashley had come a very long way. Her story is more spectacular than most. How did a child born before World War II into hardscrabble poverty — a boy whose desperate wish to be a girl alienated him from his family and almost everyone else he knew — fulfil a life's ambition, becoming a beautiful cabaret artist and top model, and marrying into the peerage?

On one level, these questions are not difficult to answer: April Ashley's life was thoroughly documented in the many newspaper, radio, and television interviews she had given since the 1960s. There are also two as-told-to autobiographies, which cover essentially the same ground while adding occasionally bawdy detail. Ashley very quickly understood what journalists and biographers wanted from her, and she was candid about herself and provided quotable comments, mostly with mordant humour and a light touch. As a result, she became a darling of the tabloids and television stations — a status she accepted and navigated with aplomb.

There is, of course, a more serious and much tougher life story to be told. Ashley was one of the very first Britons to undergo gender-affirming surgery — in Casablanca, in 1960. The decision took immense courage: the procedure was new and she was under no illusions about the possibility that she might die. Ashley went ahead because, as she often told interviewers, 'If I couldn't be a woman, I didn't want to live.'

The operation did give her what she had so wanted, but the price she paid was very high — physically, personally, and professionally.

Through no fault of her own, she was at the centre of a case that set back the cause of trans rights in Britain for more than 30 years. But, in her determination to fashion herself into the person she wanted to be, she maintained her Liverpudlian toughness.

April Ashley left a huge archive. She seems to have made a record of almost all her public appearances and comments. With the permission of her executors, that archive will in time seed further research and no doubt further books. It may also allow for a reappraisal of the characters involved in her story — not least April herself. Her handling of information about herself in her own lifetime was as much a part of her self-creation as her name and the surgery that marked her rebirth.

Paradoxically, this wealth of material can mean that the 'real' April Ashley is not easy to find. As she aged, her stories about her life became increasingly rehearsed; she was wont to describe the same events several times, word for word, dealing them out like playing cards on a table. But she rarely, if ever, allowed any public access to her inner life, she seldom explained or questioned the reasons for her actions, and she generally did not indulge in analysis or insight, written or spoken. The persona she presented to the world was careful, glossy, glamorous: *Look, but don't touch — don't try to see what lies beneath.*

It cannot be said that April Ashley was a particularly reflective person — but, in another sense, that is exactly what she was, for the polished surface she presented to the media was also a mirror. Her story reflects so much of post-war British social history — especially concerning attitudes to sex and gender — from the public repression of the 1950s and consequent flourishing of an underground culture, through the apparently casual, insouciant 1960s and the reactionary Thatcherite 1980s, to today's fractious, splintered, and sometimes contradictory debates. The suffering and experiences of many other transgender people form a vital component of — sometimes a counterpoint to — April Ashley's story. She always had an appreciative understanding of what conventional society saw as eccentricity: 'I miss all the eccentrics; everybody is so bloody PC these days,' was her lament. (Quite a number of those friends have elbowed their way into this book.)

Ashley's assertion that she was her own Pygmalion, then, is an accurate one. Henry Higgins would have approved of her success in completely changing her accent to achieve higher social status. And Eliza Doolittle — a character, incidentally, that Ashley played in Paris cabaret during the late 1950s — would have revelled in her achievement of a 'lovely life', with champagne, titled friends, and beautiful clothes.

It wasn't always lovely, of course — and the example April Ashley set with hard-earned resilience and sheer bloody-minded bravery has made her a standard-bearer for those who would follow in her footsteps.

PART ONE

Scouser

CHAPTER 1

'Please let me wake up as a girl'

April Ashley was born at Sefton General Hospital, Smithdown Road, Liverpool, on 29 April 1935. She spoke about her childhood many times, on radio, television, and in print — always with a notable lack of sentimentality. Indeed, while 'Dickensian' was the adjective most journalists plucked from their bale of clichés in describing her early life, her story has no noble working-class parents, kindly neighbours, or twinkly-eyed, sympathetic relatives — and she knew how to narrate her most unpleasant memories for best dramatic effect. Indeed, in the upper-class accent she acquired in defiance of her upbringing, she would later share stories about growing up in Liverpool during and after World War II with a certain narrative distance — as though these experiences had happened to somebody else.

Which of course, in a way, they had.

In the 1930s and 1940s, Liverpool was a difficult place for any child to grow up, let alone a child like George Jamieson. The city's history is a tough one, its wealth built on slavery in the 18th and 19th centuries. (Penny Lane, made famous by the Beatles, was supposedly named after slave trader James Penny.) After the abolition of slavery during the early 1830s, the city's development as a trading centre continued, with textiles replacing human bodies. And, as one of Britain's most prosperous maritime cities, Liverpool became home to a vast number and range of migrants from the British Isles and beyond. People who hailed from Liverpool were later known as Scousers, 'scouse' being a local word for a type of stew consisting of whatever meat and vegetables were readily at hand. Liverpool has always been a melting pot.

It's more than likely that the Jamiesons' own ancestors came from Scotland or Northern Ireland. By 1935, the sectarian street violence in Liverpool that had culminated in Catholic–Protestant clashes in 1909 had settled down, but there was always tension below the surface – tension that was reproduced between George's parents. George's father, Frederick Jamieson — born on 21 February 1904 — was a Scouser on both sides. George's mother, Ada Brown — born on 18 June 1908 and the youngest of eight (four boys and four girls) — grew up in Liverpool, the birthplace of her mother, Margaret. Her father, Edwin Brown, was from the Shropshire town of Much Wenlock.

When Frederick met Ada, she was pretty, diminutive and sharp-featured with soft brown hair, a flirtatious young woman who loved dancing. Frederick — who drifted in and out of jobs, mostly in the merchant navy but also as a tram conductor and a factory worker — was hardly taller than she, with dark hair and the delicate androgynous features that George inherited. Frederick was an attractive, feckless young man — something of a silver-tongued devil, never happier than when holding forth in the local pub. He was the first man Ashley ever heard addressing other men as 'darling' without their taking offence.

Ada and Frederick married in the Catholic Church in the spring of 1933, when Ada was 23. (Ashley later said her mother was only 16 when they married, but 1933 records of marriages in Liverpool confirm otherwise.) Frederick had been brought up Catholic, Ada was Protestant: this became a constant cause of friction in their marriage.

By the time of their wedding, the couple already had two children:

Roderick and Theresa. Roderick was probably born in 1927, although the records do not show Ada as his mother; he might have been Frederick's illegitimate child. Theresa was born on 12 December 1930. Shortly after Ada and Frederick married, their son Freddie was born. In Catholic working-class Liverpool, a young woman rarely escaped the prison of her fertility. With three children under the age of seven, Ada had to put away her dancing shoes and her dreams forever: she dragged through her days in domestic drudgery, pregnant most of the time — a wife whose husband was frequently absent in the merchant navy and who spent every penny he made on alcohol.

George, named after Ada's eldest brother, was the fourth child who survived — several of Ada's babies died — and he was followed by Ivor and Marjorie.

Ada, Frederick, and their children started family life in a cramped tenement in Pitt Street, not far from the docks and Scotland Road, one of the most violent streets in Liverpool, where knives were the weapon of choice.

Liverpool had long been known for having the worst housing records and highest mortality rates in Britain, but in the 1920s local governments recognised the strong correlation between overcrowding and bad health, and they began to invest in social housing. When George was three or four, the Jamiesons were rehoused, moving to 51 Teynham Crescent, Norris Green — a council estate on the edge of the city, for the families of skilled and semi-skilled workers.

For the Jamiesons, the move signalled much greater comfort, even luxury: Norris Green houses had three bedrooms, a bathroom, electricity, and hot water. The rent was reasonable, although tenancy agreements demanded a high standard of maintenance, not always met at a time of fluctuating unemployment. Many of the Jamiesons' neighbours had also moved to Norris Green, and life there could be nearly as violent as in Pitt Street. 'In five minutes Norris Green became a ghetto, with fist fights and brawls,' April later recalled.

Despite the extra space, the new house in Teynham Crescent soon became at least as crowded as Pitt Street had been. George's eldest brother, Roderick — who was in the merchant navy, like his father — was constantly bringing people to stay with the family, dossing down wherever they could find space. Some of these occasional lodgers paid rent, helping to keep the Jamieson family financially afloat, and some brought glimpses of another world to Norris Green. Ashley remembered Reggie Endacott, the Madras-born son of a white father and a mother who worked on a tea plantation. Reggie, like Roderick, was in the merchant navy. April also remembered that, at one point, a Mexican woman named Phyllis was found asleep with her baby in the outside lavatory and was taken in. And a lugubrious 17-year-old lad from Lancashire named Bernie Cartmell followed Roderick into the house one day. He was tall and skinny, with floppy hands and feet, and the family referred to him as 'that long streak of piss'. He stayed for years — and later became Ashley's stepfather.

Not long after the Jamiesons moved to Norris Green, Liverpool discovered what war really meant. In August 1940, the Germans started dropping bombs on the city. There were 15 small raids in September and nine in October; the first major raid came in November, when the docks were hit by 350 tonnes of high-explosive bombs, as well as land mines and incendiaries. Raids continued in December, and while the docks were the main target, the surrounding streets of terraced houses — including Pitt Street — were also devastated. Bombs fell on Merseyside almost every night for a week the following May, killing 1,900 people, seriously wounding another 1,450, and making 70,000 homeless.[1] George witnessed exactly what bombs could do when he saw two boys in his class messing around with an incendiary bomb at the edge of a playing field near Norris Green: 'I was screaming at them — and the bomb went off and they both lost an arm from the shoulder down. Bits of hands were hanging from sinews. It was horrendous.'[2]

When the bombings began, well-to-do families fled to the

basements or cellars of their houses, but many others were less fortunate. The government supplied Anderson shelters, usually huts in the back gardens of houses or apartment blocks. Made of corrugated iron and covered with earth, equipped with bunks, they were supposed to be safe from anything but a direct hit, though many were badly built. The Jamiesons' shelter was a makeshift hut with three bunks on each side. Frederick would allow George to curl up close to him for comfort and protection: this was hugely important for the young child, who idolised his father.

Even though Frederick never went to church, he insisted that all his children be brought up Catholic. George started at the local Catholic primary school, St Teresa of Lisieux, in September 1940. Ashley recalled it as a vicious and backward institution, where students were forced to their knees in prayer four times a day and spent a great deal of time cleaning floors with dusters tied to their wooden clogs. George never did well at school, partly because of dyslexia and partly because of a calcium deficiency not helped by poor diet.

George hated school life and rebelled against it. At one point, a young teacher, Canadian-born Miss Filben, gave him the job of distributing textbooks to the class. As George walked down the rows of desks, some of the other kids kicked out at him. George endured bruised legs for about two weeks before deciding enough was enough. Next time Miss Filben asked him to give out the books, he refused. She raised her voice and stood over him, becoming so angry that she slapped his face; George instinctively slapped her back. The class gasped. The teacher's eyes filled with tears, but she yielded. George was no longer required to be class monitor. It is unclear whether George was punished at home for the incident. Perhaps not: the Jamiesons never set much store by education. Nobody seemed to mind whether George went to school or not, and he was always happier away from the classroom.

There was another, overriding reason why George hated attending

St Teresa of Lisieux. He was bullied mercilessly, mostly because he was tall, slim, and dark-eyed, with a gamin look rather like a young Audrey Hepburn. Every day he was called 'pansy' or 'sissy'; sometimes physically attacked — often in the school's air raid shelter. Teachers who came into the shelter after school hours often found George tied face down to one of the bunks, his face criss-crossed by marks from the metal frame. 'I don't think a day went by without my being beaten up,' Ashley said. 'Simple as that. And once I was held down while they jumped on my legs and I was crippled for four months.' George's education, Ashley said, consisted of learning how to run fast.[3]

All of this reinforced what George had always known: he could never belong to the rough-and-ready, hypermasculine world of working-class Liverpool, no matter how hard he tried. 'My entire childhood was spent trying to conform to the male body I was born into,' said Ashley — and it was torture.[4] George would kneel beside his bed every night and pray to God, *Please let me wake up as a girl*.

While his siblings had to share bedrooms, George slept in a room by himself, occupying the tiny boxroom on the first floor. Part of the reason was that George suffered — understandably — from crippling anxiety and was a chronic bedwetter until about the age of 14. His brothers and sisters resented what appeared to them to be special treatment. If they were going somewhere and he asked whether he could come, they would turn their backs and walk off.

One day, George, then aged about ten, dragged along behind his brothers when they went to the local swimming pool, determined to make them notice him. George hated his brothers calling him names and ridiculing him because he couldn't swim, so impulsively he threw himself in at the deep end. He sank to the bottom, but surfaced and was able to pull himself out. He jumped in again — this time, at the shallow end — and watched what other people were doing: this, said April, was how George eventually learned to swim. Clearly, George was a child with both resilience and determination.

In almost every story April Ashley told about her childhood in later interviews, her mother, Ada, is the chief villain. Ashley said that George spent his whole young life trying to win his mother's love, but he never succeeded. According to Ashley, Ada beat George so badly that he was covered in scars and had a dent in his back the size of a golf ball; April claimed that the doctor even threatened Ada with imprisonment for child abuse. But when the doctor suggested that, to avoid future beatings, George should do more work around the house, such as cleaning the family silver, George couldn't stop laughing: *Silver? What silver?*

Ashley admitted that George was difficult to live with, not least because of his intractable health problems. His calcium deficiency sometimes left him unable to walk and he needed weekly injections at Alder Hey Children's Hospital. Ada would take him there on the tram, carrying him piggyback part of the way without speaking, her mouth set — challenging Ashley's assertion that Ada did not care about George. April told her first biographer, Duncan Fallowell, that George was a fussy eater: when his brother Roddy brought back the first banana after the war — a rare luxury — and it was cut into six pieces, one for each of the children, George spat his piece out, claiming he hated the taste. When he refused to eat the family's meals, Ada would make him chip butties (deep-fried, thick-cut wedges of potato between two slices of buttered white bread) — which he did eat. It is not difficult to feel sympathy for Ada Jamieson: overworked, poor, trying to do her best for an exasperating child who often behaved like a spoilt brat, all while compensating for a shiftless absentee father. Ashley saw things differently. 'I was totally rejected by the family, except for my father who was absolutely marvellous,' she recalled in 1982, 'but of course he was away at sea a lot of the time.'[5]

Ada squashed down her disappointment about the cards life had dealt her and went grimly to work, as she had to do for her family's survival. She first worked for a greengrocer, lugging around huge sacks of potatoes. Like many other Liverpool women, she took a job during the war in a munitions factory in Fazakerley, not far from Norris Green. It meant handling the explosive TNT, which can have devastating effects on health, and Ada lost most of her hair and all her teeth. In her mid-30s, she had the wizened face and bent shoulders of an old woman, but she was luckier than many of the other women at the factory. Ada's best friend, Doris Paper, who worked with her, said she felt 'odd' one day at work. Doris developed a raging fever and became so ill that an ambulance was called; it took both women back to Ada's house. Suddenly Doris ran to the back door, tearing off her clothes and saying she had to go to the lavatory. Ada found her dead on the toilet seat a while later. Doris might have succumbed to toxic jaundice — not an uncommon disease for munitions workers at the time.

Some solace came for lonely George when he was seven or eight and his eldest brother came home on shore leave with Prince, a brown-and-white pointer. The dog came straight to George to be petted: an early example of the affinity with animals that lasted Ashley's whole life. Prince swiftly became George's chief ally and defender. One day, when a classmate attempted to hit George, Prince grabbed the bully's wrist in his teeth. The word soon spread, and if George was with Prince, his tormentors left him alone.

With Prince at his side, George went rabbiting in the countryside around Liverpool, often venturing onto the 2,500-acre estate owned by Lord Derby, one of the richest landowners in England and a prominent member of the Conservative Party. This was a time when Liverpool's ruling class was both Protestant and Conservative; Lord Derby was the donor of the land on which Norris Green had been built. George usually stayed away from the house, wary of the deer roaming around the lush parkland, but one day curiosity got the better of him and he crept closer. Knowsley Hall, an enormous part-Gothic, part-Georgian pile, was the most gracious house he had ever seen. George, in his patched and darned hand-me-downs and steel-rimmed wooden clogs, was looking at a world of wealth, luxury, and elegance he could only dream about. He resolved that, whatever happened, he would join this elite: he would become part of that world.

CHAPTER 2

Ways of escape

George's sense of not belonging to the world he knew grew inexorably as he moved towards puberty. 'I had this terrible problem of growing up feminine and yet having to behave as a boy,' Ashley said. 'I knew I was unique in my environment, but it was drummed into me day after day. It was intolerable at times.'[1]

Although George never wanted to play with dolls or dress up in Ada's clothes, he was constantly taunted for being 'like a girl'. The bullying and name-calling continued, with 'Chinky' added to 'sissy' because of his almond-shaped eyes and black hair. Not much changed when he left primary school and started at St Teresa's secondary modern.

One day, Ashley later said, the headmaster, who had come into George's classroom, accused him of whispering. When he denied it, the headmaster said George was lying and pushed him in the chest so violently that he fell over. George ran home in tears and told Ada what had happened. Furious, she marched up to the school and stormed into the classroom. The headmaster had knocked her son to the ground, she said, and she was having none of it. The headmaster's patronising advice to calm down had the predictable effect: Ada immediately grew angrier and told the headmaster she would kill him if he ever touched one of her kids again. She took a swing at the headmaster, who — being much taller — easily evaded her. This didn't stop her from continuing to hit him, calling him a 'bloody Catholic' and declaring that she hadn't wanted her kids brought up Catholic anyway. With one final punch, she grabbed George by the arm, and they left. After that, Ashley said, word got around about mad Ada Jamieson of Teynham Crescent — and the teachers generally left George alone.

Ashley, who very rarely gave Ada credit for anything, told this story as an example of George's travails, not as an example of Ada's care for her son — and, indeed, Ada's reaction was more than likely driven by her conviction that no member of the church she despised had the right to punish any child of hers. The incident surely increased Ada's disdain for her children's education — and it certainly made George even more determined to leave school at the earliest opportunity: according to the law at that time, when he turned 15. His misery was being made worse by the dyslexia that caused him to fall further and further behind the rest of the class.

In a newspaper interview many years later, Ashley revealed an intimate detail for the first time. 'I didn't put anything about this in [my first autobiography, published in 1982] but I was raped when I was eleven by a friend of my family. You never get over something like that. Whenever I read a story about a young woman who has been raped I feel for her because you can never get over the pain, the suffering and the guilt.'[2]

When George was 13, a kindred spirit finally arrived in the form of Vincent Paterson. Like George, Vincent belonged to a large family — he had five older sisters and a younger brother — and his father was a labourer. Vincent was much bigger than George, with pale skin and dark hair. He was also devout, with ambitions for the priesthood. George was influenced by this religious zeal — at least for a time. There were probably several reasons for this, aside from their friendship.

When George was in church, he was safe from the school bullies, and embracing Catholicism was also a way of rebelling against Ada. The rituals of church services would also have appealed to a young child who — from an early age — was responsive to theatricality and beauty. (When Ashley visited St Teresa's in old age, she automatically dipped her fingers in holy water, crossed herself, and genuflected to the altar.) Vincent was valuable for another reason: although he seemed gentle, when angered he could beat the daylights out of anyone. George now had another protector besides his dog, Prince.

And then, after several months of friendship, Vincent drank from a polluted stream in Bromborough, Cheshire, and died three days later, probably of typhoid. He was just 14 years old.

This loss of a fellow outsider — the only friend George had made — devastated him and reinforced his hatred of school. Without Vincent, George lost any interest in religion: if God was a benign creator, why had Vincent been allowed to die? When, as an act of rebellion, George missed Sunday mass, telling the priest that he needed to think about God, the priest told him to get out of the church for good. This suited George, who never went back.

Meanwhile, Ada had had enough of Frederick's drunkenness; not long after Vincent's death, she threw her husband out. Frederick never lived with the family again; though he briefly worked as a bus driver, by and large he would survive on a very small pension from the merchant navy. Ada now set up house with Bernie Cartmell, the skinny, awkward young man from Lancashire who had lived with the Jamieson family for years. George despised Cartmell and remained devoted to Frederick against all odds. As an adult, Ashley often recalled curling up with Frederick in the family's Anderson shelter and standing beside him near the Liver Building, with his father's merchant navy uniform smelling of the sea. But now George, bereft of both his best friend and his father, blamed Ada for Frederick's absence from his life. George's list of grievances against his mother steadily grew longer.

*

One of the striking things about April Ashley's life was a constant need to earn money and consequently the development of an impressive work ethic. The pattern was established almost from the time George set foot in primary school. At the age of about six, he already had a part-time job helping the local milkman, Mr Jones, deliver milk from his horse and cart; all the money George earned he gave to his mother. Mr Jones provided Ashley with one of her favourite anecdotes:

> When I said goodbye to him before we moved to Norris Green, he said to me, 'You know, you're an extraordinary child and you have an extraordinary aura.'
>
> As soon as I got home, I asked my mother what an aura was, but she didn't know.
>
> When I asked Mr Jones, he said, 'One day you'll find out.' And he paused and put his hand on my chin and said, 'But I'm afraid you've got a difficult time ahead of you.' We shook hands very formally, as you did in those days, and he said, 'By the way, you've been calling the horse "Daisy" for the last six months. It's not Daisy, it's Dave. Didn't you ever look?'
>
> I said, 'Look at what?'
>
> He tweaked my hair and said, 'Go on – get home.'
>
> I didn't know the difference between a male and a female horse, you know.[3]

George re-entered the workforce at the age of ten, when he became a delivery boy in St John's Market. Constructed in the 1820s, this was a huge Italianate building with roof finials in the shape of liver birds, the symbols of the city. As the first covered market in the United Kingdom and the model for many others, it was one of Liverpool's most cherished civic landmarks until its demolition in 1964.

George's new employers, a husband and wife, ran one of the 60-odd stalls in the market, selling meat products and groceries. John Lundy was a large, fair-haired man who liked a joke; Edna was dark-haired, with buck teeth and a rich Devonshire accent that fascinated George, who already had an ear for different voices. The Lundys had a tenuous family connection to the Jamiesons — John's brother had been briefly engaged to George's eldest sister, Theresa — but the Lundys were much better off financially. John, Edna, and their daughters lived in a large and comfortable flat in a middle-class neighbourhood of Liverpool. They were a close, supportive family — another reason why George found them so attractive.

Like other stallholders in St John's Market, they'd had their brushes with the law. In May 1940, shortly after wartime rationing was introduced in Britain, John's father had been sentenced to three years in prison for receiving and selling 20 bales of bacon belonging to the Cunard White Star Company and worth almost 1,000 pounds. Although this was not his only conviction, his lawyers had argued for clemency on the grounds that Lundy Sr had readily confessed to the theft and had previously been 'helping police with their enquiries' — that is, helping them to recover stolen goods. They also pointed out that he had a war wound that would not heal and had fallen into heavy debt. Nevertheless, the presiding judge thundered, 'People in positions of trust who steal the country's food — which the government buys not only for the well-to-do but for the poor — at a moment like this are doing their best to stab their country in the back.'[4] John Lundy had taken over the business during his father's spells in prison and effectively ran it thereafter.

John and Edna Lundy — who called George 'Nugget' — employed him for years, choosing to ignore the amount of time he spent at work when he should have been at school. 'Another religious holiday?' John would enquire. 'Okay, the bike's round the back; here's a list of deliveries.' On the days when George skipped school, he worked from 8.00 am to 10.00 pm for half a crown (two shillings and sixpence) a day, plus tips — astonishing wealth for a ten-year-old at the time. He wobbled along on a huge bicycle, taking meat products into neighbouring villages. Once, John Lundy asked George to carry six sides of bacon to a customer — a load that was so heavy that he lost control of the bike and fell right in front of a tram. The fact that he was nearly killed worried him less than his inability to finish his deliveries, and a passer-by who worked in the market agreed to deliver some of the bacon for him.

George worked so hard because he loved being accepted by the Lundys — and John and Edna Lundy did well out of him. After a day as an errand boy, George would go back to their house, where he had dinner before the Lundys went out for the evening, leaving George to babysit. More than likely, George was also privy to some of their dodgy business activities. These included finding extra ration books for customers, at a price, and delivering goods as payment for favours without the use of ration books. There was also a flourishing trade in forged tea coupons. George would stay in the Lundys' house for days at a time, returning to Teynham Crescent only when Edna became pregnant again.

Thanks to the Lundys, George learned about the contradictions of his native city — especially its extremes of poverty and wealth. The fruit-and-vegetable markets were in St John's Precinct, a disreputable part of town with a persistent smell of rotting produce and stale urine from overflowing drains. (It was in the cellar of one of the nearby fruit-and-vegetable warehouses that the famous Cavern Club, forever associated with the early days of the Beatles, opened for trad jazz and skiffle in 1957.) There were frequent brawls around the market area, too: the nearby pubs were the epicentre of Liverpool's underground gay scene, and the 'queer-basher' gangs did not miss their aim. And his job took him out into the countryside, where he was again able to explore the lush parklands of Knowsley Hall, as well as the large and elegant houses around Princes Avenue.

Like so many unhappy children, George found his greatest solace at the movies. It wasn't just because films represented sheer escapism, although that was obviously important; rather, it was because Hollywood showed him what he thought life ought to be like — with the glamour, self-assurance, and wealth he longed to attain. Not far from Teynham Crescent was the Regal Cinema: a handsome art deco picture palace built in 1930 to serve the Norris Green estate and the first movie theatre in Liverpool built specifically for talkies. George went there as often as he possibly could. The Tarzan films with Johnny Weissmuller were his favourites for a long time. Interestingly, he did not identify with Tarzan, king of the jungle, or his beautiful wife, Jane, played by Maureen O'Sullivan; instead, George wanted to be Cheeta, the chimpanzee. Cheeta, the epitome of freedom, spent his life swinging through the jungle canopy. His job was to be a loyal lieutenant, occasionally making Tarzan or Jane laugh at his antics or saving them from dangerous villains.

After a while, George ditched Cheeta in favour of the Hollywood actor Robert Mitchum. 'I watched all the Robert Mitchum films and copied his swaggering walk,' Ashley said later. If George had to put away his dreams of being a girl, Mitchum — the laconic, cynical, and hypermasculine Hollywood star of innumerable westerns and war pictures in the 1940s and 1950s — was the kind of man he aspired to be. When George was alone, he would try to imitate Mitchum's deep voice. As a result, he once damaged his vocal cords and was unable to speak for five days.

George also thoroughly enjoyed movies in which actors emerged after hurricanes and earthquakes without so much as a hair out of place. (He was clearly developing a taste for camp — something that stood Ashley in good stead much later.)

George occasionally went to the cinema with the Lundys. They were fans of Yma Sumac, a Peruvian-born star of stage and screen. George became enraptured by her: he longed to be like her — or even to *be* her. Sumac had dark hair and flashing eyes, and she usually played a sultry jungle princess in colourful and exotic costumes. Many of her film roles involved singing, for she had a vocal range enabling her to move effortlessly from low contralto to falsetto. According to some press reports, Sumac was an Incan princess; others alleged she was a housewife from the Bronx. George revelled in the sheer brazen chutzpah of these stories: what did it matter whether you were a princess or not if people thought you were because you behaved like one?

However, of all the movies and stars George loved as a child, his favourite — judging by the number of times Ashley referred to it later — was *The Perils of Pauline*, a 1947 Hollywood musical comedy starring Betty Hutton, best remembered today for playing sharpshooter Annie Oakley in *Annie Get Your Gun*.

In *The Perils of Pauline*, Hutton played a frustrated garment worker desperate to have an acting career. The plot — a daffy, though competent, young woman from the wrong side of the tracks becomes a star — immediately appealed to George and fuelled his ambitions. One sequence made a special impression: Pauline is given voice coaching by a fellow actor, who lectures her about the importance of refined speech in making a successful career. The film also happened to feature English actress Constance Collier, who went on to become a well-known Hollywood voice coach — and whose patrician cadences were uncannily like those of the adult April Ashley.

This may be one of the ways in which George Jamieson — who grew up hearing the local Scouse accent sometimes described as 'one-third Irish, one-third Welsh and one-third catarrh' — picked up the modulated upper-class southern English voice that was so much a part of Ashley's adult persona. It is not quite enough to insist, as Ashley frequently did, that she had always spoken this way and was punished as a child for 'talking posh'. She also let slip that her father's sister, her Aunt May, had been famous in the family — perhaps also ridiculed

— for her refined way of speaking. And, in working for the Lundys, George met wealthy people whose cultivated accent separated them from the working-class society he was increasingly determined to escape. As a teenager, George wrote in a school essay that he wanted to be a film star and live a 'lovely life': consciously changing the way he spoke — speaking as movie stars or rich women did — was surely an important means of achieving this.

However, George saw no escape from certain depressing facts: he was a working-class boy, and while he hadn't forgotten his deep desire to be a girl, he had to make the best of his situation.

And yet one day, Edna Lundy told him he was incredibly beautiful. As Ashley said later, 'Why would a woman call a boy beautiful? Surely it should be "handsome"?'[5]

Sometime later, he dozed off in the tram on the way home and his travelling companion, a neighbour from Norris Green, jabbed him in the ribs. 'Wake up,' said the neighbour. 'You look like a fockin' woman when you're asleep.'

George began obsessively checking his appearance, coming up with a critical inventory. He thought he was too skinny and too short. He had greenish-brown eyes, long eyelashes, and finely arched eyebrows, but his teeth were crooked. The hair on his head was thick and black, which was all right, but he was 15 years old and — unlike his contemporaries — he had developed no facial or pubic hair. Moreover, despite attempts to mimic Robert Mitchum, George's voice had never broken properly. Perhaps most dismaying of all — and again unlike most other boys he knew — he felt absolutely no sexual desire for girls.

Who was he? George understood that he could never be a girl, so he had no choice — he was trapped: he had to live as he was. If he faced up to this — if he could show in some way that he was a man — he would have some hope of being accepted. His father, his brothers, his uncles: all of them had gone to sea, mostly in the merchant navy. This was obviously what Jamieson men did. In a panic and with immense reluctance, George decided that he must do as they had done. He would join the merchant navy and become a sailor.[6]

One of the Lundys' clients was a Mrs Rossiter, a wealthy and beautiful woman who had taken a shine to George. One day, as they were having a cup of tea together — and while George was glorying in the comfortable living room and the beautiful, uncracked china — Mrs Rossiter asked him what he wanted to do with his life. Surely, she said, he didn't want to ride round Liverpool making deliveries forever. When George told her that he wanted to be like the other men in his family and go away to sea, Mrs Rossiter asked when he wanted to do this. As soon as possible, he replied. Mrs Rossiter told him that her husband was an important man in the Cunard shipping line. Mr Rossiter would easily be able to help George join the merchant navy.

And so, very soon after this early lesson in the importance of networking, George joined the training ship *Vindicatrix*.

CHAPTER 3

All at sea

As George waited at Lime Street station for the train that would take him to Sharpness in Gloucestershire and a new life on TS *Vindicatrix*, he felt very grand in his new uniform of blue serge trousers and a boiler jacket, thick woollen socks, heavy boots, and a beret, even though everything was far too big.[1] He clutched the small brown cardboard suitcase in which he carried a single personal item: a set of rosary beads. George, nervous about this huge step he was taking, evidently felt that — whether he believed in God or not — any possibility of divine protection would not go astray.

Mr Rossiter of Cunard had made it possible for George to cut through much of the red tape usually associated with joining the merchant navy, including the medical tests and — very importantly — parental consent. George had joined without telling anybody in his family: he wanted this decision to be his and his alone. Only on the night before he left did he tell his mother what he had done. According to Ashley, Ada greeted the news with indifference.

Most of the two dozen or so cadets who joined alongside George had come straight from school: his extra experience of the world might have given him some confidence. For the first three weeks of the six-week training course, cadets lived in Nissen huts close to where the *Vindicatrix* was moored in the River Severn. George quickly adapted to the routine: up before dawn, quick wash, tidy bed and locker, polish buttons and boots, clean the washroom, marching, breakfast, formal classes in seamanship, lunch, peeling potatoes and scrubbing floors, physical exercise, lights out at 9.00 pm.[2]

After three weeks, the cadets moved on board the *Vindicatrix* — a former sailing ship used for naval training between 1939 and 1966. Now, for the first time, George was part of a team in which everybody was equal and the only thing that mattered was whether you could do the job or not. There was also companionship and the possibility of making friends; thanks to his work with the Lundys, George had been developing his social skills. The training aimed at reproducing conditions at sea, including keeping watch night and day, signalling time on the ship's bell, and using navigation lamps. Cadets learned how to handle ropes, signal, use a compass, keep the ship clean, and serve food in the mess. Although it was exhausting work, George enjoyed it. The exception was having to tie knots, which he just couldn't get right, until one of the instructors offered to teach him after class; the condition was that he would beat George whenever he made a mistake. Time and again, George was bent over and flogged with a leather strap. It was excruciating corporal punishment with a sexually abusive edge — but he learned to tie knots.

When Christmas came, George chose to stay on board: he had no wish to go home. John and Edna Lundy sent him a huge fruit cake that he shared with the few other trainees who remained on board. On Christmas Day, they all went over to the Mission House, where women volunteers wearing festive paper hats served them lemonade and buns. On Boxing Day, George and two other cadets slipped away and got drunk in Bristol pubs a short train ride away. Apart from the hangover, George had just spent the best Christmas of his life.

At the end of the course, George had done well, despite his lack of expertise in tying knots. He left the *Vindicatrix* feeling good about himself and what he had accomplished. Despite his less-than-stellar academic career, he had shown he was intelligent and a quick learner — and he had made friends. And so he went back to Liverpool and cheerfully resumed his job with the Lundys.

Not long afterwards, George heard of a job at sea. His sister Teresa's fiancé, Colin Shipley, was a ship's carpenter. Colin's ship, the SS *Pacific Fortune* — a 9,400-tonne cargo freighter bound for Kingston, Jamaica — had a vacancy for a deck boy. The job entailed working with the crew while helping the stewards look after a dozen or so passengers. Here was another chance to get away from home — and George leaped at it.

Walking up the gangplank of his new home, 'doubts crowded back' into George's mind:

> The dour old Scottish bo'sun on deck looked me up and down and commented bluntly, 'Och, I thought it was a boy we were getting.' I was shattered. But as the ship headed into the open sea, some of my confidence returned. I thought I had made it.[3]

George followed Colin aft to a small three-bunk cabin. Two of the bunks had obviously been taken, so George climbed up to the third and waited to meet his cabin mates. An hour later, Danny arrived: a skinny, mouthy 19-year-old who knew his way around and showed George where and how to stow his gear. The other occupant of the cabin was Robbie, a phlegmatic and amiable young man. George was the youngest in the cabin — the only one who had not been to sea before — and Danny was the boss.

Not long after they went to bed, three young sailors burst into the cabin, obviously the worse for drink. They headed straight for George and started to pull away his bedclothes. When one of them said, 'C'mon, girlie, let's have a look!', George realised with a sinking heart that the Scottish boatswain had mates. Danny told them to fuck off and they staggered away laughing. But for George, the damage had already been done. His only consolation was that in Danny he evidently had some kind of protector.

George soon discovered that the lower your status on board, the earlier you had to get up: deckhands always rose earlier than anyone else because they had to organise breakfast for the rest of the crew. And George, who was rapidly becoming a connoisseur of class differences, also realised that there was a sharp distinction between the sea crew, who actually made the vessel work, and the stewards in charge of service for the passengers. The sailors despised the stewards, contemptuously referring to them as 'fairies'. Most of the stewards came from a slightly more elevated social class than the sea crew and most of them were gay, Ashley said later. George wanted nothing to do with them. Even though deck boys were supposed to split their time between helping the stewards and the other sailors, George always volunteered for the arduous work on deck. He was there to prove he was a tough sailor, a man, and that meant doing the dangerous jobs — even though he was once almost decapitated by a steel cable.

But George's body was beginning to betray him. To his horror, he saw that, far from becoming muscular, his chest was growing softer: *was he developing breasts?* For someone who had already been bullied because of his feminine appearance, the thought was terrifying. Even as the *Pacific Fortune* moved south and the weather grew warmer, he never took his vest off. He used to sneak into the showers at four in the morning, when there was nobody around to see him. And so he gradually lost the carefree self-confidence he had enjoyed on the *Vindicatrix* and became increasingly remote. 'My shipmates were puzzled,' said Ashley later. 'They couldn't make me out at all. As I sat drinking beer with them and listened to their tales and backchat, and the stories of their conquests, I think they were a bit shy of me.'[4]

George increasingly needed to be alone. Work on board was

constant, but when the crew had time off and the other sailors were gambling or resting, he would climb up to a secret spot on the poop deck to gaze at the stars in the quiet darkness. Only here did he find some peace.

About two weeks into the voyage, George was thrilled to see a low, green island in the distance: he had never been outside England before, and now he was seeing palm trees! The *Pacific Fortune* glided through the Windward Passage, and they arrived in Kingston harbour at about six o'clock one evening. Immediately the ship dropped anchor, colourfully dressed hawkers thronged aboard. One was a very large Black woman named Cynthia, whose job it was to collect the ship's washing and take it on shore. George evidently still looked very young, for Cynthia grabbed him and pulled him close to her, saying, 'Aah. My baby. My baby.' She did this every time she saw George, and he adored her: she gave him the physical affection that had been missing from his life. She also did his washing free of charge.

With Colin Shipley, whose uncle was chief of police in Kingston, George went to a garden party in the grounds of Government House. A decade before Jamaica achieved independence, Kingston still had some of the trappings of Empire, including large and ornate public buildings. However, George was not impressed, thinking the place rather pretentious. Having developed an eye for style thanks to his rich Liverpool contacts, he looked askance at the women in their cheap frocks and white gloves, and the men in white dinner jackets with frayed cuffs. (As an adult, April displayed a similarly dismissive attitude towards Britons abroad.) In that tropical landscape, they looked down-at-heel, even a little shabby, he thought. But he cheered up when he drank his first Coca-Cola, which he considered an invention of genius. Unfortunately, it was spiked with rum, resulting in a very bad hangover.

The *Pacific Fortune* travelled through the blue and tranquil waters of the Panama Canal. Just before they reached the Pacific Ocean, George, exhilarated by his adventure, briefly forgot his anguish about his physical appearance and jumped overboard into the sea for a glorious swim. The *Pacific Fortune* then steamed up the Pacific coast to California and San Francisco.

In the early 1950s, San Francisco was already known as a city that catered for all erotic tastes. After World War II, many American soldiers unwilling to return to their sexually restrictive small towns had settled there and made it their own. The city had many gay and lesbian bars, among which the Black Cat was the best known thanks to José Sarria, a cocktail waiter who performed as a drag queen and who was a well-known gay rights activist. In San Francisco, drag queens could be arrested under a city ordinance forbidding men from dressing in women's clothing with an 'intent to deceive'. To get around the arcane law, Sarria had the Black Cat's performers and some of its customers wear badges proclaiming, 'I am a boy.' State law could be more enlightened. After the Black Cat's liquor licence had been suspended for 'serving known homosexuals', the bar appealed the decision. The Supreme Court of California ruled in its favour, finding that gay men had a right to assemble socially, provided that there was no evidence of illegal or 'immoral' activity on the premises.

George was not comfortable in that particular milieu: he never felt he belonged. But the relatively relaxed atmosphere might have been refreshing after the furtiveness of the gay scene in Liverpool — not that George had taken advantage of what was on offer there. While some members of the crew had their special places to visit, he preferred to go into the city by himself. He explored Chinatown and acquainted himself with diners, developing a lifelong love of the American hamburger.

After San Francisco, the *Pacific Fortune* went on to Seattle, and then on to its northernmost point in Canada — Woodfibre, British Columbia. George celebrated his 17th birthday there on 29 April 1952.

The *Pacific Fortune* began the return to England, and the crew and passengers were at sea for weeks without making landfall. After the distraction of new experiences, George's anxieties about his appearance surfaced again. At mealtimes, the bored sailors would relate interminable stories about their sexual conquests, while George stared unhappily at his plate. His body was becoming increasingly feminine. 'My hips were rounder,' said Ashley. 'My eyelashes were growing and I had no trace of a beard and my voice had not broken. More and more often I would creep away to be alone.' It was an enormous relief to George when the weather was bad, with wind and rain, so that all the crew were swathed in oilskins.

And now the bullying of George's first night was repeated, usually by the powerful young sailor who had tormented him before. He did not attack George physically, nor did his mates. Instead, they contented themselves with blowing kisses and greeting George, 'Hello, ducks' or 'Hello, girlie', usually with a wink or a slap on his bottom. This was torment for George — not least because, as Ashley admitted later, he realised he was excited as well as afraid.

After a three-month voyage, the *Pacific Fortune* returned to Manchester via Antwerp and London, and the crew was paid. George had earned the princely sum of £19 10s 3d. He was worried about not being asked to join up again — all his fears about his masculinity would be confirmed if the merchant navy were to reject him now — and so he was jubilant when he was re-engaged for the ship's next voyage, setting off a couple of months later. Going back to Teynham Crescent, even for a short time, had made George realise even more acutely how much he needed to escape. He couldn't wait to get back to the ship.

This crew, he discovered, was more or less the same as that of the previous voyage. But there was a new crewman — tall, handsome and blond — who turned out to be a friend of the chief bully. George was powerfully attracted to him — a cause for alarm that he could not admit to anyone. One of the stewards signalled interest in George, but George rejected his advances — not least because he had internalised the sailors' condescending attitudes towards the stewards. George always preferred straight men — or at least those who presented as such. He was becoming adept at evading advances — and there were several — but the absence of physical contact of any kind made him lonelier than ever.

One night, the blond sailor and two of his friends burst into George's cabin, stripped him to the waist, and made a determined attempt to kiss him. George pushed the sailor away vehemently, and the sailor and his mates sauntered off, laughing. George, meanwhile, was swamped with shame. Sitting on his bunk, close to tears, he realised how much he loathed the idea of sex with another man. More than ever, he was convinced he was in the wrong body — that the only thing that could correct this monstrous mistake would be if he were to become a woman. And when the *Pacific Fortune* reached Kingston again and Cynthia said, 'Honey, you sure is getting prettier every time I see you,' George knew his instinct was right.

The thought obsessed him: it refused to go away. One evening, when Colin took him for a drink in Jamaica's Blue Mountains, George resolved to face facts about himself and his situation. He was never going to be a woman, and he couldn't live as a man: there was no way out except oblivion. He wanted to throw himself down the escarpment to his death. He restrained himself and, shortly afterwards, left with Colin — who had noticed nothing.

Once back on board the *Pacific Fortune*, things grew worse. Anxiety caused George to vomit repeatedly — a reaction he passed off as seasickness. The new boatswain, who was not insensitive, gave George work he could do alone or with the older sailors. This man was the latest in the line of George's protectors: several times when George was being attacked, others would come to his aid. This must have been a tribute to George's personal charm. Despite his attempts to become a rough, tough sailor, he was obviously vulnerable, awakening a protective instinct among some of his peers.

When the *Pacific Fortune* reached Los Angeles, George realised he needed professional help, perhaps from a psychiatrist. He found a doctor and explained that he had been feeling suicidal because he wanted to be a woman. The doctor — a man — took one look at this slight, dark-haired, and feminine seventeen-year-old, briskly told George he would get over it, and prescribed antidepressant amphetamines and barbiturates. The doctor was presumably acting on the recent ruling of the American Psychiatric Association's *Diagnostic and Statistical Manual of Mental Disorders* that, for the first time, defined homosexuality as a mental illness.

Very early one morning, George was in his cabin when a couple of sailors barged in, stinking of alcohol, and tried to molest him yet again. George fought desperately — and once more he was saved by two of the older sailors. As he lay on the floor, he made a decision. Nothing worked. It never would. He couldn't change who he was. His only way out was to kill himself.

A few days later, George lined up the pills the doctor had given him and methodically swallowed them all. He lost consciousness and collapsed — and was appalled to wake up in the Seaside Memorial Hospital in Long Beach. It was 8 August 1952, and he was furious to still be alive. While in hospital, he was told that he was not to rejoin the *Pacific Fortune*. This cannot have been surprising, but it was a further blow. The ship had been his only home for so long.

George was transferred to the Seamen's Mission in San Pedro to convalesce. Life quickly improved. He was given meal vouchers that could be cashed in and enabled him to take bus rides out to the beach. The Samaritans from the Norwegian Seamen's Church introduced him to teenage volunteer workers, who took him to see the sights of southern California: Hollywood, baseball games, the desert, local amusement parks. He stayed in California for several months and was in heaven: he had always wanted to be a film star and now he was in the same part of the world as his movie idols. For the first time in his life, he was enjoying good food, stimulating company, and excellent medical care. George recovered amazingly quickly and decided that, when he was older, he would return to southern California to live.

He had the first aeroplane ride of his life — from the west coast of the United States to the east — when he was told to join the SS *America* in New York on its journey back to Liverpool. This was a thrill, and the *America* proved to be a magnificent surprise. Instead of being assigned a stuffy three-berth cabin below the waterline, with a permanently closed porthole, he was given a luxury stateroom with a panoramic view of the ocean. The food, too, was wonderful: it was here that Ashley's love affair with caviar began. George wasn't required to work his passage, which was just as well because he had no clothes except for the threadbare shirts and trousers he had bought in California. On his last night at sea, he went to the ship's fancy-dress ball dressed as the fictional castaway Robinson Crusoe.

George had loved every moment of his time in New York City. He had cashed in his vouchers and lived blissfully on hamburgers, hot dogs, and French fries, marvelling at the cacophony — the sheer invigorating rush of the biggest and most complex city he had ever seen. But the role of Daniel Defoe's hero — a character who, through no fault of his own, had been wrecked without resources except what fate provided or he could find for himself — would have greater resonance in his life than he could possibly have known.

CHAPTER 4

'Shouldn't they have seen
what was wrong?'

For any family other than the Jamiesons, George's return to Liverpool would have been a cheerful occasion. We don't know what he told his parents and siblings about his adventures or experiences, but nobody, it seemed, asked any questions; they simply accepted the presents he brought them. As became her regular practice in years to come, Ada thanked him and carefully put his gifts in a drawer.

In any case, his homecoming was no cause for celebration: George was told that he had been dishonourably discharged from the merchant navy, presumably because of his hospitalisation in Los Angeles. It was the final humiliation — although perhaps not a surprising one. He had tried so hard to follow the same path as the men in his family, but he just couldn't do it. The sense of failure was crushing.

George needed a job, and the obvious solution was to return to work for the Lundys, weighing out and delivering meat products. John and Edna's pleasure at seeing him again, and his own happiness in resuming a role within this affectionate family, would have been some comfort. But George had already had experiences he could not share with anyone.

Enter Roxy. He was another worker on a market stall and probably a few years older than George. Roxy was red-faced with a high forehead and a mass of ginger hair. He also regularly wore green eyeshadow — a mark of his self-confidence — and he seemed never to be still. At first, George — who had, after all, had a Catholic education — was rather shocked by Roxy's brazen use of swear words and his flamboyance. He was a new kind of person for George to know: he was tough as old boots and very obviously gay, he had no designs on George, and he apparently didn't give a damn about anyone or anything. George was mesmerised.

It was Roxy who took George into Liverpool's gay underworld. In the early 1950s, there were about half a dozen gay bars in the city, including Liverpool's oldest hotel, the Stork, and the Magic Clock, both close to the markets and the centre of the city's gay quarter. Everybody knew how dangerous being gay could be. Gay men often fell foul of the police; they could be beaten or lose their jobs. And because homosexuality was considered a psychiatric illness, and gay sex criminalised, gay men could still be blackmailed or sent to institutions or even prison. Gayness was a source of shame and not only for families: some gay men voluntarily spent time in psychiatric hospitals seeking treatment for their 'homosexual inclinations'.[1] Others led double lives out of necessity.

As it always does, the press fed the moral panic, both nationally and locally. From 17 to 20 November 1953, the *Liverpool Echo* published a series of sanctimonious articles under the heading 'The Moral Challenge' by such 'distinguished leaders of modern thought' as Lord Samuel, the Bishop of London, and Lady Cynthia Colville, DCVO, DBE. In many closely packed columns of grim prose, they all, with horror, enumerated and described the decline of the nation's moral standards, citing increasing numbers of 'sexual offences'. Judge

Emlyn Jones praised the Liverpool police for their efforts in stemming the tide of immorality, adding his belief that the increase in convictions for sexual offences, larceny, and 'homo-sexual practices' had occurred because 'trouble begins in the home'. All warned of the dangers of 'homo-sexual irregularity', mentioning the decline of ancient Rome — always a reliable benchmark in this context — and the dangers to Christian civilisation if such lax behaviour were to remain unchallenged.

At about the same time, the *Liverpool Echo* reported that 20-year-old US Airman (First Class) Donald G. Colerick had been tried in Middlesex by US court-martial and convicted of strangling US Airman (Second Class) Milton Martinez. The English barrister who defended Colerick said that 'this story began in Pennsylvania when Colerick was thirteen and was offered a lift in a car by a man of about 45 who assaulted him'. As a result, said the barrister, 'Colerick was suffering from temporary insanity and his reason had gone. If you accept this evidence, this man cannot be held responsible for premeditated murder or manslaughter of a homosexual.' This case provided further proof, if such was needed, about the scourge of homosexuality.[2]

It's not surprising that those in Liverpool's gay scene became a secretive and close-knit group. Not knowing what he wanted or needed and still at odds with his sexuality, young George Jamieson found community in this world for a time. Ashley later admitted that George had at least one affair with a man: Vic, whom George had met at the Stork hotel. Ada Jamieson quite liked Vic and allowed him to stay in the family home for a while, thinking he was just a friend of George's and that one more person paying rent could help with the household expenses.

But, even in this world, George felt like an outsider. Although he went to the gay bars, he didn't enter into the conversations, most of which concerned which men were attractive and which were not. He now wore a uniform he had devised for himself — black trousers and a dark, boxy jacket with padded shoulders — and he wore his hair in the style made popular by one of his idols, film star Tony Curtis. Known as a duck's tail, it featured a curled quiff over the forehead and the longish hair at the sides carefully combed back to meet behind the ears — the whole ruthlessly pomaded.

Unable to escape the fact that what he wanted more than anything was to be a woman, George began to drink a great deal in an attempt to dull the frustration and misery he felt about his life and his future. One evening, George went drinking with a group of friends in a hotel at the Pierhead, the area of Liverpool overlooking the Mersey. Roxy and a mate known as Little Gloria clashed over a piece of 'rough trade' they both wanted. As George, on the edge of the group, listened to them arguing, he was swamped in despair. This was hardly the 'lovely life' he had always wanted, and he was trapped: 'I had lost all reason for living, thinking *I'll never be a woman*, and I couldn't live the life that was going on around me. And so I just thought, *That's it, I'm off*.'[3] Impulsively, he jumped over the railing and into the river.

The Mersey was bitterly cold and flowing fast. George's clothes quickly became waterlogged, and he waited to sink and be dragged under. The current swept him past a line of pontoons and he plunged deeper into the river.

A few minutes later, George felt his hair being pulled, and he found himself being dragged out of the water onto one of the pontoons. His rescuer was a young man who had seen him jump. As Ashley later said:

> The poor young man! I was screaming, 'How dare you?' because I didn't want to be rescued. But I never got around to thanking him, never got his name or anything. It was extraordinary ... the water was very rough, with white caps on the waves, and the tide was whizzing along. I don't know how he had the sense or the knowledge to bolt three or four hundred yards down ahead of me and jump onto a pontoon.[4]

Ashley received her first press, the incident reported in the *Liverpool Daily Post* under the heading 'Youth saved by his hair'.

The police were called and George was sent to Ormskirk County Hospital while the authorities decided what to do with this young man who had tried to kill himself. Shortly afterwards, he was transferred to Liverpool's Walton Hospital, which at the time had one of Britain's largest psychiatric units. George protested that this was a place for mad people, and he wasn't mad; he had tried to end his life because he was so unhappy. Nobody took any notice of what he said — they had probably heard similar stories from others — and George stayed there for three days. It was a dismal place: he was not allowed a knife and fork to eat with, shaving was forbidden, and he was escorted to the lavatory by two men in white coats. On the fourth day, he had an angry visitor: his mother, with her lover, Bernie Cartmell, in tow. George, said Ada, had let the family down. He was allowed to go home if Ada consented to his psychiatric treatment as an outpatient at

Walton for a year, and this was agreed.

The Walton Centre for Neurology and Neurosurgery, one of the first psychiatric units in the country not to be housed in a designated mental hospital, was run by Charles Vaillant, a distinguished Lancashire-born psychiatrist. He was very influential in his field: a lecturer in psychiatry and forensic medicine and a member of several mental health tribunals, he also sat on panels of independent examiners in cases of capital murder.[5] Ashley later described Vaillant as a 'ferrety little madman'.

Vaillant and the other doctors found George a bit of a mystery: *Why did he want to be a woman? How active was his sex life?* Said April, 'I told them I wanted to be a woman and they said I was mad. I was told that I'd have to become a homosexual, but that wasn't what I wanted.'[6] George said that he had been molested by gay men but found gay sex repugnant. The doctors did not believe him, taking the view that his wishes and feminine figure were the result of a hormonal imbalance. Hormone therapy changed neither George's view of who he was nor his physical characteristics. The doctors tried stronger drugs, including injections of sodium amytal (a barbiturate known as the 'truth' drug), to no avail. Next, they resorted to more drastic methods.

A standard treatment for a wide range of so-called psychiatric illnesses was electro-convulsive therapy. By the 1950s it was used widely in National Health Service hospitals throughout Britain, largely because of its success in treating depression. This therapy, the Walton doctors concluded, would help George, and it would not be painful, since Dr Vaillant, unlike other practitioners, had introduced anaesthetics and relaxant drugs into the procedure. George was tied to a table with heavy canvas straps, and wires were attached to his wrists and ankles, and to his head. A doctor, hidden behind a screen, pulled a lever that administered an electric shock and caused George to convulse as he briefly lost consciousness. This therapy was repeated several times a week for months during George's time as an outpatient at Walton.

It's very possible that, because the doctors had diagnosed George 'homosexual', they might have subjected him to another fashionable treatment to modify 'deviant' behaviour: aversion therapy. Extensively used on gay men up to the age of about 40, this involved showing the patient photographs of naked men and women on a screen. When a naked man was shown, the patient received an electric shock; nothing would happen if the picture was of a woman. The idea, of course, was to associate attraction to men with unpleasant consequences.

In George's case, none of these treatments was successful. He remained adamant: he was not gay, and all he wanted was to be a woman. After about six months, the frustrated doctors, seeing that the treatment was wrecking George physically, left him alone. According to their report: 'This boy is a constituent homosexual who says he wants to become a woman. He has had numerous homosexual experiences, and his homosexuality is at the root of his depression.' Ashley's later retort was: 'My records said I was of womanish appearance with practically no body hair. Shouldn't their own words have told them about what was wrong?'[7]

During his time as an outpatient at Walton, George continued to work with the Lundys; Ashley later said that this was the only thing that kept him sane. But, though he was grateful for their support, George was coming to believe that Liverpool had nothing more to offer him. The director of a local brewery offered to send him on a catering course; this was too much like being a steward on the *Pacific Fortune*, George decided, but he had no other offers. His first assignment, at the Commercial Hotel in Chester, was not a success. Ashley did not say why; she said only that George started to attract an 'extrovert clientele' and asked for a transfer, perhaps before he was fired.

George next went to the Westminster Hotel in Rhyl, on the coast in north Wales. It was the off season, and he found it extremely boring: he knew how dining rooms and kitchens worked by now. He transferred to the Talardy Hotel in St Asaph, slightly inland, but he didn't get on with the family running it and he disliked his job as a cocktail barman. He did, however, make friends with a junior member of the kitchen staff: a young man named John Prescott, who was three years younger than George. Prescott had worked in the merchant navy as a steward, although he was also involved in union activism — the beginning of his rise through Labour politics. George and Prescott shared digs with another young hotel employee, and by all accounts they had a good time. John Prescott — later deputy prime minister, as working-class ballast in Blair's New Labour government, and a man who was to influence Ashley's life and fortunes — later said, 'I was fifteen, and on first impressions [George] looked like a woman. He waltzed into the dining room wearing an eiderdown as a long ballgown.'[8] Prescott said he found young George to be 'impressively exotic' — and Ashley liked him too: 'He was incredibly nice and very, very handsome, like a young Marlon Brando. I can see why his wife Pauline fell for him. He was more than dapper – he was strapping. He was just a lovely young man.'[9]

But the time had come for George to make another change in his life. Shortly after his time at the Talardy, he reconnected with a friend in Liverpool. Ronnie Cogan had moved to London, and he told George what a wonderful, exciting city it was. The Jamieson family had long said that anyone who lived in London was mad, which would certainly have encouraged George to give it a try. He packed a kitbag with his meagre wardrobe and left Liverpool, hoping for better things. He would never live there again.

PART TWO

Becoming April

CHAPTER 5

Bona coves and zhooshy dishes

When Ashley looked back on George's time in London during the early and mid-1950s, she clearly had mixed feelings. In 'My strange life', a three-part story published under her name in 1962, she told the *News of the World* that she bitterly regretted being in 'the twilight world of the half-men and half-women ... Drug addicts were among my friends. I went to grotesque, weird parties night after night. It was an interlude of horror that I never wanted and have always regretted.'[1] But in her second as-told-to autobiography, published in 2006, April claimed with glee that she'd had a wonderful time during those years: 'I was used to putting on the Ritz in Liverpool – now I was standing out in front of the Ritz Hotel. London and I were not just compatible, we were *en rapport*. We were made for each other, the big city and I.'[2]

So, when George Jamieson first came to London, did he have a good time or not? When Ashley's comments were published in 1962, she was a glamorous model and keen to gloss over certain aspects of her earlier life. The society London she had come to enjoy so much was very different from the gay scene she had known a scant decade before.

In any event, in mid-1953, 18-year-old George was shaky and excited about what his life might become. He was also broke: because of Ada's disdain for 'the south', she had refused to support him in any way. George might have been able to claim sickness benefits, because of his psychiatric history, but that was the last thing he wanted; he always expected to work. His friend Ronnie had friends in London, and he assured George that they would find jobs and accommodation fairly quickly.

George and Ronnie spent their first night in London on the floor of a room in Earl's Court. Before long, they moved to a very small flat in Westgate Terrace on the edge of Chelsea. It was an area less sought-after than it later became, but in a part of London for which Ashley maintained an enduring fondness. As Ronnie had said, work was easy to find: one of George's first jobs in London was slicing ham in a grocery store on Gloucester Road. It was not much different from working for the Lundys in Liverpool, but it was a start. George was good-looking, healthy, and smart. He had already survived life with his family, the merchant navy, and two attempts to end his own life. Now, he had a job and somewhere to live in London, and he was ready for whatever came next.

He and Ronnie also found work wiping down tables at the Lyons Corner House on Coventry Street, between Piccadilly Circus and Leicester Square, in the heart of the West End. Lyons Corner Houses, which had been London institutions since before World War I, were basic restaurants and tearooms. There were more than 250 in London during their heyday, providing workers with cups of tea and inexpensive and nutritious lunches. Their waiting staff was famous: personable young women resplendent in black skirts, buttoned-up black cardigans, white aprons, and frilly caps. They were known as Nippies, because they had to serve a large number of customers very quickly. Paragons of feminine service, Nippies had to follow strict rules. They were not allowed to wear high heels — medium heels only, for comfort — and their nails had to be short and well manicured. Any makeup had to be discreet.

George took to his new job, however menial, with alacrity. The five-storey Coventry Street Lyons, with its first-floor restaurant open twenty-four hours a day, was the biggest and most popular in London. Being on the edge of the theatre district and near Soho, this Lyons attracted a raffish clientele. It was also the epicentre of London's gay scene, which was vibrant and varied: clerks, shop assistants and workmen, civil servants, the metropolitan intelligentsia, and occasionally theatre stars met on the first floor to eat, drink, and socialise in the late evenings and at weekends.

For young George Jamieson, working on the first floor, this was a glamorous world — and one he wanted to be part of. Queer London in the 1950s could be a great place for a boy of 19 with George's looks, energy, and insouciance, and his social life quickly blossomed. He was already noticeable and, in defiance of the rules employees had to follow, he began wearing green eyeshadow — perhaps a nod to Roxy, his friend from the Liverpool markets. He was drinking more than ever, and his new friends introduced him to 'bennies'. These were benzedrine inhalers, cheap over-the-counter decongestants containing paper soaked in a form of amphetamine. George quickly learned to cut up the paper and swallow it with water. On bennies, George could go for days without sleep, enabling him to both work and party. And when he needed to come down from this high, he found a whole bottle of vodka useful. Years later, Ashley described the initial effect as 'wonderful':

I used to feel as if I was floating around with my feet hardly touching the ground. But after a few weeks I began to see things. I had extraordinary hallucinations. Sometimes I'd look at some very ordinary customer and be quite convinced that Humphrey Bogart or Frank Sinatra was sitting there.[3]

In later years, Ashley described being accosted by an elderly

gentleman in a Dean Street restaurant. 'Are you a boy or a girl?'
he asked. April said she recognised him as Albert Einstein, that he
nicknamed George 'Madama Butterfly' because of the length of his
eyelashes, and that George thought him 'a dear'. It is a good story, and
it seems a pity to spoil it, but in fact Albert Einstein had left England
for good in 1933. Perhaps this was one of those instances in which
the bennies belied George's own eyes; either way, Ashley's account of
meeting Einstein remained part of her own mythology.

Central London had a number of pubs where gay men congregated
and George soon discovered the Marquis of Granby in Shaftesbury
Avenue, the Bricklayers Arms, the Wheatsheaf, and — best known of
all — the Fitzroy Tavern in Charlotte Street, near Soho. In the 1920s,
this pub had been a meeting place for an assortment of London's
bohemian artists and writers — mostly men — including Dylan
Thomas, George Orwell, Jacob Epstein, and Lawrence Durrell. 'If
you haven't visited the Fitzroy, you haven't visited London,' declared
artist Augustus John. Other less salubrious habitués included public
executioner Albert Pierrepoint, who hanged between 400 and 600
people in his 25-year career, and occultist Aleister Crowley.

In the 1950s, it was commonplace for the Fitzroy to be raided
by the police, ostensibly looking for underage boys or men without
identification, who were routinely arrested. George took care always
to carry his passport as proof that he was over 18, because he looked so
much younger.

His sexual partners did not always take such good care of him.
After a night in the Fitzroy, George was raped so brutally that he needed
stitches. In an attempt to avoid inconvenient questions, the perpetrator
took him across the Channel to Paris for medical treatment.

The Fitzroy was regularly pilloried in London newspapers, who
thundered that the place was a sink of depravity and iniquity. The
police frequently fined Fitzroy licensees Charlie and Annie Allchild
for allowing drunkenness and disorderly behaviour, and for 'permitting

the premises to be the habitual resort of reputed prostitutes', as well as 'male perverts'. But the Allchilds' appeals against their convictions and penalties were always successful, and the Fitzroy continued to operate. It was rumoured that Charlie avoided prosecution for more than ten years by bribing the police, which might have been true. Bennett's Festival and the Spartan Club close to Victoria station had been gay haunts for years and it seems that, in the absence of an actual complaint, the police often ignored the law in return for cash.

The political atmosphere in Britain during the 1950s was strongly homophobic. Sex acts between two men were illegal under the Criminal Law Amendment Act 1885, and men could be arrested even if a police officer — sometimes undercover — thought they *looked* as though they were about to commit the crime of 'gross indecency'. (This was the crime for which Oscar Wilde had been sent to prison for two years in 1895.) During his time as Home Secretary between 1951 and 1954, Sir David Maxwell Fyfe made the gloomy promise to carry out 'a new drive against male vice' that would 'rid England of this plague'. Many members of the police force throughout England were alert for any hint of such behaviours; according to *The Times*, a year after Maxwell Fyfe became Home Secretary, prosecutions for 'actual or attempted sodomy or gross indecency' had risen from 1,276 in 1939 to 5,443.[4] It seemed that nobody was immune, including men who might previously have been protected by their social position: in 1954, Lord Montagu of Beaulieu was sentenced to 12 months in prison.

Perhaps the best-known use of the 1885 Act took place in 1953, when George was already in London. The celebrated actor John Gielgud, wearing a cap he fondly hoped would disguise his well-known face, had been unlucky enough to approach an undercover policeman while soliciting in a Chelsea public lavatory. When he appeared in court, Gielgud gave his real name of Arthur and said he was a clerk. The magistrate — evidently not a theatregoer — failed to recognise Gielgud, fined him £10 and ordered him to 'see your doctor the moment you leave this court'. Gielgud was, however, recognised by a sharp-eyed court reporter for the *Evening Standard*. The story made the front pages and the Conservative peer Lord Winterton called for Gielgud to be horsewhipped. Gielgud was sure his career was over and considered taking his own life.

Gielgud's fellow actors organised their own form of protest against the law that had so humiliated their friend and colleague. The next day, when Gielgud turned up in Liverpool to rehearse *A Day by the Sea*, his co-star Sybil Thorndike said severely, 'John, you've been a very naughty boy. Now let's get on with the rehearsal.' And the moment Gielgud stepped on stage for the first performance, the audience cheered him. But Gielgud's health and reputation suffered for a number of years, not only in England: he was denied entry to the United States, where he had planned to take his production of Shakespeare's *The Tempest*. While he never spoke or wrote about what had happened, it was never entirely forgotten: on Gielgud's 80th birthday in 1984, theatre critic Harold Hobson wrote that the 'sickening' episode would not have occurred if the actor had only married.

The treatment of gay men forced them to be model citizens by day, cruising by night. George Lucas, a gay public servant who lived for many years on the margins of straight society in Britain, wrote in his diary in 1948: 'The homosexual concupiscence is a very dreadful malady ... it is a sad disease that can turn one who by day is a respected and useful official into a furtive night prowler, driven by dark lusts till the fit has passed.'[5] During his time in London, George Jamieson learned that a former lover back in Liverpool had become so depressed about his life that he had drowned himself.

One widespread feature of the gay subculture, especially in mid-century London, was a language known as Polari, a code that allowed gay men to gossip and converse in public: a 'bona cove', for example, described a good friend, and a 'zhooshy dish' was slang for a stylish and good-looking man. The vocabulary was based on words from several languages and dialects, including Italian, Romani, and Cockney rhyming slang, with bits of Yiddish and thieves' cant thrown in.* Polari conveyed the community's characteristic irony, sarcasm, and camp innuendo — all ways of coping with and evading a hostile society. Speaking Polari could even serve as protection from arrest, blackmail, or violence: it was understood by others in the gay community, though not by straight men, including undercover police officers.

Polari was also widely used in the merchant navy, where George might have heard it for the first time, and he would certainly have come across it in the Coventry Street Lyons. And users of Polari — who included drag queens — often claimed feminine nicknames: in Ashley's autobiography, she mentions men named Tallulah, Audrey, and Pussy.

Ronnie moved on, and George took a room in a basement flat belonging to a sex worker named Tristram. George discovered that while he was out working, Tristram was letting George's room to other sex workers and that the police were watching the house. George left hurriedly, and next found a room in Nevern Square near Earl's Court Tube station — hardly the most salubrious part of London. This was an area of cheap hotels, hostels, and bedsits, a popular place of first settlement, including for students from former British colonies and refugees from eastern Europe, and the site of an increasingly flourishing gay scene. It was here that George renewed his acquaintance with Little Gloria, a drag queen from Liverpool's Pierhead and a shoplifter who went on spending sprees with stolen chequebooks. Visitors to Little Gloria's room usually recognised things that belonged to them and quietly reclaimed them on the way out, with no words spoken.

---

*   Linguists have concluded that Polari can be traced back at least to the 19th century and possibly as far back as Shakespeare's time. Some Polari words and expressions made their way into mainstream language, including *naff, rozzer, blag, hoofer, dishy, scarper,* and *khazi.*

At the top of the house in Nevern Square lived Scheherazade —
a very tall, red-haired lesbian from the north of England, who ran
a thriving business as a dominatrix from her bedsit. At one point, a
young man named Hilary stood to inherit a sizable sum of money
if he married. Scheherazade offered to become his wife for a fee and
so the couple, with Ashley and other friends in tow, trooped off to
Kensington Registry Office. Halfway through the ceremony, Dawn,
one of the witnesses, produced a syringe from her handbag and stuck it
into her buttock. She was wearing winter tweeds, so this needed a fair
amount of muscle and determination. The registrar paused, blinked,
and carried on.

After a while, George started work as a switchboard operator at
a theatrical agency in Charing Cross Road. This brought him into
peripheral contact with show business, and he loved meeting dancers
and actors. The agency was near Old Compton Street, the epicentre
of the jazz and skiffle craze that was sweeping the newly established
coffee bars of the mid-1950s. George joined the eager young mods and
rockers who flocked to hear the fledgling stars of the time, and several
became friends.

The most famous of these Old Compton Street coffee bars was
2i's — later described as the birthplace of British rock 'n' roll; the
ambitious tagline 'Home of the Stars' displayed in jaunty script above
its entrance. The bar's name derived from those of its first owners,
Freddie and Sammy Irani (the two 'I's), and it was later taken over
by a pair of professional wrestling entrepreneurs: Paul Lincoln, an
Australian known as 'Dr Death', and Ray Hunter. The floors above
the coffee shop provided temporary accommodation for any visiting
wrestlers Lincoln and Hunter happened to be promoting.

The basement below the coffee bar accommodated an audience
of about 20 — standing room only — in front of a low stage made
of milk crates topped with wooden planks. When skiffle — a short-
lived phenomenon heavily influenced by American folk music — gave

way to rock 'n' roll in the late 1950s, 2i's followed suit. It eventually became one of the most famous music venues in England. Several stars began their careers there, including Tommy Steele, Cliff Richard, and Adam Faith. A second branch of 2i's opened in nearby Gerrard Street in 1956, but it closed because of intimidation by organised crime; the original 2i's lasted until 1970.

Even though George had come a long way from being a skinny kid from Norris Green, and despite his success in seeking out a new and exciting life, he was still dissatisfied — a feeling that increased during his time in London. He was becoming tired of the gay scene — and, most importantly, he still had the dream of becoming a woman, a desire that had never gone away.

George decided to get out of London for a while, establishing a pattern of escape that endured for many years. With a friend, he headed for the Channel Island of Jersey, looking for hotel work. He found a job as the general manager of a hotel in La Corbière, perched on a cliff opposite a lighthouse. It was Gothically romantic, utterly different from rackety Soho and its temptations. His days were busy with making breakfasts, morning coffee, lunches, and teas, and looking after the bar, but he had the evenings to himself. Sometimes, friends arrived from London; at other times, he was alone. George enjoyed both friendship and solitude, happy to have found some peace and to take a break.

On Jersey, George continued to dress androgynously. His preferred outfit was black trousers and a sweater, with a gamin pixie haircut like that of Audrey Hepburn. He was increasingly presenting himself as femme; he had learned from his drag queen friends in London how to apply 'slap' (Polari, meaning makeup) and how to look glamorous. And when Joey — a young Cockney from the Isle of Dogs, who was working for a boatyard in St Helier and to whom George was strongly attracted — thought George was a woman, George was delighted.

It was at this point that George decided what he must do: he would undergo the surgery necessary to become a woman. He promised himself that he would do this by 29 April 1960, his 25th birthday.

Gender-affirming surgery was in its infancy. By the time of George's decision, several people had undergone it, including Christine Jorgensen, an American trans woman whose story had caused a worldwide sensation. A former military clerical worker and photographer, Jorgensen had begun taking large doses of oestrogen in young adulthood and travelled to Denmark for surgery in 1950. The news of her successful transition broke with a 1 December 1952 headline in the *New York Daily News*: 'Ex-GI becomes blonde beauty, operations transform Bronx youth'. When Jorgensen went on to tell her own story to the surprisingly sympathetic British paper the *Sunday Pictorial* in March 1953, she said of her medical transition that, 'after two and a half years of medical and surgical treatment[,] I had been changed from an apparent man into a woman.'[6]

Christine Jorgensen launched a successful nightclub act and appeared on television, radio, and in the theatre. Her autobiography, published in 1967, sold more than 400,000 copies. In the late 1950s, her new celebrity and career seemed to promise the 'lovely life' that George had always wanted. And Christine quickly became the poster child for people all over the world who did not identify with the sex they had been assigned at birth.

While Jorgensen might have become the first transgender celebrity, she was by no means the first person to receive gender-affirming healthcare. In 1935, Britain's *Reynolds Illustrated News* had carried a small story about an unnamed 'boy' in Devon taking hormone therapy to 'change into a girl'. There was also the case of a Czech athlete who had won the 1934 Women's World Games 800 metres race, as well as long jump events. She underwent successful surgery shortly afterwards and emerged as a man named Zdenek Koubkov — a man whose former sporting achievements were erased from the record books.[7] And, in March 1954, news broke about Roberta Cowell, the first named trans woman in Britain to undergo gender-affirming surgery.

Born in 1916, Cowell had a distinguished career as a racing driver, went on to serve as a Spitfire pilot and instructor in the Royal Air Force during World War II, and was a German prisoner of war for several months. After being demobbed, Cowell started several businesses, before founding a motor-racing team in 1946 and competing in events throughout Europe. Cowell married, divorced, and suffered greatly from depression. 'My conscious mind was predominantly female,' wrote Cowell in an autobiography, 'and the feminine side of my nature, which all of my life I had known of and severely repressed, was very much more fundamental and deep-rooted than I had supposed.'[8]

Cowell, who began taking oestrogen, met Michael Dillon, a British doctor who had been assigned female at birth but was more comfortable and self-assured living as a man. Dillon's 1946 book, *Self: A Study in Ethics and Endocrinology*, which explained what he referred to as 'transsexualism', was enormously important to Cowell and the two became friends. Dillon asserted that everyone should have the right to the kind of body they wanted, one better aligned to their gender identity. Dillon surgically removed Cowell's testicles — without publicity, for the procedure was illegal in the United Kingdom — and Cowell then successfully obtained, from a Harley Street gynaecologist, a document stating she was intersex. This document enabled her to acquire a new birth certificate on which her sex was recorded as female, and she affirmed this by undergoing a vaginoplasty in 1951.

Leading with the story, the *News Chronicle* headlined its front page 'Man changes into woman', and the story began:

Bob Cowell, 35-year-old war-time fighter pilot and the father of two children has changed into a woman. Somerset House has accepted the re-registration, and where was once Robert Marshall Cowell is now Roberta Elizabeth Cowell – an attractive woman with long golden hair and delicate fingers.

As well as a glamorous posed shot of Roberta and a smaller inset photograph of her younger self in racing goggles, the paper reproduced the 'altered birth certificate giving official recognition to the amazing change', captioned 'Boy is now Girl'.

Unlike Jorgensen, however, Cowell — who continued to be active in motor racing until the 1970s — was not supportive of others who sought to transition. Distinguishing herself as intersex, she disparaged people with XY chromosomes who underwent reassignment, the same surgery that had so helped her, saying that they were 'normal people who've turned themselves into freaks by means of the operation'. This is very likely why Ashley, in turn, later disparaged Cowell.

Attention-grabbing headlines aside, the coverage of Jorgensen and Cowell in the newspapers of the time emphasised the success of their social and medical transition. It's a telling contrast to the press treatment of gay men, who were frequently described as 'perverts'.

Here, then, were precedents for George to follow in his quest to become a woman. He decided not to go back to London, and when the opportunity came to travel to Cannes, a place he had never visited, he agreed. The idea of the Côte d'Azur was very appealing; George might have seen pictures of Roberta Cowell looking glamorous on the Riviera.

Shortly after he arrived, George encountered some English visitors. One of them was Eric Lindsay, the entrepreneur behind the Soho coffee bar Heaven and Hell, so named in tribute to the Cabaret du Ciel and Cabaret de l'Enfer in Paris's Pigalle area. According to Lindsay:

We met on the beach at Cannes when [April Ashley] was George Jamieson. He was lying in just a pair of swim trunks, and I said to the owner of the Plage, 'I didn't know you allowed topless bathing?' I had mistakenly taken him for a girl, he was that beautiful.[9]

It was Eric Lindsay who offered George a lift to Paris, suggesting he try to find work at Le Carrousel, a nightclub specialising in the art of drag. George took a little while to warm to the idea, but he eventually realised that a job that required him to dress as a woman would be a perfect rehearsal for actually becoming one. And when Lindsay assured George that Le Carrousel was a respectable place, patronised by some of the most famous and wealthiest people in the world — people who lived a 'lovely life' — George made the decision.

In a 1962 interview Ashley gave to the *News of the World*, she described what happened next. She presented herself late one winter night at Le Carrousel, just off the Champs-Élysées, dressed in a sports coat, a white shirt, and brown trousers. 'Sorry,' said M. Lasquin, the artistic director. 'We don't employ girls here.'

But, George protested, he was, in fact, a boy.

M. Lasquin gave him a long look and finally said, 'Well, if you really are a boy, you have found yourself a job.'[10]

And so, late in 1956, Toni April started work at Le Carrousel.

CHAPTER 6

'I felt completely at ease for the first time in my life'

Toni April was to become part of an enduring French theatrical tradition. Certainly, English theatre had long featured men dressing as women — most recently for comic effect in music halls or as pantomime dames, with little attempt made to disguise their gender. But in many parts of Europe, *travesti* cabaret had been part of the theatre and entertainment scene for many years. And, by 1950, it had emerged triumphant after two catastrophic wars and a worldwide economic depression.

In Paris, while *travesti* cabaret originally referred to male performers who took on feminine roles, it was later extended to include all trans performers. It really took off in the 1930s, in clubs such as La Petite Chaumière near Sacré-Coeur in Montmartre, and at the balls at Magic City, near the Quai d'Orsay (the latter celebrated by the famous Hungarian-born photographer Brassaï). Also very popular were Le Monocle, a lesbian cabaret and club, and Le Binocle, known for its Black musicians and for the scandalous fact that men danced together there. Every month, Le Binocle held a ball at which patrons dressed according to a particular theme and a jury, chaired by the famous singer Mistinguett, chose the most beautiful. Neither club survived the German occupation of Paris in 1940, but their spirit lived on.

One cabaret artist who triumphantly survived the war and became internationally famous was the singer and dancer Josephine Baker. Born in St Louis, Missouri, in 1906, she came to Paris at the age of 20, escaping the racism of the United States. Baker met Pepito Abatino, a former stonemason from Sicily who became her lover and manager, and he helped her become an acclaimed cabaret artist — first at the Casino de Paris and later at the Folies Bergère. As talented a self-promoter as she was a singer and dancer — she inspired a line of cosmetics called Bakerfix — Baker made headlines when she adopted a cheetah as a pet and for her erotic and cheeky burlesque *danse sauvage*, in which she danced naked except for a skirt of artificial bananas. She toured Europe and the United States, and became the first Black woman to star in a major motion picture, the 1927 silent film *Siren of the Tropics*, before appearing in several others.

In 1937, Baker became a French citizen and toured South America; when she returned to Paris in July 1939 — having divorced her third husband in Brazil — she found France preparing for war. She continued her career in Paris, and she and Maurice Chevalier performed for French troops during the early stages of World War II. But when Holland and Belgium fell to the Nazis in 1940 and refugees fled to France, Baker left the theatre, working instead at a homeless shelter and as a volunteer for the Red Cross. Baker was later recruited for undercover work and travelled to North Africa with the Resistance, while giving concerts in Paris and elsewhere. Baker also became mother to 12 children adopted from various parts of the world, whom she called her 'rainbow tribe' — and she needed to keep working to support them.

Josephine Baker remained part of the Paris cabaret scene all the time Toni April was working at Le Carrousel, and the two became good friends, with Ashley later describing her as 'one of the most responsive, warmest people' she had ever met. The fact that Baker, like her, was a determined person — an outsider who had triumphed over great odds — was the basis of a strong and enduring bond between them. Whenever Baker was in Paris, Toni would go and see her shows, and Baker would always come into the dressing room at Le Carrousel. As Ashley later commented:

> I once asked [Josephine] why she hadn't become a big star in the United States. She told me, 'They spit on me in America.' And she told me that, because of racism, she wasn't allowed to walk through the front door of the hotel where she was staying. As a Black woman she had to go through the kitchen.[1]

Like other Paris cabarets, Le Carrousel sprang to life after the war. It was the brainchild of Marcel Wuysmann, a French Algerian always known to his staff as M. Marcel — a sign of familiarity that belied the level of commitment and formality he demanded from his staff. Although he had grown up in Algeria during the years of bloody guerrilla warfare that marked the colony's struggle for independence from France, he was no stranger to running a cabaret. He and his wife had managed Madame Arthur's, a drag cabaret in Pigalle named after a song by the chanteuse Yvette Guilbert. In 1947, M. Marcel left the running of Madame Arthur's to his wife and set up Le Carrousel, close to the fashionable and wealthy Champs-Élysées. From the start, Le Carrousel was intended to be a cut above other similar cabaret shows. In Pigalle, it was not uncommon for trans performers to do escort work to pay for hormone therapy and surgery. M. Marcel made sure that this was not the case at Le Carrousel.

By the time Toni April joined the cast, Le Carrousel was the most famous of the *travesti* nightclubs. A piece in the magazine *Female*

Mimics, dating from the mid-1950s and aimed at American visitors to ooh-la-la Paris demonstrates how firmly the club had become part of the scene. A visit, wrote the correspondent in happily shocked admiration, was 'a must for all broad-minded visitors to the nite-life of the most beautiful city in Europe':

> Countless celebrities can be seen in this fabulous rendezvous. Dim lighting reigns, and the lengthy show may be seen even from the bar which is decorated magnificently. All the performers, moreover, without exception, are MALE and all are young and handsome. A few dress as virile men but most appear as beautiful girls, dressed in exquisite gowns by Fath or Dior. These gentlemen are artistes of the highest order, and sing French songs with great flair.[2]

Nicky Haslam, later a well-known English interior designer and socialite, knew Le Carrousel well as a young man. He revelled in the 'tawdry allure' of the club, with its plush banquettes and glittering stage curtain, and enjoyed the *coup de théâtre* when, at the end of their act, performers pulled off their glamorous wigs, revealing their short, masculine haircuts, as was required 'by law'. He described Toni April as 'slightly gauche'.[3]

M. Marcel's business model was a tough one. Le Carrousel was open seven nights a week, and he kept a very close eye on his employees, enforcing rigid discipline. Anyone who missed a rehearsal or a performance for no good reason was suspended without pay, no questions asked. Because most of the performers lived from hand to mouth in cheap hotels or rooming houses, this could mean ruin for them. Fighting with another performer meant suspension for ten days. No alcohol was allowed backstage, and M. Marcel had the final say about who could visit the cast in the green room after performances.

Toni April photographed for a Carrousel publicity card

M. Marcel was not a generous employer, although he did pay for costumes and even sometimes for breast enhancements and nose jobs. When Toni April started at Le Carrousel, she noticed that several of the performers had the same cute button nose, evidently because they had all gone to the same plastic surgeon. The shows, which usually consisted of a string of solos plus an elaborate finale, changed frequently, and there were rehearsals for the current show every morning. The choreographer M. Tarquin was, Toni found, almost as exacting as M. Marcel.

Ashley never described her early days with Le Carrousel in much detail, although she freely admitted that, as neither a professional singer nor dancer, she had been chosen for the troupe solely because of her looks. M. Marcel did not treat his stars with much respect. He insisted that Coccinelle, the trans performer who became one of his greatest stars, was a girl when he first met her. When Coccinelle insisted that she wasn't, he grabbed her by the hair, 'tugging it violently':

The wig was no longer on my head, but in his hand ... He freely
explored my body, starting with my teeth, then ears, then discovered my breasts were artificial and finally compared the size of
my feet with his own. He studied me as a veterinary [sic] would
examine a horse.[4]

Toni evidently got off lightly during her audition.

Life at Le Carrousel wasn't always rigorous and strict. A documentary
film by Sébastien Lifshitz presents an engaging view of playfulness
backstage, with performers chatting as they apply makeup, wigs, and
costumes, getting ready for the show.[5] They are all casually and strikingly
beautiful, for M. Marcel's standards of feminine beauty were exacting. At
Le Carrousel, there was a strong spirit of camaraderie, too: one engaging
scene in the documentary shows members of the cast lifting each other's
skirts, pulling down bras to display their breasts and giggling.

Sometimes, this *esprit de corps* involved sarcastic badinage that was
not intended to be taken seriously. Toni April was reluctant to enter
into this, perhaps because her command of French at that time was not
great. She was given the nickname 'M'Lady': she was English, tall and
reserved, with a shyness that could have been interpreted as conceit or
snobbishness. Some other members of the cast apparently decided she
needed to be brought down a peg or two. 'Look at M'Lady,' Ashley
remembered hearing. 'She's just off to Heaven to have lunch with God.'

One routine on which Toni worked with M. Lasquin was based on
the new hit musical *My Fair Lady*, with Toni as Eliza Doolittle, the role
originated on Broadway by Julie Andrews; Nicky Haslam remembered
seeing her performing a version of 'Get Me to the Church on Time' (even
though the song is not intended to be sung by that character). Ashley
later wrote that her turn involved fast and dramatic costume changes, and
she thought it was a smash hit because, unlike some of her colleagues, she
wasn't trying to copy the languid sensuality of Marlene Dietrich.

The dressing room at Le Carrousel was divided in half by a row of back-to-back makeup tables. On one side were the stars, including Coccinelle and Bambi; on the other the would-be stars, including Toni. The stars usually looked after the others: Coccinelle gave Toni lessons in applying makeup when she first started, and Bambi took her to the doctor once a week for doses of oestrogen. Toni needed very little to look convincingly feminine: her breasts, though small, were well shaped, and all she had to do to enhance her figure was to wear a tight girdle, cover her nipples with sticking plaster, and tuck her penis.

Le Carrousel performers didn't all present as women offstage. Once the show was over, Les-Lee, a headline singer from Canada, changed out of her outfit and became a handsome man, as did Kiki Moustique, a very pretty blonde, who was married with a young son. And then there was Mickey Mercer, a tall and very good-looking lounge singer from Montana. Mercer had started his career in American cabarets — often in small, rather rough nightclubs — before coming to Le Carrousel. Presumably because he was one of the few other workers at Le Carrousel whose first language was English, he and Toni became fast friends and allies, having conversations about all sorts of topics while they waited to go on stage. Ashley admitted later that she had a crush on Mickey — and her fascination increased after Les-Lee told her Mickey Mercer had started life identified as female.

The most prominent star was Coccinelle, born Jacques-Charles Dufresnoy in 1931. Her stage name, meaning 'ladybird', was an example of in-your-face defiance: the word is an insult aimed at any feminine-looking man. Like Toni, Coccinelle had spent much of her youth being teased mercilessly for her femininity, and she made her debut as a showgirl in 1953 at the Madame Arthur nightclub, where her mother was a flower seller. Because of her blonde hair, beauty, and ability to mimic French stars such as Brigitte Bardot, Coccinelle — known to her colleagues as Coxy — became a media sensation, looking so much the part that one day her own mother failed to recognise her in the street.

Coxy's act was ostentatiously vulgar in the vaudeville tradition — she would blow raspberries while singing 'Love is a Many-Splendored Thing' — and audiences adored her irreverence. Ashley wrote that Coccinelle had a whole string of male lovers who came to the club wearing women's clothes.

The other great star of Le Carrousel was Bambi, a member of the lineup for more than 20 years. Bambi, who led a quiet, respectable life with her mother in Paris, was a sultry and thoroughly professional chanteuse with several hit songs to her credit. Ashley described her as the most beautiful of the troupe, and photographs bear this out.

Backstage at Le Carrousel, with April and Bambi in the centre,
and Kiki Moustique to their left in a strapless number

Bambi's life story is a convincing riposte to some commonly
held beliefs about cabaret artists. She was smart and hard-headed
enough to realise that she would eventually cease to be young and
beautiful, and while she was still at Le Carrousel she began studying
at the Sorbonne in Paris. (There is an amusing photograph of her,
elegant, blonde, and self-possessed, in a classroom full of scowling and
chubby adolescent girls.) She went on to acquire university degrees
and became a teacher of literature — a career she maintained for 25
years. She also wrote a five-volume novelised autobiography under
the general title *J'inventais ma vie* ('I was inventing my life'), and she
appeared in several films.*

Bambi and Toni became close allies. Before going out on the town,
Toni would dress as Audrey Hepburn; Bambi as Grace Kelly. They
were united in always appearing smart and ladylike in public. After the
late show, many cast members would rush for the stage door to meet
the clamouring stage-door johnnies and older men with particular
sexual tastes. Toni and Bambi seldom joined them.

---

*   Bambi was profiled in Sébastien Lifshitz's documentary film *Bambi*, which won the Teddy Award
for Best Documentary Film at the 2013 Berlin International Film Festival.

In summer, the cast of Le Carrousel left Paris to present shows in Germany, Scandinavia, Italy, and South America, with mixed success. They appeared in small theatres, and their shows were not well publicised — perhaps because of the influence of the Catholic Church in the countries they visited. However, Toni, like her colleagues, always looked forward to their summer season in Juan-les-Pins on the Riviera, which was not quite the opulent resort it later became, though certainly elegant enough. Like other performers, Toni was feted by audiences there, and she made friends with some of the English-speaking visitors, including the English actress Margaret Lockwood and her daughter, and American comedian Bob Hope. Ashley later complained that, during breakfast with Hope and his wife, the comedian did not crack one joke, which showed how reliant he was on his scriptwriters.

The real action for the Le Carrousel troupe remained in Paris, however. It was always fun for Toni and her colleagues to peer through the curtain before the 11.00 pm show to see who was seated at the tables closest to the stage. Celebrities who came included Ginger Rogers, Claudette Colbert, Rex Harrison, and Marlene Dietrich. Toni was also introduced to Judy Garland and Anton Dolin, the star of the Ballets Russes, who had been principal dancer with the Vic-Wells ballet in the 1930s. There were many others.

Toni was particularly starstruck by the young Elvis Presley, then in the army in Germany and on leave in Paris. He never came to Le Carrousel alone, even when he was off-duty: he was always accompanied by an entourage, including his manager, Colonel Tom Parker, whom Toni considered an oaf. She really liked Presley, however, later describing him as a dazzlingly beautiful Southern gentleman, with blue-black hair, golden skin, cherry-red lips, and brilliant green eyes. They flirted, and one night one of his aides took her aside and asked her whether she would be prepared to 'go with Elvis'. Toni was very flattered, of course, but reluctantly said no: April later claimed she was not quite ready to go to bed with a man, even Elvis Presley. Despite her refusal, he always bought her champagne.

According to Ashley, the surrealist Salvador Dalí visited Le Carrousel every night for six weeks just to see Toni. He bought her chocolates and champagne, and he wanted her to pose naked for his portrait *L'ermaphrodito* (*The Hermaphrodite*). She refused, appalled at the idea of appearing somewhere like the Tate Gallery with both male and female genitals. She was a woman, she told him. Dalí was persistent, and eventually Toni introduced him to another performer, Peki, who became Dalí's muse.

Peki, who later changed her name to Amanda Lear, went on to have a very successful career as a provocative singer and occasional actress, mostly in Paris. In a playful reference to speculation about the gender she was assigned at birth, she described her background as 'a *mister*-y': her mother was English — or French, or Vietnamese, or Chinese — and her father might have been Russian or Indonesian. In the 1960s and 1970s, she was linked to a number of rock stars; according to one newspaper account, she was a kind of 'up-market groupie but with her own cachet'. While never as well known as, say, Bianca Jagger or Marianne Faithfull, she became famous for her erotic showmanship and was regularly mentioned in the gossip columns.[6]

As the 1950s were coming to an end, Toni April was thoroughly enjoying her life at Le Carrousel, but she had never forgotten her vow to become a woman by the time she turned 25, and time was passing. Her conviction that she had been born into the wrong body was underlined every time she bathed or put her clothes on in the morning and undressed at night. Taking oestrogen, as she did all the time in Paris — having her body take on softened curves — would never be enough; neither would being feted as a beautiful woman on and off stage. Toni could not feel the same self-confidence as some of her colleagues at Le Carrousel — performers such as Les-Lee or Kiki Moustique, who presented as masculine as soon as they came off stage. Toni wanted to be, and to be acknowledged as, the woman she felt she truly was.

April later commented:

> The Carrousel management refused point-blank to let me wear women's clothing in the streets, but I ignored the ban. One day I turned up there in a beautiful blue costume with a big black picture hat. All they said was, "How can we be cross with anyone who looks so beautiful?" Ever since, I have dressed as a girl.
>
> It was a wonderful change. I felt completely at ease for the first time in my life. I could go swimming again – in a bikini now – without shame. And everywhere the stares I attracted were of admiration, instead of puzzlement or scorn.[7]

Toni knew that a vaginoplasty would be expensive. Her pay at Le Carrousel was barely enough to live on and she refused to contemplate escort work, the usual way of earning extra. Instead, she made a deal with the manager of the nearby nightclub Le Bantu: if she introduced guests to his club, he would pay her a commission of one-third of what he made from them. Before long, Toni was earning as much from Le Bantu as she was at Le Carrousel, and her savings began to grow.

One day, in the summer of 1959, Coccinelle came into the dressing room and fell theatrically backwards onto a sofa, her legs wide apart. She was naked from the waist down. 'What do you think of that?' she asked Toni, pointing to the space between her legs.

Toni could see a very neat cut there, without a trace of a penis. 'Where did you get that done?' she asked eagerly.

But Coccinelle laughed and refused to tell her. Toni kept asking her; Cocinelle continued to evade the issue.

Finally, while the company was on tour in Italy, Kiki Moustique told Toni that the surgeon who had performed Coccinelle's successful operation was Georges Burou, a French-born doctor who ran a clinic in Casablanca. Coccinelle said later, 'Dr Burou rectified the mistake nature had made and I became a real woman, on the inside as well as the outside.'[8]

Toni did some research, discovering that Burou was expensive, but reliable, with a growing reputation for successful gender-affirming surgery. More determined than ever, Toni took on further work. In early 1960, while the troupe was on tour in Milan, Toni announced that she was leaving Le Carrousel to have the surgery that would make her a woman.

And so, aged 24, Toni left her 'family' in Paris and once more set out on her own.

CHAPTER 7

'Au revoir, monsieur ... Bonjour, mademoiselle'

The jaunty tone in April Ashley's two as-told-to autobiographies is particularly noticeable when she describes her gender-affirming surgery. This contrasts starkly with some later interviews she gave, in which she revealed she had known there was a 50–50 chance that she might die under the knife. When asked whether she had been afraid of what might happen to her, she said: 'No, no, no. I was never frightened because if it didn't work, I didn't want to live anyhow.'[1] But the sheer courage involved in voluntarily submitting to this invasive and risky procedure in 1960 should not be underestimated.

In early 1960, Toni April wrote to Dr Burou, who promptly agreed to see her. On 10 May, she boarded a plane at Orly airport bound for Casablanca. It was shortly after her self-imposed deadline of her 25th birthday, but M. Marcel had refused to let her leave Le Carrousel until then.

More than a decade later, the travel writer Jan Morris visited Casablanca for the same purpose as Ashley, describing the city as 'mostly modern, noisy and ugly in a pompous colonial way', totally

devoid of the romance of the Bogart/Bergman film.[2] Clutching
not letters of transit signed by General de Gaulle but her savings of
£2,000 and the address of Dr Burou, Toni April saw the place entirely
differently. Here was an exotic city she had never visited before —
and on the evening of 10 May, her last before her consultation, she
decided to embrace its glamour. She put on a black cocktail dress
and six rows of pearls, swept her hair up into a chignon, crammed
banknotes into a very small beaded handbag, and took herself off
to an expensive restaurant. Although the context was completely
different, Toni April was doing what she had done for several years,
something that reassured her until the end of her life: preparing for
showtime.

Early the next morning, she presented herself at Dr Burou's rooms
in the rue Lapébie. The clean, bare appearance of his clinic might
have reassured her a little. Dr Burou conducted his gender-related
practice in conjunction with his regular work as an obstetrician and
gynaecologist; he basically ran a maternity clinic for rich Moroccans.
His rooms consisted of several operating theatres, a surgical ward, a
15-crib nursery, and delivery and patients' rooms. Gender-affirming
surgeries took place on the fourth floor.

Dr Burou, however, did not look anything like a surgeon. He
always wore elegant suits and was very good-looking, with tanned
skin, dark hair, striking blue eyes, and a dazzling smile. In photographs,
he looks rather like the French actor Vincent Cassel. He spoke fluent
English with what Jan Morris later described as a 'delectable' Maurice
Chevalier–type French accent.[3] Ashley said that Dr Burou examined
her thoroughly — rather as though she were an exhibit in an art gallery
— and asked her to sign a paper absolving him and the clinic of all
responsibility if things went wrong. He was clearly not the kind of
doctor to give reassurance for its own sake. 'Do you realise you might
die?' he asked. When Toni said yes, she was willing to accept the risks,
Dr Burou seemed entirely unsurprised.

Burou explained that the entire procedure would be completed in a single surgery. He would remove Toni's testicles and penis, and he would create a space between the rectum and the prostate, lining this space with sensitive skin from the excised penis to create a vagina. A small portion of the penile tissue, with its nerves and blood vessels, would be dissected and preserved to create the clitoris. He described in detail exactly how he intended to do this, illustrating his explanation with photographs that left nothing to the imagination. Toni saw the results of brutal incisions along the scrotum to the root of the penis, the bloody sleeve of scrotal skin, dissected testes, the severed and tied spermatic cord, and the massive cut across the urethra.

Ashley later said, 'Believe you me, if you had had any doubt in your mind that you wanted to go through with the operation, the photographs I saw would have flushed it out.'[4] It was one thing to bid a gleeful farewell to the parts of her body she hated; it was quite another to find out exactly what getting rid of them would look like.

She added, in what seems like fairly solid understatement, that any candidate for such surgery would need not only extraordinary determination but also physical courage and the ability to withstand a great deal of pain.

Now that she was thoroughly informed, Dr Burou asked Toni, again, whether she was prepared to go through with the surgery. Again, she nodded. 'Good,' he said. 'I'll see you here tomorrow morning at seven.'

Toni was taken aback, having expected to wait a few more days at least — but clearly Dr Burou liked to work quickly, perhaps to give patients less time to worry about what they had seen.

Toni stayed in the clinic overnight, and she didn't get much sleep.

The next morning, just before the anaesthetic mask was placed over her face, Dr Burou smiled and said, 'Au revoir, monsieur.'

Seven hours later, Toni awoke in jolting pain. The first person she saw through her drugged haze was Dr Burou. Just as he had with

Coccinelle before her, he smiled and greeted his patient, 'Bonjour, mademoiselle.'

The surgery had been a complete success — and Toni had never been so happy in her life.

The next two weeks were hell. Toni, who remained in the clinic, was allowed strong painkillers only for three days because of the risk of addiction. Her black hair came out in handfuls. 'It grew back,' Ashley said later, 'but it was never the great mane that it was before.'[5] Her face was puffy; her stomach was bound with bandages. The May weather was hot. Babies in the maternity wards close to her room wailed incessantly. There was no respite from the traffic noise and the braying of donkeys in the street below. But Toni was pleased when Dr Burou came to see her with the assurance that he was very happy with the outcome of the work he had done. Toni would no longer need to take oestrogen, and Dr Burou promised that she would be able to have penetrative vaginal sex.

But all that was of little comfort when Toni was forced to endure having a speculum inserted into her new vagina to check its elasticity and that the vaginal walls were healing. This was a new level of pain — agony that was almost unendurable. At night, she lay on the bed hot and sweat-soaked, screaming and moaning in pain, her body bruised and swollen and foul-smelling with clogged blood. She stayed in bed for two weeks, unable to move, before she was allowed up to bathe. On her first morning out of the clinic, she walked, white and shaking, into the street — and fainted into the gutter.

But she did start to heal — surprisingly quickly, according to Dr Burou — and the pain gradually decreased. Julia Lockwood, the 18-year-old daughter of English actress Margaret, stayed with her in the clinic. Julia had been a well-known child star who had gone on to have a notable career in film and television. Toni had become friendly with her during a summer season at Juan-les-Pins, and the two women had giggled and gossiped together. Ashley later said that Julia, whose strength of character and vivacity she greatly admired, saved her life. Julia offered to introduce Toni to Winston Churchill's daughter Sarah, whom she said was a great friend and her adopted mother, and Sarah Churchill later became a great and valued friend of Ashley's, too. After another week or so, Julia and Toni went swimming at a local beach. As Toni lowered herself into the water, she said to Julia, 'Well, at least everything's watertight ...'

Toni was in the clinic for about four weeks in total. Dr Burou wanted to keep her there for another two, but she was worried about money and decided she could not afford the extra time. Besides, she wanted to get on with her new life. First, she returned to Paris — although not to Le Carrousel, even though M. Marcel had offered to increase her pay. Then, she travelled on to London. Julia Lockwood had offered to put her up in her flat in London for a few weeks: a good place, Toni thought, for her to decide what to do next. But who was she?

It was a question that became urgent when she landed in London and had to present her passport to the customs officer. As Ashley later said:

> He saw it was in a male name, and looked at me, and he said, *This is not you*. But I insisted, and I must have been convincing, and I said, *An awful lot of things have changed since that photo was taken*. And, finally, he let me go through. He was very kind.[6]

Toni April needed a new name and, after a great deal of thought, she decided to keep April, the month of her birth, adding Ashley as her surname. She told her first biographer that 'Ashley' was a reference to Ashley Wilkes, one of the main characters in *Gone with the Wind*, played in the movie by the urbane Leslie Howard. She later changed her story, saying that she had chosen 'Ashley' as a name because, as someone who had always enjoyed poring over maps, she had noticed there was a village or town named 'Ashley' in practically every English county. This was not quite true, but it did indicate that she intended England to be the base for the newly minted April Ashley. Now April Ashley, lover of maps, had a whole new life to navigate.

PART THREE

When Her Face Was Her Fortune

CHAPTER 8

'I always carried a spare pair of eyelashes'

The first thing April Ashley did when she returned to London was to change her name by deed poll. For the trifling sum of £13 she now had a legal identity as a woman. And she was more beautiful than most: five feet ten inches tall, long-legged and slim, with delicately tilted grey-green eyes, full lips, and black hair. Her voice was husky — slightly deeper than that of most women — and she had schooled herself to speak slowly and deliberately with aristocratically rounded vowels. All of this, she knew, added up to an attractive — even sexy — package. And yet beneath the self-assurance and confidence April now projected ran a vein of insecurity. Not because of her surgery. To the end of her life, Ashley knew that, whatever medical problems might result, she had made the right, the only, decision for herself. But what would happen now?

April knew she had the support of her new friends, Julia Lockwood and Sarah Churchill. Churchill's whole life had been dominated by her father — especially the conflict between her need to rebel against his influence and her equally strong wish to please him.

During World War II — when she had been married to comedian Vic
Oliver — she had joined the Women's Auxiliary Air Force, working
closely on interpreting photographs for the 1942 British invasion of
North Africa. She had travelled extensively with her father, especially
in the Middle East, and was his aide-de-camp at the Yalta conference in
February 1945.[1] After the war and until the early 1960s, Sarah worked
as an actor — much to her parents' dismay — on radio, American and
British television, and in film. With her red hair and deep-set blue
eyes, she was striking, although not conventionally beautiful, and April
admired and respected Sarah's intelligence and professionalism.

Churchill lived in Dolphin Square, an imposing block of
apartments overlooking the Thames. The largest such development in
Europe and surrounded by a huge garden, it comprised 13 blocks in
all, each named after a famous navigator or admiral. Within easy reach
of the Palace of Westminster and the intelligence agencies MI5 and
MI6 on the Thames Embankment, its residents included politicians,
peers, and civil servants. (The blocks were known as 'houses', perhaps
as a reassuring echo of the wealthy private schools most of the residents
had attended.) Apartments varied in size from one-bedroom suites to
family homes with five bedrooms, a maid's room, and three bathrooms.
There were also shops, a nursery, a restaurant, a library, and a basement
garage with space for 200 cars.

April's friendship with Sarah Churchill gave her entrée into
this affluent upper-class world. Sarah proved to be a good friend,
but knowing her could be a mixed blessing, for she had developed a
problem with alcohol. Ashley wrote that the Dolphin Square porter
would occasionally telephone her and say, 'Miss Churchill's gone out
again, can you help?' and Ashley would go in search of her friend.
Once, she discovered Churchill directing traffic on the Embankment
in her nightdress.

April saw less of Julia Lockwood, who was working in the theatre,
playing Peter Pan at the Scala Theatre, best known these days as the site

of the concert sequences in the Beatles' film *A Hard Day's Night*. But it was Lockwood and her friends who helped April to determine her future career.

One evening, a colleague of Lockwood's asked April, abruptly, 'Well, what are you? An actress or a model?'

April did not quite know how to reply, but Julia Lockwood stepped in: 'She's a model,' she said.

The confidence of that comment must have impressed April and, after the words had sunk in, she thought, *Why not?* She knew she had the right 'look', and she had just spent the last four years of her life on stage, with some success. And surely the fact that she had done so in Paris — home of haute couture by the likes of Givenchy and Schiaparelli — would give her some credibility once she started looking for modelling work. Aided by Lockwood, April duly put together a portfolio of photographs and, at Lockwood's suggestion, presented herself at Cherry Marshall's model agency in Jermyn Street.

British fashion in 1960 was a few years away from the miniskirts and cheeky, casual clothes associated with the Swinging Sixties. It was still a time of long gowns, twinsets, tartan skirts, pleated shirts, stockings, and high-heeled shoes with pointed toes. Modelling was a relatively new industry, with upper-class overtones, and Cherry Marshall — born Irene Pearson in Dorset — was an astute businesswoman. She ran one of the most successful model agencies in London and was also a fashion journalist for the *Sunday Express*.

Marshall saw that April had the dignified, imperious look required of models wearing the formally upholstered clothes from Paris, and quickly hired her. However, a day or two later, Marshall contacted April and asked: 'Did you work at Le Carrousel?' April had not made a secret of her previous career: although she had not exactly advertised it, she had dropped heavy hints about working in Paris. Clearly, Marshall had carried out some background checks. When April admitted that, yes, she had been employed at Le Carrousel, Marshall abruptly cancelled their deal, explaining that she only employed 'real' women.

This was a heavy blow — and indeed became something of an omen — but April rallied quickly. She realised she would probably do better at an agency that was smaller — one that offered a wider range of modelling opportunities, though perhaps with less cachet. She tried Signon Fashion Models, whose proprietor, Mme Signon, was equally impressed by April's appearance and assurance and by what she said about her Parisian experience. April confessed that British modelling was new to her, and Mme Signon warned her new recruit about the dangers of life as a model: drugs including amphetamines, too much alcohol, and the perils of the casting couch. Given her previous life, April might have found difficulty in keeping a straight face through all of this. But she dutifully thanked Signon for her advice, and so April's career as a model began.

Before long, April realised that being a fashion model involved rather more than striking poses in fashionable clothes. Like Jean Shrimpton — the first English supermodel, whose career began at about the same time as April's — she learned that the most important part of the job was interpreting the clothes for customers, as well as displaying them. Some acting skill was necessary, and April learned to perform the appropriate stances and expressions: carefree for sportswear; relaxed and cheerful for beachwear; haughty and elegant for evening gowns and some daywear. The rules were strict and precise, and April, always a fast learner, picked them up without much trouble. She found the precise tilt of the head necessary to best show off a hat, and on the catwalk she picked up the trick of looking down at the lapel of a jacket and feeling the material — to demonstrate the quality of the fabric — before slipping it off her shoulders. And she learned the necessity of always keeping herself immaculate, including carrying a spare set of false eyelashes in case of emergency.

April's first job, a three-day fashion show in the Stratford Court Hotel on London's Oxford Street, was highly successful. But catwalk modelling was, she found, both boring and highly competitive. Her slim waist and long legs made her suitable as an underwear model. A colleague warned her that if she became known for modelling underwear, she would never graduate to couture, where the real money and kudos were, but April didn't care. She was being paid eight guineas an hour — a fortune for her — and soon she started working for *Vogue* magazine, which paid even better. She appeared in television advertisements — crude and amateurish productions that paid £160 a day. April enjoyed this work, not only because of the money, but also because she hoped television might be a stepping stone to the goal she had had since childhood: to be a movie star.

And so she was delighted when, late in 1960, word went out that United Artists was looking for young women to appear as extras in a movie, *The Road to Hong Kong.* It was the seventh in a series of comedy-adventure movies featuring Bob Hope, Bing Crosby, and Dorothy Lamour, and set in distant locations — most recently, Bali and Brazil. The series had a tried-and-true formula: Crosby and Hope had to carry out some impossible task, with the suave Crosby making plans and the bumbling Hope failing to help him carry them out, while Lamour played a femme fatale. The scripts bristled with Hope's wisecracks about current events or issues, and Crosby and Lamour took care of the musical numbers.

The Road to Hong Kong was no exception: the plot involved mistaken identity, a rare Tibetan herb, and Crosby and Hope trying to defeat a secret organisation that sought world domination and was led by a criminal mastermind. (Years before the *Austin Powers* series, it was a satirical take on Ian Fleming's enormously popular James Bond novels; *Dr No*, the first film in the Bond series, was released in the same year.) In this latest *Road* movie, the femme fatale part was to be taken by Joan Collins — Lamour, at 48, was considered too old, even though Hope and Crosby were both pushing 60 — and the cast included other English actors, as well as extras. Every model or would-be actress in

London picked up her photographic portfolio, put on her sharp-toed high heels and tottered towards Shepperton Studios in west London.

April was crestfallen to find that she was one of about 200 women auditioning for six parts. She was delighted to be chosen and perhaps also surprised: not only was she taller than most of the applicants, but the script called for the women to be Chinese. This was at a time when 'Asian' in a Western film was a synonym for 'sinister' or, if a woman, subservient to villainous types. According to the script, April's character was supposed to sit at Bob Hope's feet before she and her colleagues clustered around him and carried him away on their shoulders. She knew that this was hardly the stuff of which movie careers were made, but it was a start.[2]

Ashley gave few details about her experience of working on the movie. She did later say that, because she had once breakfasted with Bob Hope in her Le Carrousel days, she was worried that he might remember where and how they had first met. It was a possibility — although a remote one — and perhaps her anxiety was reinforced by her experience of rejection at the Cherry Marshall agency. Hope did not recognise her, of course, and April appears to have relaxed and enjoyed herself for the brief time — likely no more than a day — they were on the set together.

April returned to modelling with greater confidence, knowing she could now add 'film experience' to her résumé. She was now appearing in a range of increasingly lavish charity fashion shows in such places as the Dorchester hotel. At one such show, she found herself parading before royalty, in the form of the Duchess of Gloucester, while wearing £150,000 worth of jewellery and furs.

April's career as a model was fulfilling her dream of entering the world of the upper-class rich. Wealthy and well-connected men loved being seen with beautiful models — young women who bolstered their egos and made excellent trophy wives. April was well aware of this, and she knew that marriage to someone rich and aristocratic would give her permanent entrée to that world. She could think of nothing better than a successful career that showcased the beauty for which she had suffered so much, with the extra reward of a marriage to a rich and titled man.

She had the examples of several of her contemporaries to follow. In 1956, Fiona Campbell-Walter, a well-known New Zealand–born photographic and fashion model, had become the third wife of Baron Heinrich von Thyssen, a Swiss billionaire who had amassed one of the greatest private art collections in the world. After their divorce in 1965, the now-very-wealthy Campbell-Walter continued her jet-set life, embarking on a relationship with Alexander Onassis, the son of Greek shipping magnate Aristotle. The model Maggie Simmonds had become the Countess of Kimberley, Sandra Paul had married aristocrat and author Robin Douglas-Home, and — perhaps most spectacularly of all — Bronwen Pugh had become the wife of William Waldorf, the third Viscount Astor. (This was a few years before MP John Profumo's extramarital and scandalous affair with 19-year-old Christine Keeler made the word 'model' synonymous with 'call-girl' in the tabloid press.)

Late in 1960, April was a guest at a Sunday buffet lunch in honour of the Italian actor and director Vittorio De Sica, famous for his movies *Bicycle Thieves* and *Two Women*. It was a stellar occasion, with guests including Shirley Bassey, Lucian Freud, Lionel Bart, and the Maharani of Cooch Behar. A solidly built, deeply tanned, dark-haired, and handsome young man kept plying April with drinks. She noticed that he was stylishly dressed in a casual shirt and trousers with a scarf around his neck, while most of the other men wore suits and ties — and asked whether he was an actor. No, he said, his name was Tim, and he invited her to dinner.

April and Tim went back to his house in Belgravia. The front door was opened by a manservant who addressed April's host as 'm'lord'. The house was full of modern paintings, which April disdained, although she liked the study and especially the writing paper embossed with the words 'Lord Timothy Willoughby de Eresby'. Over dinner, April discovered that Lord Timothy Willoughby was a year younger than she, heir to former Lord Great Chamberlain of England the Earl of Ancaster, and the grandson of Nancy Astor, the first woman to take a seat as a Member of Parliament in the House of Commons. Lord Timothy was, then, a bona fide English aristocrat, with lineage, good looks, assurance, and enormous wealth, and he moved easily between sexual, class, and social boundaries. In his *Who's Who* entry he had listed, under 'Recreations', 'Collecting: very nearly anything' and 'Travelling'. The biographer of artist Lucian Freud commented of Willoughby that he 'conducted himself as a neo-Regency buck, his dissipation so extravagant that, marvelling at it, Freud felt moved to compete'.[3] Nicky Haslam described him as 'a courageous daredevil and gambler', as well as 'a beautiful young Casanova who collected paintings for his many stately homes, as well as girls'.[4] It is hardly surprising that April was dazzled by him almost from the moment they met.

Lord Timothy and April began spending time together. On Sundays, they sometimes went to the Stork Club, drinking expensive champagne from plain water jugs and glasses because of the liquor licensing laws. They often went to the exclusive Mirabelle restaurant for caviar, they might go to the greyhound races, and sometimes April would find herself in a grand house, meeting other titled members of Lord Timothy's circle, resplendent in tiaras and tails. It was enormous fun, and she loved every second of it.

From the start, however, April sensed that she was dealing with a complex man. Lord Timothy's moods were mercurial: he could move from anxiety to despair, annoyance or teasing urbanity. He was, she thought, a stranger to peace of mind. And he was chronically restless: April could never be sure where he was. He was likely to turn up after several weeks in the South China Sea, or South America, or New York (where he seemed to spend a great deal of time), or as a guest at a fancy-dress ball in Venice. Ashley wrote that he had 'the blues' about once a week: he suffered from constant depression. At such times, he would invite April to his house for cups of tea, or perhaps to the Grenadier pub for shepherd's pie and to watch the transactions between young Guardsmen and older men. Ashley said that she enjoyed these quiet days perhaps more than all the grand parties, and she felt very close to him.

April probably knew little about Lord Timothy's business activities. He was one of three investors — another being the Queen's racehorse trainer — who financially supported John Aspinall's Clermont Club. Aspinall was a somewhat questionable character who had moved into British high society thanks to his expertise in running high-stakes gambling establishments. He had begun his career by hosting private gaming parties in London, using the proceeds to establish two wild animal parks in rural England. He bought a flat in Belgravia, where he built a garden enclosure for a tiger, two bears, and a capuchin monkey, of which he was very fond. In the 1950s he had wanted to run a gaming house, but this was illegal — the definition of 'gaming house' being an establishment where gambling had taken place more than three times — so he had worked around the law by using upper-class flats and houses, acquired on short and complicated leases. Bribery sorted out possible problems with the Metropolitan Police.

Aspinall's Clermont Club, founded in 1962 after the law was

relaxed, was an exclusive establishment. It was a success from the start, its devoted members including five dukes, five marquesses, a scattering of earls, and two Cabinet ministers. Enthusiastic players of blackjack, baccarat, or roulette included Peter Sellers, Ian Fleming, Lucian Freud, James Goldsmith, and Tiny Roland. Aspinall's patrons regularly bet amounts in excess of £25,000. It was later alleged that Aspinall worked with gangster Billy Hill to employ criminals who would cheat the players, and indeed some of the wealthiest people in Britain lost millions of pounds. April was never a big gambler — she was too financially canny for that; as to Lord Timothy's finances, there was no doubt a reason why his father had failed to follow the then-common practice of minimising death duties by handing his vast estate over to his son.

Ashley wrote that she and Lord Timothy lunched at the Mirabelle restaurant more often than they went to bed together. She knew he had other lovers, and she said her recent 'emergence' as a woman gave her no right to be jealous. This could have been disingenuous on her part. In fact, Lord Timothy's most constant lover was the American-born pop artist Harold Stevenson. Seven years older than Lord Timothy, Stevenson was a prominent member of the art scene, a friend of Andy Warhol — he had a minor part in Warhol's movie *Heat* — and an associate of Robert Rauschenberg and Jasper Johns. (Modern art was not something April enjoyed or knew much about: she described the art on the walls of Lord Timothy's house as 'splodges'.)

Stevenson was making a name for himself as a painter of large-scale portraits of nude men. At the time Lord Timothy and April were seeing each other, Stevenson was preparing *The New Adam*, a massive, nine-panelled mural that he dedicated to Lord Timothy. It was eight feet high and 30 feet long, featuring a reclining male nude with sensually large nipples and genitals: an exercise in gigantism that required two panels to contain testicles and penis alone. The painting was exhibited in January 1963 in Paris, and while it was at first deemed too risqué for New York's Guggenheim Museum, it later entered the collection and is now regarded as a modern masterpiece.[5]

Nothing Ashley ever published, either in her autobiographies or her many press interviews, mentions the more complex aspects of Lord Timothy's business or personal life; in her telling, he sounds like a titled upper-class wastrel from a novel by Evelyn Waugh. She enveloped her relationship with him in a romantic haze — to the point of declaring that he would have married her if she had been able to have children. How much did she really know about Lord Timothy? How did she feel about the existence of Stevenson's painting and its dedication to her lover? Perhaps she cared little about it. After all, she had secrets of her own — and the subject matter of *The New Adam* struck right at their heart.

CHAPTER 9

'"Her" secret is out'

Being a successful model meant hard work and a great deal of it. It required April to get up at the crack of dawn for photo shoots, rush to jobs with long, unpredictable working hours, model winter clothes in summer, evade creepy photographers and exploitative agents, and look immaculately turned out at all times, regardless of how she felt — and she still had intermittent pain from her surgery. Not much of this added up to the 'lovely life' she so craved. But April prided herself on her professionalism, and she took it all in her stride.

It could be irritating, however, to mix with members of the aristocracy who did not understand or share her need to earn a living — or, indeed, to work at all. Lord Timothy Willoughby and his friends came into this category: people born to wealth and privilege, with nothing much to do except spend the money they had inherited. While April enjoyed being part of this world — the knowledge that most material things anyone could desire were there for the asking, including champagne — her Liverpool-born tough, hard-headed, and occasionally puritanical streak surfaced from time to time. Lord Timothy's addiction to gambling, for instance, was something she certainly did not share; she was unimpressed when he and several friends were hauled before Marylebone Magistrates' Court in connection with John Aspinall's illegal gaming activities. April was fond of Lord Timothy and being with him was always great fun, but she had little idea of what he took seriously.

She soon had more pressing matters to think about. One Saturday morning late in 1961, there was a knock at the door of her apartment in Kensington. The caller introduced himself as Roy Earl, reporter for *The People*, a Sunday newspaper. Was it true, he asked, that she used to be a man?

April immediately told him to go to hell, but Earl held firm, claiming he had discovered her secret thanks to 'a reader' — later alleged to be a former housemate — who had recognised her in a photo accompanying *The People*'s investigation into *la dolce vita* in Rome, that is, the 'shadow of vice that has fallen across the Eternal City'. Under the headline 'The Wickedest Street in the World', a photograph showed April, resplendent in ropes of pearls above a plunging neckline. It was captioned: 'You never dare take things at face value on the Via Veneto. The girls ... turned out to be MALE BALLET DANCERS, one of them British!'[1]

April recognised the photo as dating from a visit to Italy with Kiki Moustique during their time at Le Carrousel. They had been asked by the hotel to show their passports; unhappy with the mismatch between their names and their clothing, management had asked them to leave. The two dancers had refused and made a fuss; the incident had caused something of a local sensation, with photographs appearing in the local press. Whoever had tipped off *The People* had seen the photograph reproduced in the British paper and recognised April from her modelling stint at the Dorchester; Roy Earl had contacted April's agent, and now here he was.

April knew she was in trouble and might have been in two minds about what to do. If she shut the door on Earl, she could be sure that *The People* would print the story anyway. If she agreed to an interview, she would at least have some chance to influence what *The People* printed. She could reasonably point out that she had never tried to hide or deny her history, and, while she had not particularly wanted it to be publicised, the possibility of extensive publicity might have been too tempting to resist. And so she let Roy Earl into her apartment.

The story appeared in *The People* on Sunday 19 November 1961 under the heading 'The extraordinary case of top model April Ashley: "Her" secret is out'. April gave a brief account of her own story, toning down certain aspects: 'At school I was a real boy and after I left school I was still a boy at heart,' she said, glossing over the bullying George had endured and his longing to be a girl:

> But long before I was 21 there had been a great change in me. Not at that time so much of a physical change, but there was a very great mental change. All my ideas and thoughts were a woman's. That's why when I reached 21 I decided to live as a woman, dress as a woman and be known to my friends as a woman ...
>
> [I]t could have gone on like this. But I met so many people with the same problem as I had who seemed so lost. They lived in a world of neither one thing nor another. I suppose it was seeing others suffering in their own minds that made me set my heart on having an operation.[2]

The sole reason she had taken up modelling, said April, was that the surgery had been very expensive.

'Look around my flat,' she added. 'You'll see it is the house of a woman ... The only omission in my own life is the fact that I know I can never have children.' But, as she pointed out, 'there are lots of girls who have been female all their lives who can't have children. I want to do just what they would do. Adopt a couple of kids.' This last was perhaps a sop to the newspaper's conservative readership, though April did mention the same idea from time to time.

While the interview concluded with Roy Earl wondering solemnly whether April had been wise to have the surgery, 'because no complete man can ever be a complete woman', he clearly admired April. The tone of the article is thoughtful, without sensationalism (except for the headline), and Earl praised Ashley for her courage in talking candidly about 'her two lives' (at the time, frank discussion of sexual matters in newspapers was still off limits). April came across as dignified, self-contained, and assured.

However, if April had hoped the interview might arouse sympathy for her, she was soon disillusioned. The day after publication she was told that all her bookings — every single one — had been cancelled. It was a huge shock: she had had jobs lined up months in advance. The clients' reasons were depressingly similar: they had suddenly discovered she 'was not quite right' for what they had in mind and, reluctantly, they would have to let her go. Only one client told her bluntly that they would not have their name associated with a model who had 'had a sex change'. Over the following weeks and months, April realised that her career as a model in London, so successfully begun, was over.

April was by no means the first trans woman to be outed by the British press. When Roberta Cowell's gender-affirming surgery became public in 1954, *The People*'s headline had been 'Roberta: The ghastly truth at last "He is still a man"'. The tone of that article had been strikingly hostile:

> There was no physical condition that existed for the operations ... They were done purely to meet his abnormal craving and because the psychiatrists thought his mental condition justified them. For two years Cowell had operation after operation in a London nursing home. These would be revolting to describe in detail, but in effect they merely removed parts of his body and substituted a form of female sex mechanism. The change was purely outward and artificial. No actual female organs were added to him, and in the end Cowell was without any kind of natural female attribute ... When all of this work was complete, this horror that was Robert Cowell released himself on the world as 'Roberta'.[3]

According to *The People*, then, Roberta Cowell was neither a sexually functional man nor any kind of woman.

Yet Christine Jorgensen's case two years earlier had not been reported with anything like the same prurient disgust — perhaps because Jorgensen was a foreigner and therefore a curiosity, rather than some kind of threat. And the tabloids had published other 'sex change' stories — though as oddities at about pub-quiz level — without fuss or comment.[4]

One of the more interesting of these was the story of Ewan Forbes-Sempill. On 22 September 1952, *Time* magazine had reported on a paid advertisement in the *Aberdeen Press and Journal* announcing that 'Dr E. Forbes-Sempill, Brux Lodge, Alford, wishes to intimate that in future he will be known as Dr Ewan Forbes-Sempill. All legal formalities have been completed.' Born in 1912, Ewan Forbes-Sempill had been christened Elizabeth, the youngest child of a Scottish lord, but had identified as a boy from an early age. In 1952, he re-registered his birth and changed his name, became a medical general practitioner, and married. He lived quietly with his wife, avoiding any publicity, until 1965, when his elder brother died. As the next in line, Forbes stood to inherit the estate and title; his cousin John challenged this, arguing that the title could go only to someone assigned male and that Ewan Forbes's 1952 re-registration of his birth had been invalid. It took three years for a ruling at the Court of Session to recognise Ewan Forbes's right to the title. At the time, this case was not given much publicity — not only because it was held in a closed court, but also perhaps because certain very private affairs of the upper classes were not released to the tabloids. Some years later, however, the case of Ewan Forbes became a significant factor in April's own life.[5]

April's interview with *The People* in 1961 was the first time someone with an established public profile — and a beautiful model at that — had discussed transgender issues frankly. The story didn't make the front page — indeed, the first interview was on page 7 — but, in Ashley's understandably bitter memory, it might as well have done. Losing her career as a model was only part of her ordeal; over the next few months, she had to endure abusive phone calls and letters. People would shy away from her at parties. It seemed that her London life, as well as her livelihood, had collapsed overnight.

Loyal friends and colleagues rallied round but could do little to change things. Lord Timothy seems to have been too preoccupied with his own social life and business interests to support her, and perhaps he had troubles of his own. There was, however, one friend who did what he could to help: the Honourable Arthur Cameron Corbett.

April had been introduced to Arthur Corbett at the London restaurant Le Caprice in November 1960, not long after her modelling career began. Tall and thin, and in his early 40s, Arthur was handsome in a bony-faced way; in photographs, he looks rather like the 1950s English actor Michael Rennie. He was the eldest son and heir of Lord Rowallan, owner of Rowallan Castle in south-western Scotland.

Arthur Corbett's status as 'a peer's son' (as the tabloid newspapers

always referred to him) was relatively recent: his social position and
wealth had come from his grandfather. In 1885, Cameron Corbett,
then in his early 30s, had entered politics as the Liberal Member of
Parliament for Tradeston in central Glasgow. Two years later, he
married the exceedingly wealthy Alice Polson, aged 17, whose father,
John, had made a fortune from Brown & Polson's Original Patent
Cornflour. Cameron and Alice bought a 6,000-acre estate in Ayrshire,
including the crumbling castle of Rowallan, and decided to build
their own massive house nearby. Alice's death in 1902 almost caused
Cameron to abandon the project, but four years later he and his three
children moved into the new house: a Victorian Gothic pile he named,
rather grandiloquently, Rowallan Castle.

In 1911, Cameron Corbett, now a successful and influential
Liberal politician, was created Baron Rowallan of Rowallan in the
County of Ayr — a new hereditary title that entitled its bearer to a
seat in Parliament's upper chamber, the House of Lords. As the family's
coat of arms he chose a design featuring several crows, or corvids —
more than likely a reference to the family name.

Cameron's son Thomas inherited the family's money and property
on his father's death in 1933. In 1918, he had married Gwyn Grimond,
sister of Joseph Grimond, leader of the parliamentary Liberal Party
from 1956 to 1967. They had four sons and a daughter; Arthur was the
eldest son and Thomas's heir.

In his many photographs, Thomas Baron Rowallan looks less like an
intimidating parent than a nervy, bespectacled bank manager, but he was
a man of energy and ability. He became a prizewinning cattle breeder
— indeed, in the House of Lords, he seldom resisted the temptation
to speak at length about cattle infections — served in the Ayrshire
Yeomanry, raising a new battalion of the Royal Scots Fusiliers during
World War II, and became a governor of the National Bank of Scotland.

Thomas was a lifelong member of the Boy Scout movement,
eventually becoming Chief Scout of the British Commonwealth

and Empire. His youngest son, Bobby, took perennial pleasure in teasing him: 'Wouldn't read the *News of the World* this morning if I were you, Daddy — another naughty scoutmaster.' And, with great delight, Bobby Corbett let it be known that, when his father retired, his waxwork effigy at Madame Tussaud's was melted down to make way for a new Chief Scout. Bobby's teasing never let up. He became joint master of the Eglington Hunt in 1975 solely to annoy his father, who disapproved of blood sports. 'It gave him a new lease of life,' said Bobby. 'Fury is a great adrenalin.'*

Lord Rowallan with Princess Elizabeth during her review
of British Commonwealth Scouts, 1951

The pinnacle of the second Baron Rowallan's career was becoming governor of the Australian state of Tasmania in 1959. This role gave him the opportunity to deck himself out in florid uniforms, much like the character Sir Joseph Porter, KCB, in Gilbert and Sullivan's *HMS*

---

*   Bobby Corbett was a man whose keen wit, intelligence, and zest for life made him enormously
      successful socially. His obituary in *The Times*, 3 April 1999, is well worth reading and, fittingly,
      he is given its punchline: 'Asked recently in an interview in *Horse and Hound* whether he had
      children, he replied: "I doubt it." '

Pinafore. Lord Rowallan evidently enjoyed dressing up: photographs show him resplendent in various outfits for official occasions as Chief Scout, including an impressive number of kilts. He also evidently revelled in exerting the authority of the British Crown. His daughter, Fiona, later commented that he expected his own children to bow or curtsey to him. Thomas's public life left little room for any kind of domestic life, and Arthur's father was a distant parent. Fiona later said that he probably wanted to be more affectionate towards his children but did not know how.[6]

Conscious of the Corbett title's relative newness, Thomas adhered strongly to what he saw as aristocratic principles. In his 1976 autobiography, he said that his father, Cameron, had 'believed that men must look up to others for moral guidance [presumably to himself and possibly other aristocrats], a philosophy I have faithfully tried to follow.'[7]

Thomas Baron Rowallan's view of moral guidance was lavishly displayed in House of Lords debates about the bill that sought to decriminalise some acts of gay sex in the mid-1960s. 'I am not prepared to ... cause even one foot to stumble and be driven into homosexuality because we have not the decency to keep the country clean,' he declared:

> The acceptance of this Bill ... will inevitably lead to an increase of homosexuality ... There are certain types of homosexuals whose delight it is to seduce young heterosexuals and lead them down the garden path which, as we have been told, leads to nothing but frustration, sorrow and degradation.[8]

Thomas's immediate family lost no time in rebelling against him in as many ways as possible. Fiona, the anti-debutante, would abandon her long dress and gloves on the way to a formal ball, climb into jeans and boots, and go clubbing, resuming her formal clothes before she came home. Three of Arthur's brothers cheerfully embraced sex and drugs (and likely rock 'n' roll). And Thomas's wife had several affairs with men outside her marriage.[9]

Arthur Corbett, born in December 1919, was never allowed to forget that his destiny was to become the third Baron Rowallan. His own rebellion against his upbringing took another form, a clue to which may be seen in his wedding photograph. In 1945 he married Eleanor Boyle, the wealthy granddaughter of a Scottish nobleman: a tall and very attractive woman with masses of red hair, a long chin, and a sensuous mouth. In the photo, Arthur looks pleased — even relieved; Eleanor's expression is both sceptical and determined. Perhaps she knew more about her new husband than she was admitting at the time.

Arthur's defiance was particularly pointed, given his father's views on sexuality. From adolescence, he had worn women's clothing, and he was a well-known habitué of brothels where male prostitutes dressed him as a woman. Eleanor and Arthur managed to keep this a secret without too much trouble — one of the benefits, presumably, of being rich and aristocratic.

April and Arthur had been introduced in 1960 by Louise Lawrence, an American-born trans woman who had worked with sex researcher Alfred Kinsey. As well as being an advocate for transgender rights, Louise had built a strong and extensive network of gender-nonconforming people over many years. She had introduced Kinsey to cross-dressers, professional drag queens, and eventually trans women. It is unclear whether Lawrence was a friend of Arthur's or April's. However, if April hadn't known about Arthur's tastes before they met, she soon found out.

Arthur speedily became April's most reliable escort and her knight-errant: he even visited the editor of *The People* to try to persuade him not to print April's interview. April liked him for his obvious intelligence — he was a product of Eton and Balliol — and his kindness, and their relationship continued, on and off, for some time. Arthur even introduced April to his wife, Eleanor, and family.

Naturally, April was apprehensive about this, but Eleanor was cordial and even friendly, apparently not considering April a danger to her marriage or social position. In her autobiography, Ashley later wrote that Arthur and Eleanor seemed comfortable with each other, although she described Eleanor as 'overcontrolled', which might have been an understatement.

According to Ashley, Eleanor asked her to go on seeing Arthur 'if it stops him going off for the other thing'. Her wish for April to be assimilated into the Corbett family as a kind of distraction for Arthur suggests that she knew how besotted her husband was. April went along with this for a while, even spending some time with the Corbett children in Hampstead. By her account, they all got on famously — except for Arthur's son Johnny, who clearly disliked April.

As so often happens, this noble behaviour soon showed its limits. Arthur's infatuation with April grew with the passing of time and, after some months, he made a drastic decision: he left his home, wife and family, and moved into the Vanderbilt Hotel in South Kensington, not far from where April lived. April might have tried to dissuade him — it's easy to imagine that she felt guilty about Eleanor and the children — but Arthur was determined to seek a divorce, and his wealth and position might well have been irresistible to April.

And so, at the end of 1961, with April's modelling career at an end and her London life compromised, April Ashley and Arthur Corbett climbed into a white Zephyr convertible, together with Arthur's Great Dane puppy, and headed off to Marbella in southern Spain, where Arthur proposed to extend his business interests by running a club. Both, for different reasons, were eager for a new start.

CHAPTER 10

Bombshells

Life in Marbella was very pleasant. Indeed, Ashley described it as 'bliss – just what I seemed to need after the hectic years of my strange life'.[1] Arthur had a devoted Spanish maid who did all the cooking and housework, and April — true to her lifelong love of animals — doted on Mr Blue, the Great Dane pup. After *The People* episode and the miserable London weather, April revelled in the Spanish sunshine, the sea, and the mountains — and, above all, being cosseted, admired, and looked after.

But there were problems. Abject devotion was all very well, but Arthur's adoration soon became little short of claustrophobic. In all fairness, he had given up a great deal to be with her and only her, but it seemed to April that he became irrationally angry when she wanted time to herself or to meet other people.

Gradually, April's worries and misgivings about her life — *what would she do now?* — resurfaced. Now, not only was a London modelling career closed to her, but so was her long-cherished hope of a movie career. When *The Road to Hong Kong* was released in April 1962, she discovered to her chagrin that not only was she uncredited but also she hardly appeared. Blink and you would miss her: she didn't even get a close-up. Ashley later said that she was convinced the film-makers had deliberately cut her name from the credits because of the article in *The People*, but this may not be true: none of the women she shared a scene with was credited either. While the years have not been kind to *The Road to Hong Kong*, it was the fifth biggest film at the British box office that year — largely because of the enduring popularity of Bing Crosby and Bob Hope. April was hugely disappointed at missing out on its success.

She had to face the fact that modelling and film stardom were now out of her reach. She had little education and now no career. She had only her extraordinary good looks and her innate Scouse toughness — the resilience and ability to bounce back she had shown so often.

Apart from these qualities, the only constant in her life was Arthur's devotion. April accepted it gracefully, while knowing — as he did — that she was not in love with him. At least he was on course to inherit a title and considerable wealth, not to mention a castle in Scotland. Moreover, he was in the process of divorcing his wife. He had also declared that he wanted to marry her.

Pragmatism won over doubt: April told Arthur she would accept his offer of marriage. He was overjoyed, and they became engaged.

April's hard-headed decision was allied with another. After the sensational story in *The People*, various tabloids had offered to pay April if she would tell them her whole life story in full. The proposition was attractive. The news of April's engagement to Arthur would certainly become public knowledge very quickly, and now she would meet the press not as 'model girl April Ashley' but as the fiancée of an aristocrat. She was sure that the deference journalists usually gave to the upper classes could be counted on to insulate her from further unpleasant publicity.

What Arthur thought about all this has not been recorded, but April left Spain soon afterwards and returned to London. In a lime-coloured skirt that showed off her spectacular long legs, and resplendent in a glamorous turban and chunky jewellery, she invited tabloid journalists to the Dolphin Square flat on her birthday — 29 April 1962 — and offered them champagne. All were aware that this was not so much a press call as the opening of an auction for the tabloid rights to her story.

Patricia Clough, then a young journalist who worked for Reuters, attended. She later wrote:

> I remember April very much as in the photos, very glamorous – full of apparent self-confidence and purring an obviously very carefully prepared spiel. She was a simply terrific tabloid story, and a total one-off ... She was so attractive and well spoken, but definitely not a figure almost anyone would try to emulate.[2]

The *News of the World* was the highest bidder, first offering to pay April £3,000 for a six-part serialisation of her life. She asked for £15,000 and, in the end, they agreed on £10,000 — at a time when the average manual worker was paid less than £1,000 a year.

The tabloid press carried the news of April's engagement under headlines such as 'Peer's son loves a sex-change girl' and 'April: Yes, I want to wed Arthur'. (The headline on Patricia Clough's brief story, 'Once man, April's aim aristocracy', was particularly succinct.[3]) To promote its upcoming series, the *News of the World* carried on its front page a head-and-shoulders photograph of an unclothed April, showing the tops of well-developed breasts, with a headline proclaiming: 'April Ashley was a boy. Peer's son says I want to wed her when free.' Arthur's divorce from his wife, Eleanor, had not yet been finalised.

Quoting interviews with Arthur in Spain, the tabloids made much of his love for April and his hopes of making her the next Lady Rowallan. April's comments were more restrained: 'I want to marry Arthur. I'm aware of the difficulties we would have to face, and I want a long engagement.'[4] This was a precise summary of the situation. At no stage, then or thereafter, did Ashley declare — despite a *Daily Mirror* headline 'Sex-change girl talks of love' — that she was in love with Arthur Corbett.

The *News of the World* made an unexpected request. In accordance with their readership's family values, they wanted to interview and picture April with her mother. This was probably following the lead, several years earlier, of Christine Jorgensen, who had given a cosy and reassuring press interview with her parents. In April's case, the idea was presumably that Ada Jamieson would confirm how lovely it was that her daughter was marrying a peer.

This must have been an interesting situation for April. For the sake of the story, she had to agree — even though she'd had nothing to do with Ada for almost a decade. April's mother was now living with Bernie Cartmell in Manchester. We do not know whether she had kept up with her daughter's career — although Ada had more than likely read the exposé in *The People*. It would be fascinating to know how she felt about being asked to be part of the story and to have some insight into Ada Jamieson's mind when she was confronted by the impudent kid who was now the glamorous April Ashley. In her autobiographies, Ashley says little about this particular photo shoot.

According to the *News of the World*, the reunion of mother and daughter was the epitome of goodwill and familial love. This is not exactly borne out by the accompanying photograph: April, in a dashing broad-brimmed black hat, looks straight ahead into the camera, while Ada, in a fussy hat and glasses, and short enough to fit under April's arm, gazes up at her daughter adoringly. It is a thoroughly staged, and thoroughly unconvincing, picture.

MY STRANGE LIFE
By April Ashley
HER OWN AMAZING STORY STARTS TODAY ON PAGES 2 AND 3

April's accompanying interview glossed over the knottier parts of life in Norris Green:

One day my younger brother and sister came home from school looking sad and bewildered. When I questioned them, they admitted that other kids were saying things about me. So now the finger of scorn was pointing even more into my home, threatening to poison the lives of my mother, brothers and sisters, too. It was more than I could stand.[5]

Accordingly, April said, she had nobly left home to spare them further misery.

April insisted how happy she was to be reunited after eight years with Ada:

... the mother who last saw me when I was George Jamieson, deck hand in a British cargo ship. The mother, so dearly beloved, from whom I had deliberately kept apart all this time to spare her the agony of my gradual transformation from manhood to womanhood. The mother to whom at long last I was ready – even proud – to present myself anew as a daughter.[6]

Not to mention, of course, a daughter who had been a successful model and was now engaged to marry a peer of the realm.

Whatever might have been the *News of the World*'s intention, some of this incongruous nonsense reads as comical. An admiring Ada is reported as saying, 'You look so young and beautiful, so very beautiful.' However, at the same time, she persistently referred to her tall, dark-haired, and elegant daughter as 'George'. April apparently laughed this off, reminding her mother, 'Not George now, Mother. It's April, always April.' And, presumably at the behest of the *News of the World*, April took her mother to Asprey's jewellers to help her choose an engagement ring: rubies surrounded by diamonds.

'My strange life' is an odd serialisation. It loops backwards and forwards through April's life, and there is not much of a connected narrative. The journalist — not given a byline but later identified as Noyes Thomas, one of the *News of the World*'s most distinguished reporters, who had made his name as a foreign correspondent — manages to strike a tone that is both bland and overwritten, even when describing difficult issues. Here, for example, is April, providing emotive details of her early life:

> [I was] a youngster always walking alone. Subconsciously shunning yet coveting the rough-and-tumble games and friendship of my fellows. I was determined, at the time and for long after, to make a man of myself. I tried to excel at games. I broke the rules and bravely took my beatings. I made my three brothers teach me to box.[7]

In line with contemporary expectations, April duly describes her life in London as 'bizarre', saying she lived in 'the twilight world of the half-men and half-women'. She presents her time in Le Carrousel as exceedingly 'exotic' and vaguely mentions being toasted by celebrities with names unfamiliar to British readers. This was all of a piece with the staunch Britishness and indifference towards foreigners that were staples of the *News of the World*: on the front page of one issue in which April's story ran was a piece about an Italian accused of sexually assaulting two young English women, with the heading, 'Weren't used to his Italian ways'.[8]

The trip to Casablanca for the surgery, says April, was 'a flight into terror and abject loneliness ... away from all I had ever known as a man into a new, unknown world as a woman'. Dr Burou, she made clear, had not encouraged her to have the procedure and had made her aware of its dangers — but he had promised that what he did with his scalpel would give April 'all a normal woman's feelings and sensitivity, that in fact I would be able to enjoy being a girl'. The echoes of nudge-nudge titillation are never far away. But, importantly and rightly, Noyes Thomas emphasises April's courage and determination: she never regretted what she had done, she says, and never would. And she had only to think of the rewards:

> Soon afterwards I set out on a new and most feminine career that was to lead me into exciting new spheres. Photographers and national advertisers vied for my services as a model. I became a pinup girl. Top people wined and dined me. And no one ever suspected that I had once been a man.[9]

The well-crafted innuendo in this story suggests that the *News of the World*, and perhaps Fleet Street generally, didn't quite know what to make of April Ashley. The women who appeared in its pages were generally one of two archetypes: beautiful, quiescent models and actors or, after they married, homemakers. April's experience fitted comfortably into neither of these categories, but nor could she be ignored (not least because she had announced her engagement to an aristocrat). It is easy to sense the journalists' confusion when we read their interviews with April at this time: she was obviously a confident personality, someone to be reckoned with, and she had model looks. How much could the cosy, middle-England readers of *The People*, the *News of the World*, the *Daily Mail*, or the *Daily Express* understand about her life, and how much did they sympathise with her? How could she help them to identify with her? To some extent, April colluded with journalists in inviting readers to feel sorry for her because of her struggles, while also — sometimes — asking them to admire her beauty and chutzpah.

But staying in the shadows or portraying herself as some sort of domestic goddess was not April's style: she didn't wish to rely on Arthur and still needed to earn her own living. The Astor Club near Berkeley Square offered her the chance to renew her career as a cabaret artist: a one-week trial, with a five-week season to follow if the trial was successful. It was recognition of a kind — although not entirely desirable.

The show was tawdry. Ashley described coming down the stairs to the tune 'April Love' onto a stage covered in dry ice, on which a chorus line stretched their arms towards her. People flocked to see her and, feeling like some kind of circus sideshow, she decided not to complete her contract. When she told the management her opinion of the show, they pointed out that if she were to go on stage and simply say, 'Shit' — the explosive antithesis of polite language at the time — she would still attract audiences. And so, the following evening, she went on and did just that: 'Ladies and gentlemen,' she said, 'I hear from the management that even if I only said "Shit" you'd still come and see me. So ... *shit*!' — and she walked off the stage. Such a word pronounced in April's rounded aristocratic tones caused a sensation. However, her manager had booked her to appear in Manchester, Dudley, and Weston-super-Mare, and she had to honour her commitments. At one venue, she was billed as 'The Most Talked about Woman in the World'. She said she hated every minute, but at least she was paid.

April Ashley's love/hate relationship with publicity and earning money as a celebrity — sometimes as a curiosity — lasted throughout her life. But she was beginning to discover another role for herself. She began getting mail — thousands of letters, she said. Many were insulting and offensive. But some were written by people who, having read her interviews and knowing her story, felt she knew and understood how it felt to be tormented by one's sexuality or gender identity. She always replied to such letters, continuing to do so for the rest of her life.

In June, the press began to circulate stories that April was about to break off her engagement to Arthur Corbett — rumours that she confirmed at the end of July. April had decided that, even if she didn't want a renewed career as a cabaret artist, she didn't want to stay with Arthur either. She told the press that he had been 'upset' by her decision — still in Spain, he wasn't interviewed — and, when asked why she had decided to call it off after less than three months, she said, rather coyly, that she would rather not talk about it.

However, it is not difficult to work out what had happened. April had gone to Marbella several times to be with Arthur, and she had even managed to find an agent in Madrid, who offered to take her on as a model — no mean feat in strongly Catholic Franco-era Spain — but she was finding the insular bubble of expatriates and jet-setters increasingly claustrophobic and she frequently escaped to London. Arthur's possessive neediness was another factor: it exasperated April, and they quarrelled. April insisted on having some kind of life of her own, independently of Arthur — and he was furiously jealous of her male friends.

Prominent among these was Lord Timothy Willoughby, who came to London from time to time. It was impossible not to compare him with Arthur: here was a young, attractive, top-drawer aristocrat, with more money than the Rowallans could dream of — someone who was intelligent and stimulating and fun to be with. True, he had shown little sign of wanting to marry April, but she often said she put that down to his desire for an heir. (She must have realised that he wasn't really interested in marrying anybody.) Lord Timothy added a great deal of spice to her life, both in London and when she visited his place in Morocco, and she was not about to give that up.

April during her quest for modelling work in Madrid

In summer 1963, she accepted his invitation to spend a week with him in Tangier. It was not a great success. Lord Timothy, April thought, was depressed: he and his valet spent most of the time sitting around, listening to Moroccan pop music on the radio and smoking hashish, which made her feel sick. There were no visitors; they didn't go anywhere. For the first time, April was bored in his company. She did not extend her stay and arranged to see him later.

In August, Lord Timothy finished overseeing renovations to a private members' bar off Leicester Square that he co-owned — one that featured fur-lined walls and a tank of piranhas (another aspect of his life that could have been written by Evelyn Waugh) — and he decided to go to the south of France. In bad weather and against advice, he and a sailor friend decided to risk a 100-mile crossing of open sea from Cap Ferrat to Corsica in an open-cabined motorboat he had christened *Zero* after his lucky number on the roulette wheel. But Lord Timothy's luck ran out. The boat, with Lord Timothy and his friend, was never seen again. All that was found was a floating mattress.

It was a terrible, unexpected blow. For a while, April wondered whether Lord Timothy had arranged his own disappearance in order to vanish to Tahiti: he had repeatedly mentioned buying an island in the south Pacific, where he could conduct a wild sex life free from any interference. His distraught sister Jane hired an aeroplane and spent a great deal of time and money exploring the Mediterranean without success. He was eventually pronounced dead, although sightings of Lord Timothy — like Lord Lucan — were reported for some years. Lord Timothy's death meant that the main title, the earldom, became extinct.

And so the man April had perhaps come to consider her best means of entrée into the privileged lifestyle of the nobility — her ambition since her impoverished childhood in Liverpool — was gone, leaving her bereft. She would have to make do with Arthur.

CHAPTER 11

Spanish fantasy

When April first decided to flee London and make her home in Marbella with Arthur, the town was shedding its status as a typical Spanish village of whitewashed houses, orange trees, and fishing boats. It was becoming a resort for what was known as the 'international jet set', attracted by its climate and picturesque views as well as its accessibility to the rest of Europe. Wealthy foreigners built villas along the slopes of the low hills behind the town and bought up the small farms set back from the shoreline; the main street sprouted cafés, bars, and shops. Marbella was a strange little bubble of wealth and hedonism that had very little to do with the increasingly grim fascist dictatorship that was Spain under Franco.

Arthur's ambition in Marbella was to run a club for British expatriates with April by his side. His Jacaranda Club was part bar, part travel agency, and part real estate agency, and it even included a small subscription library. The English expatriates who frequented the Jacaranda were mostly retirees from the British civil service who had come to Spain to make their pensions go further. April found them mostly amusing: like the British who had stayed on in India after independence, they were, she thought, trying to maintain an imperial lifestyle that had long since disappeared elsewhere. There were also the women she dubbed the 'English widows', who came to the Jacaranda for cocktails and who, sometimes to their alarm, were chatted up by the local young Spanish men. Arthur and April both knew that her notoriety — Marbella residents tended to be avid readers of English newspapers — was excellent for business.

With Arthur at the Jacaranda Club, 1962

More to April's taste than the Jacaranda was the Marbella Club. This had been opened in 1954 as a not-particularly-humble hideaway for the rich and aristocratic friends of Prince Alfonso. The prince had demonstrated his talent for real estate development and resort management after much of his family wealth disappeared behind the Iron Curtain upon the fall of the Third Reich. His own financial problems had become less pressing after his scandalous 1955 marriage to 15-year-old Ira von Fürstenberg, heir to the Fiat fortune: as a devout Catholic more than twice her age, he had needed a papal dispensation. (Five years later, he applied for another one to divorce Ira, who had left him for another playboy, 'Baby' Pignatari.)

The Marbella Club attracted the titled rich, as well as deracinated members of European royal and noble houses with little but their money and former titles to recommend them. There were also the *miembros del jet set*: film stars and wealthy business executives, and occasionally the career expatriates the Duke and Duchess of Windsor. Some of the Marbella Club habitués were part of Arthur's social circle; he had known wealthy, titled, and influential people all his life, and took them for granted. April revelled in her burgeoning friendships with members of the upper classes, some of whom had questionable pasts.

Shortly after their arrival, April and Arthur moved into the Villa Antoinette, a house Arthur bought and that he promised to give to April in due course. At April's insistence, they kept separate rooms: she said she wanted to preserve her independence. This arrangement greatly impressed the staff they hired: for the local people, separate bedrooms indicated wealth and gentility. April was perhaps not surprised to realise that separate sleeping quarters suited Arthur too; he was, she said, strangely prim about his sexual relationship with her. 'You will never be my mistress, only my wife,' he told her, adding that when she was Lady Rowallan, they would sleep together, but not before. This, she came to realise, was part of his worship of her. As Ashley acidly observed, Arthur wanted her on a pedestal, not a bar stool.

When they moved to Marbella, April was 26 and Arthur was 42. At first, their daily life together ran smoothly. Arthur, having shaken off the shackles of his former life and living with the woman he loved and whose beauty he admired — the perfect trophy wife, he evidently thought — was happy. As was April, relieved to be with an aristocrat who was not only rich and influential but who also adored her and to whom she was grateful for his kindness and generosity, at least at first. But there had already been problems in their relationship, and because, for the first time, April and Arthur were together for extended periods, life in the Villa Antoinette soon became less than ideal.

Most of Ashley's recollections of her life with Arthur Corbett in Marbella — written many years later, when their story had taken several disastrous turns — are scarcely flattering to either of them. April's first problem with Arthur — a recurring one — was the appearance of 'she'. Liberated from the constraints of the life and expectations he had always known, Arthur felt confident enough to acknowledge the other, feminine, side of his nature. Ashley wrote that he never changed into women's clothing while they were together, but quite often for a short time he would adopt parodic 'feminine' characteristics: crossed legs, a cigarette held between his first two fingers, coquettish sidelong glances, pursed lips, a high voice. And when he was like this, Ashley wrote, he lashed out at her, calling her 'whore!' — which, understandably, led to hot words and recriminations. In print, Ashley never analysed the possible reasons for Arthur's behaviour, but he was clearly conflicted, troubled by self-loathing and misogyny. And perhaps he also wanted to show April that, however he fantasised about her, deep down he did not believe that she was a real woman — as later became clear.

Arthur was always remorseful after they quarrelled, and he would shower April with presents he chose himself. 'He used to give me little teeny tiny bits of jewellery,' she said. 'I told him, this is the sixties, it's chandelier earrings, big knockers on your hands. Why don't you save up for Christmas or my birthday and buy me something big?'[1]

Arthur's need for April to be with him all the time continued to make her feel thoroughly claustrophobic and, within a few months of their arrival, she was organising expeditions away from the Villa Antoinette. In April 1962, she and two women friends went to a house halfway up the nearby mountain for drinks with the actor Shirley MacLaine, who had recently appeared in *The Apartment* and would shortly star in *The Children's Hour*, a movie about a lesbian affair. April, who had no licence, was driving, and her passengers became alarmed by her independent approach to the rules of the road. She turned to reassure them and, at that moment, the car — a Morris Minor — shot over a cliff, landing with a sickening crunch on a narrow ledge about five metres down. Shaken, the three women successfully clambered out with nothing worse than a few cuts and bruises; they managed to find a phone and call the police, who were lenient, fining them the equivalent of six pounds. Ashley made light of this accident, but it could have been so much worse: this was the third time she had come close to dying. The accident made the London papers — another sign that April Ashley's life remained newsworthy back in Britain.

After the accident, Arthur's devotion to April — his need to look after her — became increasingly intense. April spent more and more time at the Marbella Club, and she quickly became one of its most frequent guests. She enjoyed holding court among the wealthy and titled, not to mention people from the entertainment world, who were discovering Spain as a cheap and convenient location for making movies.

They included the young stage and film actor Peter O'Toole. He was starring in David Lean's movie *Lawrence of Arabia*, in which Spain was standing in for various bits of Cairo. O'Toole was portraying the enigmatic T. E. Lawrence, the British Army officer who had played an important role in the British-backed Arab revolt against the Ottoman Empire during World War I. Standing six feet tall, he had seemed a less-than-obvious choice for the five-feet-five-inch Lawrence. (As critics have since noted, the movie skated over perennial questions about Lawrence's sexuality, although it acknowledged him to be a loner who forged his own myth and identity.)

The pressures involved in filming *Lawrence* were enormous: the movie took two years to film — in Jordan, as well as Spain — and involved 3,000 extras. Furthermore, O'Toole — on whom the entire enterprise depended — had what he described as a 'delicate Irish arse', by which he meant that he was unable to stay on a camel for more than a couple of minutes. He solved the problem by sitting on foam rubber cushions invisible to the cameras; many of the Arab extras thought this was a great idea and requested foam rubber for themselves.

Not surprisingly, O'Toole fled the set whenever possible in pursuit of the high life. He liked Marbella, though he described it as 'Pontefract with sunshine'. April had already met him in London, but in the Marbella Club she failed to recognise him at first: he had had his nose straightened and his hair dyed blond to emphasise his extraordinarily blue eyes. (According to Noël Coward, had O'Toole been any prettier, he would have been 'Florence of Arabia'.) But April quickly recognised his prodigious appetite for strong drink. According to his biographer, O'Toole could down three bottles of burgundy at a time, declaring that he would otherwise be unable to sleep at night.

He and April took to one another immediately, soon becoming each other's preferred drinking companion. O'Toole was enchanted by April's beauty and femininity, and she described him as '[o]ne of the most sensitive men I have ever met, devastatingly attractive and intelligent. Even playing the hell-raiser, he would open his mouth and speak with a command of the language Shakespeare would have admired.'[2] She was insistent, however, that, though they were very fond of each other, their relationship was not sexual; they shared a bed very occasionally, but only because, April said, O'Toole liked a cuddle as much as anybody. 'He talked about Sian [Phillips, his actor wife] all the time, how much he adored and worshipped her.'

Drink often made O'Toole emotional. On one occasion, April found him sobbing his heart out at the Marbella Club bar. When he could speak, he said, 'At least six people have come up to me in the past half-hour, telling me about your background. I really can't understand how people can be so cruel ...' April told him not to worry about it, but he refused to be consoled, and he threatened to punch anyone who looked sideways at her. She was forced to pull him aside more than once, but she was touched to have such a champion.

They were often joined at the bar by O'Toole's co-star Omar Sharif, playing his first major English-language film role as Lawrence's Arab supporter and friend: O'Toole always referred to Sharif as 'Cairo Fred'.[3] The three of them turned heads wherever they went together. April, with Sharif on one arm and O'Toole on the other, once made a spectacular entrance at the opening of a lavish new bodega. The Spanish royal family were the guests of honour, but the photographers were much more interested in April and her escorts.

Sharif's interest in April was certainly not platonic. More than once, they left O'Toole sleeping off the booze and went to Sharif's room. Ashley said later that Sharif lived up to all her expectations as a lover, and she hoped she lived up to some of his. She was surprised to discover that he had known nothing about her surgery: O'Toole hadn't bothered to mention it to him. When Ashley was asked how Sharif reacted when he found out, she was rather coy. 'He was a very gracious man,' she said.[4]

April, O'Toole, and Sharif went off on three- and four-night binges, drinking at a succession of local bars; Ashley said they would end up at a nightclub, dancing and boozing the night away. There were times when April and Sharif combined forces to look after O'Toole, who could become very aggressive if told to stop drinking. They would grab hold of his arms and take him back to his hotel, standing guard in case he tried to sneak back to the bar. April would sometimes climb into his bed with him just to be sure he wouldn't escape. The following morning, she and Sharif would be physical wrecks; O'Toole was always impressively calm and lucid. As Ashley later told his biographer:

> Even when he was drunk, he would know exactly what was going on. Even when he'd been out all night, he'd be on the set next morning, line perfect. I don't think for a minute there was any inner reason for his drinking like that. Certainly he wasn't unhappy ... I think he just loved to drink.[5]

April also welcomed her chum Sarah Churchill as an occasional visitor to Marbella; they spent time together in a villa Churchill rented close to the ocean. Churchill was happily in love with Lord Henry Audley, the man who became her third husband and who was staying nearby. Her first two marriages had been greeted with frosty disdain by her parents — particularly her father, Winston, who thought neither of his sons-in-law was good enough for his beloved second daughter — but he approved of Lord Henry. Sarah married Henry in Gibraltar in April 1962.

When April confided to Peter O'Toole that she wanted to follow in Churchill's footsteps and become an actor, he said: 'Don't, darling. Those bastards would never let you alone.'[6] April had seen that Sarah Churchill needed every bit of grit and talent she possessed to transcend her family background and to succeed in her chosen profession, and regretfully decided that O'Toole was right. But April also thought that Churchill sometimes lacked focus on her career. As a young girl, Sarah had trained as a ballet dancer — something that always came to the fore after a few drinks. Arthur changed the tabletops at the Jacaranda from wood to glass because of Sarah's tendency — and April's too — to dance on them.

Sarah Churchill and Arthur Corbett didn't really form a bond, despite both coming from aristocratic backgrounds and having overbearing fathers. Churchill knew about what April called Arthur's 'bad spells': especially after drinking, he accused April of making him unhappy enough to kill himself, and he would give her a copy of his will and his keys. April thought this behaviour was simply emotional blackmail and shrugged it off, but Churchill was unable to be so casual. She once found Arthur drunk and wandering along the road to Gibraltar, looking utterly miserable; she rescued him and returned him to April. When April greeted his reappearance with indifference, Churchill grew alarmed and angry with her friend, accusing her of being cruel and heartless. Ashley told this story in her autobiography matter-of-factly; this, she wrote, was just the way things were — and she was finding them, and him, increasingly tedious.

Arthur's jealousy was a huge problem for them both. Ashley wrote that she tried to understand the complexity of his feelings for her but his uncritical adoration — and his occasional corrosive anger — were too much. Like Eliza Doolittle, the part she had played on stage at Le Carrousel and the main character in Shaw's *Pygmalion*, if she couldn't have kindness, she needed independence. She found it impossible to meet the kind of trust and wish for control that Arthur demanded.

When Ashley was looking back at this part of her life, she wrote that she had come to realise that, although Arthur had the advantages of birth, education, influence, and wealth, her inner strength was greater than his. Perhaps Arthur knew this, because he continued to cling to her, and resented doing so.

April Ashley was still not used to being the person she had always longed to become. There were times, Ashley said, when she asked herself how a kid from her scrubby, often squalid background, without hope or money or prospects, had managed to move into a world where lineage, money, and privilege were taken for granted. She knew that it was because of her beauty: some who knew her felt that her excessive pride in her looks was her great weakness. Ashley knew some people thought so, but she wrote rather movingly that the great gift of her transformation was that she now felt beautiful for the first time. In that, her transformation was a continuing source of strength. And if she was unduly focused on the way she looked, well, that was surely a minor failing.

In her attempts to escape Arthur's grip, April was now encouraging the attentions of young men, mostly the upper-class patrons of the Marbella Club and their friends. But the more she tried to get away, the more tightly Arthur attempted to hold on to her. Their life together dwindled into accusation, counter-accusation, and hysteria. April was on the point of packing her bags and walking out more than once. But she could not do so without Arthur's money.

After less than two years and an on-again, off-again engagement, April's relationship with Arthur seemed to be going nowhere. The very thought of her leaving made Arthur increasingly panic-stricken: without his family, without April, who was he? April, too, was beginning to tire of her social round, even though she now had social position and relative financial security. Ashley wrote later that she had thought she might adopt children with Arthur but had realised that the occasional reappearance of his feminine alter ego made the idea impossible.

And then, after some months, during a dinner *à deux* at the Marbella Club, Arthur proposed a date for their wedding: 10 September 1963. April finally relented: she had no plans to go elsewhere and perhaps their relationship would benefit from some structure. Despite Arthur's clinginess, she did appreciate his support, and he could be thoughtful and kind.

Nevertheless, when the date of the marriage was announced, some of April's friends were appalled. She had told them often enough that she didn't love Arthur, and they thought she had agreed to the marriage solely for her own social advancement. This suggests quite a lot of sympathy for Arthur in Marbella and elsewhere. Nothing Ashley wrote or said satisfactorily explores her own reasons for going ahead with her wedding to Arthur Corbett, and it is easy to assume that the promise of being Lady Rowallan overcame any scruples she might have had. Ashley did claim to feel guilty about her responsibility for Arthur's leaving his wife and family, but there is little evidence of this — and, of course, his divorce was his decision, not hers. One of the striking things about Ashley's presentation of herself, both then and later, is her refusal to justify her actions — even when her behaviour left something to be desired. As far as she was concerned, people could say and believe what they liked.

Lord Rowallan's response to his son's impending marriage to April was swift. He was ill, receiving treatment for cancer of the palate, but he contacted Arthur from his hospital bed, pleading with him to change his mind. When Arthur refused, his father angrily promised to cut him out of the succession and to cancel his inheritance, putting Arthur's son, Johnny, in his place. He was as good as his word. As Arthur's sister, Fiona, said later, '[Arthur] never really was in the family after that.'[7] This was a blow, and the only cheerful note from the Rowallans was provided by Bobby Corbett — he had been a pageboy at Arthur's wedding to Eleanor — who sent a telegram, asking: 'Can I be bridesmaid?' (Bobby's previous reaction to Arthur's choice of bride had been: 'A snip here, a snip there, and Bob's your auntie.')[8]

Arthur continued to protest that he loved April quite enough for them both, and he asserted that they would manage somehow: he did have some money of his own. But April, who had told Arthur she did not love him, had ceased to believe in him. 'He would say to me, "You're going to be the most beautiful Lady Rowallan that ever was," and I'd say, "Yes, but where's the castle? What's the point?"' And yet, even though Arthur would no longer have the Rowallan estate or the castle, April decided to go through with the wedding, perhaps in the hope that Lord Rowallan might change his mind.

Arthur had decided that they would be married in Gibraltar, the British territory closest to Marbella. On the day of the wedding, which had been brought forward 24 hours, they duly travelled there by car: April in a skirt and jacket, and a wide-brimmed black hat; Arthur, beaming, in a dark suit and tie. A large crowd greeted them on their arrival, complete with camera flashbulbs: word of the impending wedding had spread quickly. But the registrar who was to marry them had no sense of occasion and had gone to lunch, so April and her three witnesses drank whisky until he returned. April, who had been drinking steadily to the point of anaesthesia, said she remembered very little about that day. After signing the registry, they were driven back to Marbella, April waving a white glove on their departure — a patrician gesture befitting the newly minted Honourable Mrs Arthur Corbett.

CHAPTER 12

La dolce vita matrimoniale

April's agreement to marry Arthur Corbett had come with a set of conditions. If he failed to understand or refused to comply with them, she told him, the marriage was off.

She would not live with him in Marbella, a place she now regarded as a glass coffin. She was tired of being notorious in a small town, with gossip about her fuelled by the stories in the *News of the World* and other English papers. Instead, she would base herself in London and travel to Spain from time to time. As Arthur had no desire to return to England to live, he would have to come over and visit her if he wanted to see her more often.

She proposed to adopt children in Arthur's name. Ashley never gave details about how this would have worked. Given how much she disliked Arthur's indulgence of his feminine alter ego, and her wish not to expose any of their adopted children to it, she probably intended to look after them in London, supported by Arthur — who, after all, already had four children of his own. She asked him to give her an allowance of £2,000 a year.

The last thing she asked — which sounds trivial, but certainly wasn't in April's eyes — was that Arthur should get himself a new set of false teeth, because those he had were old and discoloured, and he had a maddening habit of sucking on them to keep them in.

So besotted was Arthur with April, so desperate not to lose her, that he agreed to everything.

Not long after the wedding ceremony, April flew to London. Almost immediately, she found an attractive apartment in Cheyne Walk, overlooking the Thames, in her beloved Chelsea. Arthur did not quibble about the rent for this: he had decided that, though he wanted to remain in Marbella, he didn't wish to continue running the Jacaranda Club, and a developer had given him a handsome price for selling it, so he had some spare cash. After several weeks, Arthur did come to London for a short time, and he and April belatedly exchanged wedding presents: an oyster mink coat for her; gold cufflinks set with pearls for him.

These gifts aside, the reunion was dismal. Arthur was now ready to go to bed with his new wife, but April rejected him when they returned to Marbella, saying that she was suffering from vaginal abscesses. She and Arthur slept apart — she at the villa; he at the club — for the next three or four nights. April then left for London again. Despite agreeing with Peter O'Toole's advice, she had not quite given up the idea of acting, and she had arranged to have drama lessons before applying to an acting school. Arthur joined her in the flat and stayed with her for a week. He and April later gave conflicting accounts of their sexual relationship. Arthur said that April continued to complain about abscesses; according to April, they had cleared up and she and Arthur often slept in the same bed. April says that when they attempted to have sex, Arthur was unable to play his role and burst into tears.[1]

Arthur sadly went back to Marbella, leaving April in sole occupation of her apartment. She soon moved from there to another in Lennox Gardens, one of Knightsbridge's most exclusive addresses. With continued access to Arthur's money, April developed the habit of telephoning Le Caprice in fashionable St James's — her favourite restaurant, and the place where she and Arthur had met — after they had closed, asking them to send two dozen oysters in a taxi. She knew this indulgence was likely to be temporary and that she would soon have to develop less expensive tastes, as well as find a cheaper place to live — but she enjoyed it while it lasted.

In December, April reluctantly returned to Spain, to discover that Arthur was miserable — and for good reason: with no club to run and no work to do, cut out of the family and without April, he was drinking and smoking more than ever. He and April resumed their bickering, and Arthur once more adopted his feminine persona. For April, that was the last straw: she instructed the maid to pack her bags and called a cab to the airport. This time, she decided, she wasn't coming back — not even for a visit.

Back in Lennox Gardens, April decided that their marriage was never going to work. She would have to leave Arthur — and, to her far deeper regret, Mr Blue, the Great Dane:

Dear Arthur,

A letter from me. A none too happy one I'm afraid. I have thought and thought, not slept for days. But from all the pain and torture on my mind I see only one thing very very clear. That is I will not ever be coming back to you. I don't know what I will do. I don't know how I will live. But I know I won't be back.

The last three years have been the longest, the unhappiest, the most horrible of my short twenty eight years. In those three years I have known you!!!! So you must understand that although I don't put all the blame on you, you do seem to have been a terrible jinks [*sic*] on me.

I am paying dearly for my sin of marrying you. The worry and anguish I have felt in the past three years is making me ill. So the only thing I can do is to try to cut you out of my life completely. Then all I have are my earthly problems. A job, a less expensive place to live. Arthur don't think I expect any money from you I don't. Because I know I should never have married you. But I do hope you will either let the house or pay whatever rent you think. At least that.

It's so funny but I feel so much more (although I never really did) secure before I married you than I did after. Then you denying what you had so promised made me feel so sick to the stomach. I could never have stood myself, let alone you afterwards. Then I seem to remember you trying to convince me of other lies of yours in the past. I don't want to sound bitter, but I suppose I am a little. At the moment my life seems a wreck all over again. I hope this time I have a little more strength.

Arthur as I am quite a nice person I will say, and do nothing about getting an annulment until you let me know. I can respect that you would not like to hurt your family any more with cheap publicity in that I hope should I ever want my freedom you will respect my wishes.

I hope you sell your land. In brief Arthur I hope you will find happiness. Although my heart is breaking I think you had better have Mr Blue. Give my kindest thoughts to Rogelia, Pepe and Jose Luis.

God bless you
April

Arthur made no comment about April's assumption that he had signed the Villa Antoinette over to her nor did he attempt to defend himself against her accusation that he had reneged on the promises he had made. His only response to this ruthless letter was to tell April not to be silly and to return to Spain as his wife – which showed, Ashley later commented, that he understood little about himself and nothing about her.

Ashley was not particularly given to introspection, either in what she wrote or the life she lived. She had failed to get into a drama school and, to make matters worse, her jewellery was stolen soon after she moved into Lennox Gardens. These were setbacks underlining that her ambitions — first, to embrace masculinity in the merchant navy; then, to become famous as a cabaret artist and model; next, to make a career in films; most recently, to have a successful, wealthy, and triumphant marriage — had all collapsed. Now, she had to take stock of her life.

Ashley sometimes described herself as a romantic, as well as a natural optimist. But, as a tough Liverpudlian, she had always had to walk alone. This had its contradictions, perhaps — her entire career to date had depended on attracting the admiration and approval of other people — but, as she always insisted, she was used to being thrown back on her own resources, she liked her own company, and she was hardly ever lonely. Nor, it must be said, was she prone to self-pity: now, as always, April's valiant spirit prevailed.

She found a cheaper place to live. This was a flat close to the King's Road, Chelsea, and she shared it with a friend, Cecilia Johnson. Cecilia was a well-known party girl; according to the *Daily Mail*, her main occupations were 'modelling, filming ... being a croupier and getting up for lunch'.[2] The two women promptly embarked on a hectic social life, including regular visits to the newly formed Ad Lib Club near Leicester Square, which catered to the pop music crowd. 'That was the nightclub where the good music played, mainly Black American,' said one of its regulars, Paul McCartney, of a time just before the Beatles' 'British invasion' tour of the United States in August 1964, when he was not quite the adored pop star he was to become. 'It was a shouty, lively scene. Lots of silly things happened there.' Once, somebody bet Cecilia that she wouldn't have the nerve to ask Freddie Garrity, vocalist of the group Freddie and the Dreamers, for a dance. She won the bet and collected the prize: a greyhound.

Paul McCartney remembered seeing April at the Ad Lib Club quite frequently. Although they were, of course, both Liverpudlians, this seems to have been the first time they had actually met:

She was definitely a sort of woman, but we all knew from the newspapers that she was a man. I'd sit and talk to her, and I guess people could tell that it wasn't worth pulling me. I think you've got to give off scents, and respond correctly to certain things, whereas with me it was just flirting. She used to flirt and I'd be flirted with, quite happily. But when it got to, 'Do you want to come and feed the ducks in St James's Park?' I'd say, 'No, I'll give that a miss.'[3]

'People were often rude,' said Ashley years later, singling out John Lennon:

He would say [adopting a Liverpool accent], 'Here comes the f***ing duchess.' I became quite good friends with him in the end. With all the Beatles. Years later George Harrison burst into tears when we met because he felt guilty about how rude they had been to me. I said, 'George, darling, it didn't matter. I took it to be a bit of fun.'

Of course, I was terribly arrogant as well. I happened to have this haughty approach to life and it intimidated people, even the Beatles.[4]

In an interview for *Playboy* magazine, Ringo Starr commented, 'She swears at me, you know. But when she sobers up, she apologises.'[5]

April made further attempts to get modelling work but without success, and then applied for jobs as an assistant in posh London department stores. Harrods, Fortnum & Mason, and Harvey Nichols all turned her down. Ashley assumed this was because she was so well known to the tabloid press.

Thanks to Sarah Churchill, she eventually found a temporary job under an assumed name as an assistant stage manager at the Ashcroft, a small but prestigious professional theatre in the London suburb of Croydon, which had opened in 1962 and was named for the well-known actor Peggy Ashcroft. April started working there in 1964, during the run of a play starring Sarah Churchill and David Hemmings, a former child actor and boy soprano who had taken small parts in British films.* This was a couple of years before he hit the big time playing a mod photographer in Michelangelo Antonioni's film *Blowup*.

Sarah Churchill's parents came to the last matinee of the season and April, whose politics were generally conservative and who had always revered Sir Winston, was overwhelmed when she finally met him. The photograph taken on this occasion shows the much taller April bending over Sir Winston with a reverent expression on her face, while he looks rather puzzled. Sir Winston was no passive member of the theatre audience. Every time his daughter left the stage, there was a deep rumble from the front row of the stalls: 'Where's she gone? What's she up to now?' And if a quip or comedy scene pleased him, he would say — at the same volume he adopted for his wartime speeches — 'That was a jolly amusing bit, yes, very good.' It got to the point, Ashley said, where the rest of the audience waited for him to comment. (Churchill was notorious for this sort of thing: once, Richard Burton, playing the lead role in *Hamlet* at the Old Vic, was thoroughly put off when he realised that Churchill in the front row was saying Hamlet's soliloquies along with him.)

The highlight of April's theatrical career: greeting Winston Churchill, with David Hemmings on Churchill's left

---

* David Hemmings created the role of the boy Miles in Benjamin Britten's chamber opera *The Turn of the Screw*. But his operatic career had ceased as soon as his voice broke, and Britten took no further notice of him.

The Ashcroft job lasted only a few weeks, and April was soon at a loose end again. When she was invited to stay with friends in Italy, she accepted with alacrity. In Rome, she renewed her acquaintance with the painter Francis Bacon, who had been a friend of Lord Tim Willoughby's; she had never liked him much, describing him as sullen, with dirty curly hair, and his work did nothing for her. But she travelled around, enjoyed the high life in Naples, and later boasted of a brief affair with a gigolo. Italy, with its freewheeling casualness, suited April, and she also thought she might find work there.

Sea bathing in Italy, 1964

Clearly, the fashion industry was booming, and so was the film industry. This was the time when Italian films and their directors — Rossellini, Fellini, and De Sica — were internationally acclaimed, and actors such as Sophia Loren and Marcello Mastroianni were known to audiences around the world. *Time* magazine had already nicknamed Rome 'Hollywood on the Tiber'. Here, April thought, was her best chance of getting into the movies.

With some English friends, she went to the studios at Cinecittà, where the celebrated director Federico Fellini was casting *Juliet of the Spirits*. Ashley later wrote that as soon as he saw her, he announced that she had to be in his film. Nothing came of that — but, at about the same time, she met the Italian actor Monica Vitti, then at the height of her career as a star in the films of Michelangelo Antonioni. Vitti said she wanted to check April out for a part in one of her movies — this one set in outer space — and organised for April to be taken in a limousine to a Renaissance palazzo in the country outside Rome. When April arrived, Vitti greeted her and made April stand still while Vitti walked around her. Vitti then nodded curtly and said goodbye; at no point during the visit, Ashley said, did Vitti mention the movie role. Ashley was pretty sure that Vitti had wanted only to satisfy her curiosity about April's transition: to see whether April looked better than Vitti herself.

April decided that the British expatriates in Rome were generally more sophisticated than those in Marbella — although many were also there for the sunshine and the lower cost of living. Even wealthy businessmen whom she thought should have known better had no scruples in asking her personal questions, including details of her gender-affirming surgery. She realised that people were expecting her to have large hands, a prominent Adam's apple, a deep voice, and silicone breasts. Ashley had endured this kind of behaviour before: trans people, she later observed, probably went through this kind of intrusive observation several times a week.

Nevertheless, April decided to stay in Italy for a while. She found an apartment owned by friends, who rented it to her while they were out of Rome. Not long after she moved in, Sarah Churchill — who had finished her stint at the Ashcroft and was similarly at a loose end — turned up. She suggested that she and April should live together, but April refused: although she was fond of Sarah, she knew that two big personalities with large and fragile egos were bound to clash. Churchill took the refusal in good part. She was still drinking prodigiously — probably even more than April herself — and she went on late-night binges to the Hilton hotel, a long way from where she was staying. Churchill sometimes asked April to bring her a change of day clothes after she had ruined her evening dress, and April, the stalwart friend, always came to the rescue. They renewed their friendship over breakfasts of Bloody Marys, followed by saunas.

Thanks to some English friends, in Rome, April met Captain Lenny Plugge. A charming, wealthy man in his 70s, whose social set included Princess Margaret, her husband Anthony Armstrong-Jones, and the broadcaster Julian Pettifer, Plugge had had an extraordinary career as an engineer, a soldier, and an inventor. (He was credited with inventing the two-way car radio telephone.) In the early 1930s, wishing to break the British Broadcasting Corporation's radio broadcasting monopoly, he had started broadcasting in English from a makeshift transmitter on the northern coast of France. Within two years, the station, known as Radio Normandy, sometimes had a larger audience than the BBC, especially on Sundays.

Plugge's star was on the rise. He married, became the Conservative Member of Parliament for Chatham in Kent, and bought a luxury motor yacht. He was a skilled entrepreneur: the verb 'to plug', meaning to increase advertising for something, is said to be derived from his name. But his expertise in radio and knowledge of French were ignored during World War II, he was defeated in the Labour landslide of 1945, and his luxury yacht sank. His business affairs fell into disorder and his marriage failed. By the time he met April, he still had some money, however, which he used for moving around Europe and lavishly entertaining those in his social set.

Plugge and April became fast friends. When they were both in London one night, he took her to a performance of the Bolshoi Ballet at Covent Garden. At the end, when the curtain calls began, he pulled flowers out of a carrier bag and started throwing them at the stage. It was a charming gesture, except that the flowers, which came from his garden, still had clods of earth attached. As the ballerinas flinched and dodged, Plugge explained to April that he found a little weight made the flowers easier to throw and increased their velocity. April always enjoyed her time with Plugge, not least because of his eccentricities; one of the themes of her later interviews was the lament that true English eccentrics were a dying breed.

The relative harmony of April's life in Rome was thoroughly disrupted early in October 1964. 'Model April is arrested' was the headline in *The Daily Telegraph*, echoed in English tabloids. As Ashley told the story later, she had been in a car with two English friends when the driver negotiated a roundabout and sped into the Via Veneto. They were stopped by police, and April got out of the car. She had walked a short distance when a policeman grabbed her by the arm and swung her round. She slapped his face and he accused her of being drunk — which she probably was. According to the tabloids, she used 'insulting language and swore like a drunken sailor in a deep male voice'. Although the English tabloids were generally respectful towards April, when she didn't behave well they were quick to remind readers of her history. She was promptly charged with abusing a policeman.

After she refused to back off, the police decided to send her to prison. The question was, to which section? One of the policemen, who had recognised her and knew her story, said that she should be with the men, but the state medical board ruled that she should be taken to the women's section, which was run by nuns (a fact that sent shudders down her spine because of her experiences at St Teresa of Lisieux primary school). Because April was on remand awaiting sentencing, she was not required to put on the uniform of women prisoners, so she continued to wear her sleeveless gold lamé dress and mink stole. She had been picked up close to the Via Veneto and the other women assumed she was a sex worker, which did not improve her temper.

Ashley hated her five days in prison. The food was appalling, and some of her fellow inmates, who were mostly sex workers and petty thieves, had been waiting months to go to trial. However, the authorities wasted no time in sending her before a magistrate. She was told to expect the worst: she was a visitor to Rome, and the police were unlikely to be found guilty at the hands of a foreigner. And so it proved: the magistrate ruled that April could either leave Italy within three days and not return for five years, or she could pay a massive fine and go to prison. April decided there was little point in arguing. She left Rome for London shortly afterwards.

Throughout the 1960s, April's life remained of great interest to the English tabloids. Almost every article of any length commented favourably on her clothes, makeup, and general appearance. In short, April Ashley had become a personality — even a celebrity.

Her publicity, as we have seen, was certainly not always favourable — but other transgender people had a much rougher time. Journalists lost few opportunities to portray them as outcasts, in prose that was at best disapproving and at worst salacious, especially if they were trans women.[6] One story concerned Kim, a 25-year-old trans woman who, in 1962, declared that she would never marry because she would not 'deceive' a boy into thinking she could have children, and that she wanted to be a 'career girl'. However, she appeared in the press a few months later under an accusing headline: 'Just how low can you get? Sex-change Kim is a stripper.'

Kim was appearing at the White Monkey club in Soho, several rungs down the social ladder, and declared that she wasn't at all ashamed about taking her clothes off, because she was proud of her body and knew that men admired it. The club manager, who called himself Johnny de Maine, added, 'This will be the greatest thing the strip clubs ever saw, just the thing to bring in the crowds. And don't get the wrong idea. Kim's act is artistic. There is nothing smutty about it.'

After a couple of years, Kim married. 'At last I'm a wife,' she said. 'I've longed for this ever since I became a girl.' Kim, defiant to the last, was usually presented in the press as misguided, or even pathetic.[7]

There was also the case of the woman known as Barbara or Robin Ashton Rose. She passed herself off as Countess Rowena de Silva of Greece — a signal for the tabloid journalists to start digging, which they did with alacrity. *The People* journalist Patrick Kent declared Ashton Rose to be 'The Vilest Creature in Town', who was 'running a monstrous establishment of depravity', and the paper declared that the person who now said she was Lady Barbara Ashton had, under her original identity, been convicted of 'masquerading as a female prostitute' and fined almost £400. *The People* was outraged at the deception — especially as Ashton had continued with this 'vile trade' after her surgery. Exactly what constituted Ashton's depravity was not spelled out, although *The People* dropped dark hints that she undertook 'the most perverted sex practices'.

In the theatre, trans issues were generally treated as comic adjuncts to the old farcical tropes of disguise and mistaken identity. Well publicised at this time was John Osborne's *The World of Paul Slickey*, a 1959 musical in which a young man and woman decide to resolve a marital impasse by undergoing dual operations to swap genders. *Aunt Edwina* by William Douglas-Home was a 1959 farce in which a family tried to convince visitors that a father was really a long-lost woman relative. Neither of these pieces was conspicuously successful and their 'jokes' fell decidedly flat. *The Stage* magazine commented, tersely: 'If you must try to get fun out of these rare surgical phenomena, you must give some convincing explanation at the start.' But 1959 was also the year of the movie *Some Like It Hot,* starring Jack Lemmon, Tony Curtis, and Marilyn Monroe, and written and directed by Billy Wilder. This story — of two struggling musicians (Lemmon and Curtis) who, on the run from gangsters, disguise themselves as women and join an all-girl band — was considered risqué by the US National League of Decency. However, the sheer brilliance of the movie, including the great comic double act of Lemmon and Curtis, overcame all criticism. And the movie is still celebrated for its last line: 'Nobody's perfect!' delivered by a lovestruck Joe E. Brown after Jack Lemmon, dressed as a woman, takes off his wig and announces that they cannot marry because he is a man.

A ground-breaking novel was *I Want What I Want* by Geoff Brown, published in the United Kingdom by Weidenfeld & Nicolson in 1966 and subsequently in the United States. It is the first-person story of young Roy Clark, who thinks of himself as Wendy Ross and is determined to live as a woman. Young Roy, shunned and misunderstood by his family, is committed to a mental hospital for stealing frilly knickers from a neighbour's washing line. He insists he is not gay but is forced to undergo brutal treatment. Although unable to have the surgery he longs for, he inherits £500, which he uses to embark on life as a woman in 1960s England. This becomes complicated when a handsome man named Frank enters the picture.

The book's reviews — in *Punch*, *The Sunday Times*, the *New Statesman* and the *Saturday Review* — were highly admiring. The

Sunday Times critic praised the novel for typifying 'the problem of all who feel themselves irrevocably alienated from their ideal selves':

> Mr Brown writes extremely well, and describes the most intimate details of this case history without in any way giving offence ... it is done with a coolness and honesty that is admirable ... [T]o remain as objective as he does while writing such a story is quite an accomplishment.[8]

I Want What I Want was subsequently made into a movie of the same name starring Anne Heywood, and it is still occasionally seen on late-night television.

A year later came *Christine Jorgensen: A Personal Autobiography*. It was the story of Jorgensen's life, from her beginnings to her transformation and her subsequent career as a celebrity. Straightforwardly written, although clumsily expressed in places, it was praised for its poignancy and sincerity, and it sold well — particularly in the United States.

But undoubtedly the best publicised and most notorious examination of transgender issues at the time was Gore Vidal's 1968 novel *Myra Breckinridge*, made two years later into an exuberant, chaotic movie starring Raquel Welch, the sex bomb of the era. In his memoir, *Palimpsest*, Vidal described the novel — a flamboyantly camp satire set in the Hollywood of the 1960s, and the first in which the main character undergoes gender-affirming surgery — as his favourite. Vidal's view, explored in several ways that were considered scandalously pornographic at the time, was that gender roles and sexual orientation were simply conventions that most people recognised, and that they were both fluid and changeable. *Myra Breckinridge* takes aim at many targets — feminism, American machismo, sexual practices considered deviant, patriarchy — and it's more than somewhat hit-and-miss. But its assault on gender and sexuality as social constructs made the novel a worldwide bestseller and, in some circles, it is still considered a classic. It would be interesting to know what April thought of *Myra Breckenridge*, as well as the other works mentioned here.

CHAPTER 13

Youthquake

When April returned to London in 1964, she was met at the airport by the journalist Noyes Thomas, author of the six-part profile published in the *News of the World* the previous year. She quickly brought him up to date with the details of her prison experience and expulsion from Rome. Thomas, who owed his first name to his uncle, the poet Alfred Noyes, was no mere Fleet Street hack; for many years, he had been a well-known foreign correspondent, and he later became political editor of the *News of the World*. For all her protestations of annoyance with the British press, Ashley, in common with most celebrities, had learned to cultivate a journalist who could be trusted to tell her story in the terms she chose. The press reports of April's adventures in Italy had been 'news in brief' items or simple cable reports; now, she had the opportunity to tell her story in detail. Thomas's treatment of Ashley's life story was published in the English paper, with a circulation of eight million and a readership estimated to be half the country's population. If favourable press attention was the oxygen April Ashley breathed, Noyes Thomas provided a superior supply.

Although April was unsure what her life would now be, she was happily surprised by London's generally upbeat feeling and energy. 'I never really knew what the [youth] revolution was all about,' Ashley said later, 'but the vitality was fun.'[1] Thanks to the British economic boom, in a few short years London had become the playground of the young people born just after the war and who had money to spend. The epicentre was Chelsea, and April felt she was seeing it for the first time. Gone were the small, grimy grocers' shops and ironmongers and haberdashers, replaced by fashionable hairdressers and dress shops selling psychedelic clothes and exaggerated platform shoes, with a whole raft of new names above their doors, Mary Quant and Vidal Sassoon among them. And in the streets were girls in miniskirts with flirty bobs and spidery lashes.

The idle rich remained, of course, but there were probably fewer of them: more often, now, young aristocrats were entering the working world, as photographers or designers or managers of pop groups. Class structures were breaking down. Those who remained true to their roots, such as the Beatles, had fun mocking this. At a Royal Variety Performance in November 1963, John Lennon famously said to the audience: 'For our last number I'd like to ask for your help. The people in the cheaper seats, clap your hands. And the rest of you, if you'd just rattle your jewellery.' This was Swinging London, and it was evidently the place to be — and this was true for April, too. Her notoriety seems to have faded to some extent: she managed to get a modelling gig for the fashionable hairdressing salon Claude. She was still April Ashley, after all: she rarely used the name 'Mrs Corbett', let alone broadcast the fact that she was married (still) to the Honourable Arthur Corbett.

The Labour government, coming to office under Harold Wilson in 1964, would shortly take advantage of the post-war energy and affluence to enact some liberal laws. In the next few years, divorce laws were relaxed, capital punishment was abolished, and censorship of the theatre became a thing of the past. These things were hard-won, as was the most important sexually liberating measure that — surprisingly, perhaps — Ashley does not mention in her autobiographies: the passing of the Sexual Offences Act 1967.

The 1950s had seen an increase in the numbers of men in England and Wales prosecuted and imprisoned for gay sex acts. There had been several significant trials, including that of Lord Montagu of Beaulieu. As a result, in 1954, the Conservative government had set up a committee to consider whether the existing law condemning 'gross indecency' — in place since 1885 — should be changed. Its report, named after the committee's chair, Sir John Wolfenden, was published in September 1957.[2] All but one of the 13 committee members recommended that private acts between consenting men over the age of 21, who were not members of the armed forces or the merchant navy, should be decriminalised.

The committee's thinking was not based on compassion, although the report included some heart-rending and sympathetically reported case histories (such as the story of Peter Wildeblood, Lord Montagu's co-defendant), but on the principles of civil liberties. The Wolfenden Report argued that the law had no business with questions of private morality and sexual behaviour. The law's function was to:

> ... preserve public order and decency, to protect the citizen from what is offensive or injurious, and to provide sufficient safeguards against exploitation and corruption of others, particularly those who are specially vulnerable ...
>
> It is not, in our view, the function of the law to intervene in the private life of citizens, or to seek to enforce any particular pattern of behaviour further than is necessary to carry out the purposes we have outlined.[3]

The government of the day decided not to act on the Report's recommendations for fear of a public backlash. The debates in Parliament had been heated, and the same was true when the issue was raised again in the mid-1960s. This time, more Members of Parliament were strikingly in favour of a change to the law. There were, however, strenuous objections, especially in the House of Lords. Two notable peers who spoke against the changes were Arthur Corbett's father, Lord Rowallan, and World War II hero Viscount Montgomery of Alamein. The latter called the proposed new law a 'charter for buggery', declaring: 'This sort of thing may be tolerated by the French but we are British — thank God.'* He was, of course, rabidly seconded by Lord Rowallan, now permanently estranged from his cross-dressing, male-brothel-frequenting son and heir. After a great deal of discussion, the matter was put to a conscience vote and the Sexual Offences Act was passed. (Lord Rowallan's attempt to vote against it in the House of Lords was stymied when his train from Scotland was delayed by bad weather — a source of great delight to his son Bobby.) But this did not mean that most Members of Parliament who voted in its favour were supportive of gay men — far from it. Chancellor of the Exchequer Roy Jenkins spoke for many of his colleagues when he argued that 'those who suffer from this disability carry a great weight of shame all their lives' and that this should not be increased by the legal system.

On behalf of many of her friends, April must have welcomed this legislation. However, in some respects, the 1960s — refreshingly hedonistic as they might have been for her — were not really her time. She had flourished and learned her craft as a model in an era of carefully curated glamour, but many of the people around her — models Penelope Tree and Twiggy, musicians, up-and-coming photographers such as David Bailey and Helmut Newton — dressed like overgrown children in play clothes. Their style was coltish and gawky, and they had little apparent interest in the kind of studied attractiveness and charm April had spent so much money, time, and effort cultivating. The

---

*   The irony is that rumours about Viscount Montgomery's own sexuality have swirled around him ever since, with at least one biographer drawing attention to them. See theguardian.com/uk/2001/feb/26/books.booksnews.

celebration of youth for its own sake, as seen in newspapers, magazines, music, and fashion, could hardly appeal to someone whose own youth had been so difficult and traumatic. Besides, she had needed to change the way she spoke in order to succeed, and it must have been galling that middle-class celebrities such as Mick Jagger and Paul McCartney were now allowed to affect Cockney speech or admired for keeping their own Liverpudlian accent.

So, while April was invigorated by the energy and possibility she saw all around her, she missed the grandeur — the kind of elegant style — she had known. She often quoted the extraordinarily wealthy Lady Docker, one of the superstars of Britain's post-war years, who had a gold-plated cream Daimler. The Britain Ashley had known was that of the Rolls-Royce and the Bentley, not the Mini Cooper.*

Another remarkable feature of the 1960s — in London, at least — was the growing number of people who used their new wealth to gain influence of various kinds. During a wedding reception at the Hyde Park hotel one evening, April met Clive Raphael, an ebullient man whose money came from a string of garages he owned in the Midlands. 'He was wearing a carnation, smoking a cigar and driving a Bentley,' she later said.[4] 'I told him two of them had got to go. I was so pleased he kept the Bentley.'

April rather liked Clive Raphael and quickly picked up on his insecurity, expressed in his pushiness and need to impress people: 'When I met him he looked 45, although he was only in his early thirties. I got him to give up drinking and smoking. I soon had him looking much healthier.' April gave him instructions about public behaviour: do be friendly, but not overfamiliar, to waiters; don't tip lavishly, because that was no guarantee of good service; don't attempt to ingratiate himself to celebrities, who would despise him. She even

---

*   The life of Lady Docker, born Norah Turner in a working-class family and ennobled thanks to
     her third marriage, has some striking parallels with Ashley's own. See Tim Hogarth, *The Dazzling
     Lady Docker*, Scratching Shed, London, 2018.

corrected his language: 'sitting room' instead of 'lounge'; 'napkin' instead of 'serviette'. She became a combination, then, of Henry Higgins and Nancy Mitford: a nicely ironic reversal of her own life's journey. Unfortunately, she could do nothing about his taste in interior design: Raphael's flat near Harley Street had orange wallpaper, highly decorated kitchen cupboards, and chairs upholstered in nylon plush. She contented herself by telling him gently that it would be better if the pictures in the living room were worth more than their frames.

Raphael fell in love with April and they became a couple; they lived together for about six months. He enjoyed going to showy, expensive restaurants, whereas she preferred somewhere elegant and expensive, such as Le Caprice. She did not much like his friends: nouveaux riches types like Raphael, they were all far too keen, she thought, on exploiting other people for their money. But Raphael and April went on holiday together: he took her to Beirut, which she enjoyed. He told her he had altered his will in her favour and asked her to marry him. He even suggested they travel to Mexico together, so she could get a quick divorce from Arthur Corbett and they could pick up a marriage licence. April was unsure about this: she had not been in touch with Arthur since she walked out on their marriage. But Raphael insisted that he wanted to be part of her life and to know all about her. As a result, April made a bizarre decision. She took Raphael to Manchester for lunch with her mother.

April hadn't seen Ada Jamieson since the awkward reunion engineered by the *News of the World* a couple of years before. Was she trying for some kind of reconciliation with her mother, in spite of everything? Whatever her motive, the meeting was less than successful. April, Raphael, and Ada had an awkward meal in Ada's local Chinese restaurant, during which Ada smoked incessantly, said very little, and didn't introduce April to anyone she knew, let alone as her daughter. April was indignant about this, but Ada could simply have been embarrassed, with no idea how to deal with the situation.

Raphael suggested that he and April should live together in Montrose House, a new block of flats behind Belgrave Square. He bought up the block and started to remodel it; he and April, he said, would have the penthouse, and April agreed. But she soon discovered that Raphael could be violent. One night he beat her up. He was pitifully repentant afterwards, declaring he would never do it again, and he took her on holiday to Majorca for a week. However, in Majorca, he attacked her once more — and this time she walked out. She did not give the press these details, of course: 'I left him because I found him too much,' she said. 'He was always busy on the social scene, which I wasn't.'[5]

Raphael moved on. He married a very young model named Penny Brahms, with whom he had been having a relationship since she was 16. After less than two years, she left him on the grounds that he was cruel and violent. 'I think Clive needs someone who is deaf and dumb,' she told the press.[6] After they parted, Raphael renewed contact with April, who for some reason agreed to have dinner with him at the Montrose penthouse. The apartment remained a monument to his horrible taste, she wrote, with gold fringes and purple walls. Raphael played the piano for a long time, ignoring her, and April left without her dinner. That was the end of that.

Raphael died in March 1970. It was thought he had been gunrunning in the Middle East, and his plane had exploded — perhaps because of a bomb on board. He bequeathed his estranged wife, Penny Brahms, a shilling and some revealing photographs of her, leaving in his will the rest of his considerable estate to his lawyer Ronald Shulman. Penny Brahms contested the will, which was found to be a forgery with Shulman a conspirator; the lawyer quietly left the country and was never heard of again, and Brahms inherited about £12 million.

April was now short of money again. To make ends meet, she sold the mink Arthur had given her and some of her jewellery. But life in London remained too expensive, and she decided to leave. This time, she went to Ibiza.

This island off the east coast of Spain wasn't yet the massive tourist destination it became a few years later; April was offered a shared house with no electricity or running water and with a carpet of black beetles. As usual, it took her little time to make friends and useful contacts, and to upgrade her living arrangements. She spent time with a young eccentric German painter named Klaus Schmidt, who was spending the summer in Ibiza. Ashley gave few details about their relationship except to say that they were both broke and lazed around together. (He liked cracking jokes in English, declaring that 'a German joke is no laughing matter'.)

When he left, April drifted into the small show-business colony. Chief among the actors and writers was the English comedian Terry-Thomas, who April thought was a loudmouthed boor. (Thomas's career trajectory was similar to hers: famous for playing aristocrats in movies, he had started life as the son of a Smithfield butcher.) Other British visitors were the actors Diana Rigg, who had just made her mark as Emma Peel in the television series *The Avengers*, and David Warner. He was about to play the title role in *Hamlet* for the Royal Shakespeare Company and, said Ashley, he would recite his lines to anyone he bumped into. (That production, featuring Hamlet as a 1960s dropout — catching 'the radical spirit of a turbulent age', according to one review — became famous and made Warner's name. It was directed by Peter Hall, and it also starred Glenda Jackson, Elizabeth Spriggs, and Brewster Mason.)

April also became friendly with the writer Robin Maugham, nephew of the more famous W. Somerset Maugham. In an odd echo of Arthur Corbett's father, 'Uncle Willie' had advised his nephew not to be a writer but to marry a rich woman and to end up as governor of a remote island. But Robin Maugham wanted to be as celebrated a man of letters as his uncle. His big success was the novella *The Servant*, made into an excellent, unsettling film in 1963, with a script by Harold Pinter, directed by Joseph Losey, and starring Dirk Bogarde and James Fox.

Maugham recalled April as excellent company at parties on Ibiza: both 'amusing and quick-witted', with a vitality that 'never seemed to flag':

> But sometimes I felt I could detect a sadness beneath her apparent cheerfulness. One evening – after a small party in my villa – I asked her if she had any hidden reason to be unhappy.

April was hesitant. 'Not exactly,' she replied, though she was concerned about what people were thinking about her and what they might remember of her past:

> 'They're thinking what an attractive woman you are,' I said.
>   'I hope so,' she answered. 'Because I don't want them to remember. I'm a woman now. I want to be accepted as such. That's why I'm more at ease with people who don't know anything about me.'[7]

Maugham wanted April to write her life story under his guidance, but she refused — at which point he flew into a rage, as he frequently did when displeased. However, a few years later, when April really needed support, he helped her.

One of the most prominent characters holidaying on Ibiza was Sir Michael Duff, Lord Lieutenant of Caernarfonshire and godfather to Lord Snowdon. After Armstrong-Jones had married Princess Margaret, Sir Michael grumbled that Armstrong-Jones had taken the Snowdon name without his permission, because Snowdon was on the Duff family estate. Sir Michael once held a reverse dinner party for the local councillors, starting with liqueurs and fruit, and ending with soup and rolls. So intimidatingly aristocratic was his demeanour that none of the councillors ever mentioned the oddity of the meal to him. He enjoyed practical jokes: as a young man, he would dress up as his godmother Queen Mary and make surprise visits to stately homes in a royal car

— until one day, while he was staying at a friend's house, the real Queen Mary arrived. Sir Michael, who was gay, had what Isaiah Berlin called a 'very peculiar marriage' with Lady Caroline Paget, a beautiful woman who continued to have affairs with men and women.[8] Much of this would have been known to the summer visitors on Ibiza, and his more unpleasant characteristics were spelled out in the memoir by his adopted son. April's decision to stay clear of him was a sound one.

April returned to London at the end of the summer, still needing money. Thanks to a friend, she found temporary work with a man who ran a sales consultancy employing out-of-work actors and models; her job was keeping track of sales representatives for Cadbury's chocolate and the Gallaher tobacco company. The office was above a decrepit porn shop near Charing Cross station — April had to wear a headscarf because plaster flaked down from the ceiling — and because so many pretty young women came in and out, the patrons of the porn shop assumed the office was a brothel and kept making unwelcome visits.

At about this time, April began a warm and important friendship that endured for many years. Viva King, born in 1893 in Argentina, was the daughter of an English railway manager. She had been prominent in English bohemian circles since the 1920s and was known variously as 'The Queen of Bohemia' or even 'The Scarlet Woman'. Her social circle included such luminaries as Augustus John, Cecil Beaton, Ronald Firbank, Rebecca West, and Philip Heseltine (also known as composer and arranger Peter Warlock). Viva's husband, Willie King, with whom she had an unconventional relationship (both were said to proposition young gay men), had left her a handsome house in Thurloe Square, close to the Victoria and Albert Museum, where he had been the keeper of ceramics. From the 1940s, Viva King had conducted a highly successful salon there.

Viva was, Ashley wrote, the epitome of the elderly upper-class Englishwoman, with white hair, china-blue eyes, and a sharp tongue, and April greatly admired her intelligence, beauty, and wit. Having such a wide and sometimes raffish circle of friends, Viva was immediately attracted to April. For ten years, Viva threw birthday parties in her house for April, with a long and varied guest list: invitations were much prized. April's biographer Duncan Fallowell, an Oxford student friend, was also a guest at Viva's house: 'I met Diana Cooper in a camel trouser suit and big cream Stetson. In the course of our conversation Diana casually reached up into the brim of her hat and took down a little dog which had been hidden there all along.'[9]

April's life had now become a balancing act between her contacts in London's bohemian society and her parlous financial position. She joined forces with a tall and boyishly attractive young man named Edward Maddock — he was still in his teens; she was in her 30s — whom she met via Robin Maugham. She and Edward shared an apartment, first as flatmates — having told the landlord they were brother and sister — but later as lovers. Their flat was in Elm Park Gardens near the Fulham Road, not particularly close to the sophisticated part of Chelsea. Neither of them had regular work. At one stage they lived on boiled potatoes for three weeks, punctuated with smart parties where they could fill up on oysters and lobster. April eventually found another job, helping out in a shop at the 'wrong' end of the King's Road, which turned, at night, into a cheap restaurant. She wore a crepe evening dress and two ropes of pearls, and was paid 30 shillings a night, with no tips.

'He was a brilliant boy,' remembered April in a 1982 interview:

He was the youngest lawyer in England and he gave it up to study acting. He was a Taurean, like myself, and one of the few people I couldn't get around, bully or talk into a corner. We were both solitary people in a physical sense. We touched when we made love but we weren't physically demonstrative out of bed. We didn't even hold hands in the cinema. But we understood each other.[10]

One of Edward's attractions for April was his background. His parents came from Preston in Lancashire, not so far from Liverpool. April enjoyed visiting them with Edward and tucking into hearty northern food. Everybody seemed to get on well, at least on the surface. However, after a few months, Edward announced that he did not want to be with April or have sex with her any longer, and he had made up his mind to leave and to study law.

Perhaps April was not entirely surprised: Edward was young and might have been exploring his sexuality; he had, after all, been part of the Robin Maugham set. April also knew that Edward's parents, who were strict Catholics, disapproved of his relationship with her. Edward was the product of a boarding school for boys, run by Benedictine monks, and it seems likely that he saw in April a mother figure or a sister. Although he had been happy to be living with such a self-assured celebrity, he had hated being introduced as her boyfriend. Nevertheless, his decision saddened April. For the first time, she had found someone to share misfortune with, and she had enjoyed being a protector and guide to a young and vulnerable man. But she dealt with it graciously, and so they parted amicably.

April was now free to take up an invitation from one of Edward's friends to visit Oxford for the first time. The cobbled streets, bicycles, arches, colleges, and ancient gardens all enchanted her: she adored being there — although she was hard-headed enough to see that living among such splendour might give undergraduates lifelong delusions of grandeur. Oxford was far more Brideshead than Bolshevik: like Britain's other universities, its students were middle-class or wealthy, largely from all-boy public schools. Magdalen, where April spent most of her time in Oxford and whose alumni had included Howard Florey, Oscar Wilde, Wilfred Thesiger, and Dudley Moore, was probably the grandest of all the colleges. She enjoyed the company of the young men studying there. They were so sophisticated, so intellectually assured — although she noticed that the polish tended to slip after a few bottles of champagne. Duncan Fallowell, who became April's first biographer, was among them.

He and his friends loved hearing her stories about wild times in Paris, Rome, and Marbella and enjoyed her occasional flamboyance: at the end of one evening in Magdalen College, presumably after drinking a fair amount, she jumped up on the table and 'danced the flamenco among the candlesticks'.[11] Oxford was altogether a cheering experience — one she felt she truly needed.

April returned her new friends' hospitality by introducing them to smart London parties and giving them a taste of a wider world. Fallowell later told the gossip blog *Madame Arcati* that he and April went to bed together a few times, and rather coyly mentioned Johnson's baby lotion on the windowsill of an unheated West London bedroom in 1969.[12]

As well as having a good time with her Oxford friends, April continued to enjoy the high life in London. At a party organised by her friend Viva King, she met James Bailey, whom she described as short, gay, neurotic, and rich. As a young man, Bailey had learned his craft from Oliver Messel, the foremost theatre and costume designer of the 1920s and 1930s, and Bailey went on to work at La Scala and Covent Garden. Like Messel, Bailey came from a well-connected and distinguished family: his father was a lieutenant colonel in the British Army; his mother, the daughter of an earl. He was also a deeply unhappy alcoholic, moody and unpredictable. He was a painter, and Ashley described his pictures of Venice as magnificent, with something haunted and mysterious about them. The windows and heavy silk curtains of his flat were never opened; he lived, said Ashley, in an eternal evening of lavender light, the walls of his flat hidden by huge banks of artificial flowers, presided over by a massive golden statue of Buddha. But he bought April designer clothes which he chose himself, and she approved of his taste. Like Captain Lenny Plugge before him, Bailey became April's opera partner: they went to performances at

Covent Garden together, always in a limousine.

On 10 June 1966, James Bailey called for April to go to the opera as usual, and she was about to go down, dressed to the nines, when the telephone rang. It was the hospital at Fazakerley, Liverpool, and April was told that her father was there and was dying. She said nothing to Bailey — they went to the opera (Verdi's *Don Carlos*) — and she caught a train to Liverpool the following morning.

April was met at the hospital by her sister Theresa, who told her Frederick Jamieson was dying of tuberculosis and that he would be unlikely to recognise her. But, when she approached the hospital bed and saw the small, wizened man lying there, he opened his eyes and smiled at her.

It was a small gift of comfort from the father who had delivered precious little to his family. The short, good-looking man with a puckish smile who had allowed young George to crouch close to him in the Anderson shelter during wartime air raids; the sailor whose uniform always smelled of the sea — he had vanished a long time ago, morphing into a drifter around Liverpool, existing on a tiny pension, and scrounging what money he could. When George had worked with the Lundys, his father had repeatedly asked him for small change. George would give him what he had and watch him walk off to the nearest pub. But none of that mattered to April right then. All she remembered was that her father was the only person in the family who had made her feel that she was loved.

Frederick Jamieson died three days after April came to see him. With a fierce determination to preserve the decencies, April called her mother, who told her that an insurance policy would cover the funeral expenses. With help from the hospital, April made the necessary arrangements for a Catholic funeral. Theresa, who loathed their mother, was furious that April had been in contact with Ada and refused to speak to April again.

April ordered a plain coffin for her father, arguing that he would have preferred the money to be spent on oysters, Guinness, and mushrooms warmed in cream for the mourners. In the same spirit of defiance, she wore a canary-yellow dress to the funeral, sure that her father would have approved. It was a quiet, dismal service. The only mourners were April, Theresa, Frederick's sister Auntie May (she of the refined accent), and his sister-in-law Auntie Frances; Ada did not attend the funeral. The priest, who hurried through the service, had never met Frederick and sucked his dentures in a way that reminded April of Arthur Corbett.

Shortly after the funeral, Ada Jamieson married Bernie Cartmell, the Lancashire man with whom she had been living for years. By all accounts, Cartmell was a quiet individual, not one to push himself forward. During the war, he had served on the Arctic convoys — the merchant ships that delivered essential supplies to the Soviet Union: incredibly dangerous and brutal missions that he rarely mentioned.* Together, he and Ada had opened a grocery shop on the outskirts of Manchester.

Ada was still woven into the fabric of her daughter's life. When April and Viva King were travelling to Malta on one occasion, an Englishwoman on the plane said to April: 'I'm sure I know your face. Do you mind my asking your name?' April replied: 'Ada Brown. I used to be quite a well-known model.' Using her mother's name in reference to a 'lovely life' Ada had never enjoyed must have given April ironic satisfaction.

---

* The Arctic convoys sailed from the United Kingdom, Iceland, and North America to northern ports in the Soviet Union. There were 78 such convoys between August 1941 and May 1945; 85 merchant vessels, 16 warships, and 30 submarines were lost.

CHAPTER 14

Corbett v Corbett: the trial

Although April's social contacts and her own confidence ensured that she appeared to be a smart, sophisticated woman, she continued to struggle financially. She had told Arthur Corbett that she did not want any money from him, but in 1965, after two years of hand-to-mouth temporary jobs and accommodation, she decided she was entitled to make a claim on his estate.

Arthur had repeatedly promised her the Villa Antoinette and she believed that the deed to the property was in her name, even though Arthur had the papers. She engaged Terry Walton, the solicitor of her manager, Ken Johnstone — the same manager who had organised her unhappy cabaret performances in several English towns — and set the claim in motion. April could not have known what a Pandora's box she was about to open, nor how that devastation would affect not only her own life, but also the rights of other transgender people.

Arthur was still in Marbella, working in a new bar in the centre of town. His pleasant manner had made him popular, though the clientele were apparently too intimidated by his aristocratic background to do anything as plebeian as offer him a tip. He was not earning much, but he could still draw on his assets, so he led a reasonably comfortable bachelor existence. His former wife, Eleanor, had swiftly remarried, to Lieutenant-Colonel Richard Cardiff; they now had a two-year-old son.

Serving a statement of claim on Arthur was tricky: he was living outside the jurisdiction of an English court, and the Villa Antoinette had been purchased in Spain. Because Arthur's assets were held in England and were therefore more easily accessible, April was advised to sue for maintenance instead, and she agreed. Months of stonewalling followed, and Arthur developed hepatitis, causing further delays.

In the end, Arthur and his lawyers decided on a brutal and conclusive course of action: to end the marriage altogether. Not until 1973 were separation and mutual consent considered sufficient reason for a marriage to be dissolved; in 1967, blame had to be given to one or other of the parties. (Arthur had had experience of this: Eleanor had agreed to divorce him for adultery with another woman, not April — a put-up job for legal purposes.)

On 15 May 1967, Arthur Corbett filed a petition to divorce April Ashley, requesting a declaration that the marriage was 'null and void ... because [April] at the time of the ceremony was a person of the male sex, or in the alternative for a decree of nullity on the ground that the marriage was never consummated owing to the incapacity or wilful refusal of the respondent to consummate it.' Arthur was claiming that, because marriage was between a man and a woman and April had been born male, their marriage was invalid.

April responded that Arthur had been the one who refused to consummate the marriage. Her position was that, as a result of her 1960 surgery, she was a 'fully functional woman' and that she could engage with the world in no other way.

April never wrote about her feelings about the case at this point, but it is probably safe to assume that she was outraged by Arthur's behaviour. On the recommendation of her solicitor, she made a successful application for legal aid, and she engaged a legal team consisting of two Queen's Counsel and three professors of medicine. Her lawyers applied to Arthur for maintenance of £6 a week: a third of his salary as a barman. April thought this was paltry, considering that he still had significant assets.

April's solicitor, Terry Walton, asked her to visit Ada to see whether she would be a useful character witness. With great reluctance, April telephoned her mother at the grocery shop she and Bernie Cartmell ran in Manchester; a few days later, April visited Ada at her house — a bungalow of which Ada was inordinately proud. We do not have Ada Cartmell's version of their meeting, but Ashley said it had been almost baroquely frustrating. She tried to explain to her mother why she was there, but Ada wanted only to complain about members of the family. April quickly realised how much fonder Ada was of Arthur than of her: Ada repeatedly said she couldn't understand why April was divorcing such a 'lovely man'. April said Ada was too scatterbrained to understand the divorce proceedings or to follow a line of questioning under cross-examination; her mother was concerned only with protecting Bernie — worried that he might have to come to court for some reason. Although April's solicitor wanted Ada to give evidence, April refused to call her to the stand.

The case was finally set down for hearing in the Probate, Divorce and Admiralty Division of London's High Court of Justice for 16 days in November and December 1969. The announcement caused a sensation. As *The Times* pointed out, a divorce court judge was being asked to decide a case that raised legal and medical questions, including 'perhaps the oldest question in the world: what is a woman?' April was described as a 34-year-old spinster, while 50-year-old Arthur was inevitably described as 'son and heir of Lord Rowallan the former Chief Scout'.[1]

Because *Corbett v Corbett* was a dispute between parties, not a criminal matter, it was heard in a closed court with a single judge and no jury. The presiding judge was Sir Roger Fray Greenwood Ormrod,

QC. To April and her legal team, he seemed an excellent choice. In a case that would depend heavily upon both medical and legal evidence, it was reassuring that Mr Justice Ormrod was a doctor. Uniquely among his judicial colleagues, he had served in the Royal Army Medical Corps during World War II, and he wore his service medals on his judge's robes. He was also respected for his fairness in judging divorce cases, and he had a crisp, no-nonsense turn of phrase that he occasionally indulged from the bench. 'When a woman marries a man of thirty-one who has never done a day's work in his life, she must accept that she is marrying a considerable problem,' he had declared in 1962. He had already used complicated medical evidence in the service of justice, having been the first High Court judge to order a blood test to determine which of two men was a child's father.

April's lawyers had heard of a case that they thought might serve as a useful precedent — one that had begun on the same day in 1967 that Arthur Corbett filed his petition to divorce April. Scottish baronet Sir Ewan Forbes had won the right to inherit his family's estate despite having been assigned female at birth. (Forbes had formally re-registered as a man in 1952.) However, the judgment, upheld by the Home Secretary, had been that, at birth, Ewan Forbes had been 'of indeterminate, not male, sex'; it was therefore of limited use in April's case. And because the Ewan Forbes case had been held in great secrecy, with very few details publicly released, April and her lawyers were prohibited from quoting it in any way.*

April was feeling vulnerable even before the proceedings began. The end of her relationship with Edward Maddock had thoroughly upset her and preparing for the trial had been exhausting. Overarching all this was the dread of knowing that her whole life as a trans woman, including intimate details of her anatomy and her sexual history, were about to be picked apart and examined in a court of law, regardless of ethical considerations or privacy. In an unpleasant echo of her

---

*   See Chapter 9 for further details.

experiences as a teenager in Liverpool's Ormskirk County Hospital, she also had to endure a battery of tests run by a succession of male doctors. At no point was Arthur Corbett required to submit to any kind of physical or psychological examination, even though April had declared that he was unable to function sexually.

The first day of the case, to be tried in the Law Courts in the Strand, was 10 November 1969. April gave careful thought to what she should wear in the courtroom. She was aware that if her clothes were too masculine in style, then the media would say she was inauthentic; too feminine, and she would be accused of trying too hard. On the day, she emerged from a limousine (supplied by friends) to greet the reporters and their flashbulbs in a black velvet maxicoat, black boots, and a white fur hat: not severe, but well groomed and elegant. She was ushered past the Great Hall — a Victorian Gothic structure designed, Ashley said, to reduce any human to the size of a mouse — to No. 2 Court. As the case was heard *in camera*, without journalists or even a court reporter taking down a transcript, Ashley's account of the trial, given in her two autobiographies, and the published summing-up by Mr Justice Ormrod are the only records of the case.

Arriving at court

Any remaining shred of self-assurance April might have had dwindled almost to nothing when she went inside the vaulted courtroom and saw Arthur, surrounded by a huddle of lawyers. Not having seen him for some time, she was shocked to notice how old he looked. She wanted to go over and greet him, but he did not acknowledge her presence. For the first time, she realised that she was simply a tiny cog in a huge and inexorable legal machine — the machine that would decide her fate.

The first question to be decided was how April should be addressed. Her own view was that 'Miss Ashley' was fine, but the court settled on 'Mrs Corbett', which she found ludicrous. Almost from the beginning, she knew that Mr Justice Ormrod did not like her. He never looked her in the eye; he just glanced at her from time to time and mumbled his references to her as if he found them, and her, distasteful. She realised he would be impossible to charm when she gave evidence. In his full wig and gown, with heavy horn-rimmed glasses and a grim expression, he seemed the embodiment of British law's awful majesty.

Arthur was asked to give his evidence first: another means, Ashley thought, of putting her at a disadvantage. As soon as he started speaking, his fluency astonished April. Gone was the neurotic, semi-apologetic, spiky Arthur Corbett she had known. This man, in his immaculate dark suit, with his polished diction and the assurance of his social class, was both relaxed and rueful. More surprisingly, perhaps, he gave considerable detail about his sexual experiences, including some April hadn't known about. Yes, he had had sexual relations with women before, during, and after his first marriage. Yes, he had felt compelled to dress in women's clothes from an early age, even sometimes in front of his wife. From the late 1940s, he admitted, he had sought to express what he described as his 'deviant tendencies' with increasing urgency: first by going to bookshops that sold pornography and then by contacting people with similar compulsions. He had also, he said, begun going to male brothels.

Arthur mentioned his visits to Le Carrousel, where he had seen and admired the cabaret artist then known as Toni April, and he said that he had met her for the first time in London in November 1960, after her emergence as April Ashley, when they had lunch at Le Caprice restaurant. Yes, he said, he had been aware that she had been 'born a man' but had undergone an operation to 'change her sex', and he said that he was mesmerised by her. 'The reality was far greater than my fantasy,' he said. 'It far outstripped any fantasy for myself.' He said that, when he and Ashley met, she looked like, dressed, and acted as a woman. He added — and it is easy to imagine him directing a frank and regretful smile at Mr Justice Ormrod — that he had been caught up in a fantasy he now regretted.

April and her legal team quickly realised how effective this confessional mode of Arthur's was. In vivid detail, he was presenting himself as a 'deviate' whose contrition was both candid and sincere. He was therefore implying that his marriage had been nothing more than a squalid pretence. Even more damning for April was that, by defining himself as deviant, Corbett was positioning her as a freak. She had lived so long as a woman, and this was the ultimate betrayal. Because of Arthur's testimony, the case had become something quite different from an objective assessment of her status for the purposes of marriage; now, she was being forced to defend herself against the allegation that the marriage itself was a sham — because she herself was one.

April's impression was reinforced by Mr Justice Ormrod himself: after a couple of days, he testily questioned whether it was necessary to let the case continue to waste taxpayers' money. Both sides protested that the evidence had to be presented in full, particularly the medical evidence, and Ormrod grumpily agreed to continue.

April and her team were becoming more worried every minute: they could not help believing that the judge had already made his decision.

As April sat at the front of the courtroom in her carefully chosen outfits, makeup and hair impeccable, she had to listen to long clinical discussions about her sexuality, her sexual development, and her anatomy from no fewer than nine doctors, some of whom gave long disquisitions about exactly what constituted sex — what factors (chromosomal, gonadal, genital, or psychological, or a combination of all) constituted the definitions of 'a man' and 'a woman'. All the doctors agreed that sexual 'abnormalities' were primarily physical, though they could also be psychological. Psychologically 'abnormal' people were either 'transvestites' or 'transsexuals', and they gave definitions of both. The difference, they said, was that 'transvestites' did not want to live as 'the opposite sex', while 'transsexuals' wanted to become members of 'the opposite sex' to the fullest extent possible. They said that 'men who wanted to be women' considered themselves to be imprisoned in their male bodies, intensely disliking their own sexual organs, which reminded them of their 'biological sex'. Unfortunately, said the doctors, these people did not seem to respond favourably to any form of psychological treatment.

One doctor testified that he thought April should be properly classified as 'a male homosexual transsexualist'; another agreed and added that the description 'a castrated male' was correct. Two of the doctors argued that 'transsexuals' could not be classified as properly 'male or female' but as intersex.

In an attempt to rebut their claims, April had taken the Terman-Miles M–F test: a battery of 455 questions that aimed at determining psychological gender.* She had been judged as 'emphatically female', and her high scores had formed an important part of her response — so she was despondent when Ormrod ruled the test inadmissible because it had not been carried out under legal supervision.

April's legal team had tried to call Dr Burou to give evidence

---

* This test, which has been thoroughly discredited, is nothing short of ludicrous. Among other questions, April was asked: whether she thought it was better to drink tea from a cup, a saucer, or a spoon; whether she was more scared of the end of the world, Black people, or tiger snakes; and whether she believed being a Bolshevik (a communist) was very bad or only mildly so.

but had been unsuccessful. April was dismayed when the report of the unnamed consultant psychiatrist who had treated her as George Jamieson in Ormskirk County Hospital was quoted instead: 'The boy is a constitutional homosexual who says he wants to become a woman. He has had numerous homosexual experiences and his homosexuality is at the root of his depression. On examination, apart from his womanish appearance, there was no abnormal finding.'

The two medical inspectors to the court, who had physically examined April prior to the court hearing, gave evidence:

We find that the breasts are well developed, though the nipples are of the masculine type. The voice is rather low pitched. There are almost no penile remains and there is a normally placed urethral office. The vagina is of ample size to admit a normal and erect penis ... The walls are skin-covered and moist. There is no impediment on 'her part' [the significant quotation marks are in the original] to sexual intercourse. Rectal examination does not reveal any uterus or ovaries or testes.

Furthermore, they said, a chromosomal test had revealed that 'all the cells ... were of the male type'.

It was now April's turn to be cross-examined. It was torture. When she was asked about her anatomy before her 1960 surgery, she broke down and wept. But she composed herself and answered the questions. She described her male genitals as 'meagre', and she agreed with one consultant psychiatrist that she had always looked more like a woman than a man. She was unable to give anatomically specific details such as penile length and stepped out of the witness box convinced that her lack of precision had counted against her.

Arthur's barrister insinuated that April had deceived his client into marrying her, even though Corbett had previously testified that he had known about April's history before they married. April's legal team declared that Arthur could not deny the existence of the marriage, considering that he had gone into the ceremony knowing Ashley's whole history.

Outside the courtroom, one of April's legal team, Ivor Mills, professor of medicine at the University of Cambridge, summed up an obvious aspect of the proceedings. 'There is a great deal of snobbery in this case, April,' he said, something she had known from the beginning. April had seen the subtle deference that the men — lawyers and petitioner alike — displayed towards one another, bound together by the certainty and confidence of their class and education. It was also abundantly clear to her that these men would never question the implications of their privilege because of a parvenue scrubber who had been born into a Liverpool slum and who hadn't had the grace to stay there but had had the effrontery to marry into the peerage.

April's court ordeal finished on 9 December 1969, when the trial was adjourned pending the judgment of Mr Justice Ormrod. This was scheduled for early February of the following year. Arthur flew back to Spain, but not before April's lawyer, Terry Walton, had pursued him down the Strand and delivered a writ seeking a court declaration that Arthur held the Villa Antoinette in trust for April. And then, thoroughly shaken, April went to Oxford to spend time with her new undergraduate friends: excellent therapy, she said, because they were much more interested in their own lives and concerns than in anything to do with *Corbett v Corbett*.

One of their number, Duncan Fallowell, now a fledgling journalist, took her to the *Spectator*'s Christmas party as a diversion from the looming judgment. '*Spectator* owner Harry Creighton and his chums were delighted,' he recalled, 'demonstrating an alternative, highly sympathetic face from the Establishment.'[2] This must have comforted April, who, Fallowell added, 'somehow retained her *jeu d'esprit* as well as her native Liverpudlian grit'. She would need every bit she could muster of both.

CHAPTER 15

Corbett v Corbett: the verdict

The judgment of Mr Justice Ormrod was handed down on Monday 2 February 1970.

On that morning, a Spanish maid who had come to Arthur's Marbella villa to take his dogs for a walk found him lying unconscious on the living-room floor. He had apparently been there for about 16 hours. His friend Guy Sitwell told the *Daily Mirror* that Arthur had planned to fly from Málaga to London on the Sunday night to attend court the following morning but had not caught the plane.[1] Arthur was rushed to hospital in Marbella, where he remained in a coma for several days.

Exactly what had happened is unknown, but concealed by the calm and lucid frankness Arthur displayed in court was the considerable stress of having to describe and explain his sexual history. Perhaps, said one newspaper report, he had suffered a heart attack as a result. Nobody mentioned the possibility that he might have tried to kill himself. And while April might have wondered where Arthur was that morning, she was too preoccupied — and probably too worried — to think about him for long.

Clutching a large wad of paper, Mr Justice Ormrod began to read in measured tones. In its entirety, the judgment ran to almost 20 pages of carefully worded prose. We do not know what he emphasised or hurried over, but a study of this transcript reveals a great deal not only about his legal interpretation but also about his own attitudes and prejudices.[2]

Ormrod said that the primary issue to be decided was whether the marriage was valid and that this question depended upon the 'true sex' of April Ashley. The secondary issue was the question of non-consummation — assuming, added the judge, that there had indeed been a marriage to consummate.

He first addressed the facts of April's early life. There had never been any suggestion, he said, that April Ashley, registered at birth as George Jamieson, had been mistakenly recorded as a boy. Ormrod briefly described Jamieson's life in the merchant navy, George's attempts to kill himself, and his time in Ormskirk and Walton. Examination by doctors there left no doubt that George Jamieson was a man, although he presented a 'womanish appearance' and had 'little bodily and facial hair'. During 'several therapeutic interviews, some under the influence of small doses of amytal or ether', said Ormrod, George had expressed an intense desire to be a woman, even though he spoke of numerous gay experiences. The Walton doctors had concluded that 'homosexuality' was at the root of his depression.

After alluding to April's time in London and Jersey and George's joining Le Carrousel for about four years, Ormrod described what had happened with Dr Burou in Casablanca.

This part of his written summary was heavily hedged about with quotation marks.

Jamieson, said Ormrod, had undergone, 'at Dr Burou's hands, a so-called "sex change operation" ... and the construction of a so-called "artificial vagina"' — and, he said, 'I have been at some pains to avoid the use of emotive expressions such as "castration" and "artificial vagina" without the qualification "so-called" because the association of ideas connected with these words or phrases are so powerful that they tend to cloud clear thinking.'

Dr Burou himself, Ormrod confirmed, had refused to supply any information or even to answer letters from April Ashley's lawyers. And April Ashley herself, said Ormrod, had been 'almost as unhelpful', claiming that she 'thought' she had a penis while in the merchant navy but that she 'hadn't the foggiest idea' of its size.

Ormrod agreed with what the doctors had said: 'In cross-examination, she was asked whether she had ever had an erection, and whether she had had ejaculations. She simply refused to answer either question and wept a little.' Although the surgery was said to have removed a 'vestigial' penis, he continued, no definition of its size was given and there was no evidence that 'the respondent's' penis or testicles were in any way abnormal.

Here, Mr Justice Ormrod offered his own insight: that people who suffer from the intense desire to belong to the 'opposite sex' often become emotional when asked about the genitalia they dislike so much. He conceded that April had given evidence that after the surgery she had used her 'artificial vaginal cavity' quite successfully.

Turning now to the plaintiff, Ormrod said that Arthur had described his sexual experience 'in considerable detail with apparent frankness and without obvious embarrassment'. In contrast to April, he said, Arthur had been an unusually good witness, answering all questions carefully without attempting to evade or prevaricate.

The judge briskly summarised Arthur's sexual history: his increasing interest in 'transvestism' and eventually his increasing involvement in 'the society of sexual deviants'. He gave Arthur special praise for his insight, quoting Arthur's observation that dressing as a woman had ceased to be entirely satisfying because he didn't like what he saw: 'You want the fantasy to appear right. It utterly failed to appear right in my eyes.'

If April or her legal team had been uncertain about Mr Justice

Ormrod's biases, this must surely have confirmed them — and worse was to come.

Arthur's meeting with April Ashley at Le Caprice restaurant was the key, Ormrod said, to the rest of 'this essentially pathetic but almost incredible story'.

At first, he said, Arthur had been interested in April as a fantasy object, but quite soon he had developed 'the interest of a man for a woman' because she looked, dressed, and acted like a woman. She had told him her story, including details of the surgery; Arthur had shared his own story because he was a 'full' man in love with a woman, not 'a transvestite in love with a transsexual' — and Ormrod repeated this point several times.

April and Arthur did not have 'full sex' together, said the judge, for April did not permit Arthur to touch her. Arthur's letters to April were affectionate, but quite without passion, emphasising marriage and his pleasure in thinking of April as the future Lady Rowallan. 'This is not at all the sort of relationship which one would expect to satisfy a man of such extensive and varied sexual experience as [Arthur] claims,' declared Ormrod. And April had agreed in court with Arthur's account of their relationship: she said she had never had any real feeling for Arthur and had been his 'nurse' for three years. Ormrod concluded that April obviously found Arthur to be a difficult person who experienced mood swings. Arthur, he added, was jealous of April as a woman, but was also jealous of other men who were attracted to her.

In summary, said Ormrod, he thought this 'strange relationship' had little or nothing in common with any 'heterosexual' relationship he had heard about in that court. Because Arthur was a man 'especially prone to all kinds of sexual fantasies and practices', it would be unwise to attempt to assess April's 'feminine characteristics' based on the impression he said she made on him. And it was a further example of the unreal nature of Arthur's feelings, said Ormrod, that he had introduced her to his wife and family.

Next, the judge observed that April had successfully changed her name by deed poll and had been given a passport in the name of April Ashley — both with Arthur's assistance. She already had a National Insurance card in that name — but, he said, she could not persuade the registrar to change her birth certificate. (Ashley later stated only that she had not changed her birth certificate, which leaves open the question of whether she thought it was unnecessary or whether permission had been refused.)

Ormrod summarised the rest of April's story until her marriage. Arthur, he said, had been happy to support her in Marbella even though she slept at the villa while he stayed at the club. After Arthur had been divorced from his first wife, he repeatedly asked April to marry him, and she would not agree: she continually came and went from Marbella, even though he remained there. Arthur estimated that they had been together for less than six months of the year between July 1962 and July 1963, and nothing of a sexual nature took place. However, in July 1963, Arthur took the first steps towards marriage, consulting a lawyer in Gibraltar and discussing financial arrangements with April.

Both Arthur and April, said Ormrod, obviously had considerable doubts about whether they could marry or whether they could find anyone to marry them. They did not ask for or receive any legal advice about the validity of the marriage. April had suddenly agreed to go through with it, and they married in Gibraltar. In this, Ormrod said, 'I think there can be little doubt that [Arthur] was still in the grip of his fantasies and that [April] had much more sense of reality.'

He emphasised that April's realism was demonstrated by the long letter she had written to Arthur declaring she would never return to live with him: 'It shows, I think, that reality had broken in on her and that she, quite understandably, could not face the intolerably false position into which they had got themselves.' But Arthur had not taken the letter seriously; as far as he was concerned, the love affair was continuing.

So much for the marriage.

Mr Justice Ormrod now turned to the medical evidence — and he took his time. As a former medical man, he praised the quality of the evidence on both sides, describing it as 'quite outstanding', in terms not only of the clarity of the doctors' explanations but also their scientific and intellectual objectivity. 'The cause of justice is deeply indebted to them,' he said. Because April Ashley had XY chromosomes and was born without internal or external female sex organs, she was chromosomally and genitally male. However, she was 'psychologically transsexual' and '[s]ocially, by which I mean the manner in which [she] is living in the community, she is living as, and passing as, a woman more or less successfully'.

To emphasise this last phrase, the judge said that April had looked convincingly feminine at first sight, but that as her cross-examination continued, 'the voice, manner, gestures and attitude became increasingly reminiscent of the accomplished female impersonator'.

Nevertheless, the medical professionals who examined April had agreed that she had had the benefit of very skilful surgery: one specialist had said that 'the pastiche of femininity was convincing'. This, said Mr Justice Ormrod, was an accurate description. All the medical witnesses agreed that 'the biological constitution of an individual is fixed at birth [at the latest] and cannot be changed, either by the natural development of organs of the opposite sex, or by medical or surgical means. [Ashley's] operation, therefore, cannot affect her true sex.' And the term 'change of sex' was applicable only when a mistake about sex, made at birth, was revealed after further investigation.

Appalled — devastated — April was being forced to listen to the demolition of her whole sense of self.

And still Ormrod continued. The question of sex, he said, was most relevant on the question of marriage, where it was an 'essential determinant':

[B]ecause [marriage] is, and has always been recognised as, the union of man and woman. It is the institution on which the family is built, and in which the capacity for natural heterosexual intercourse is an essential element. It has, of course, many other characteristics, of which companionship and mutual support is an important one, but the characteristics which distinguish it from all other relationship can only be met by two persons of opposite sex.

It thus followed that, because marriage was essentially a relationship between a man and a woman, the case depended on April Ashley's womanhood.

Ormrod explored in some detail various definitions of the word, but in the end he poured scorn on April for asserting that she was a woman. If, he said, the law recognised that April had been 'assigned' female as a result of the surgery, what was her sex immediately before it? If her womanhood depended on the results of her surgery, she would have to be regarded as a woman with only male sex organs — and, '[f]rom this it would follow that if a 50-year-old male transsexual, married and the father of children, underwent the operation, he would then have to be regarded as a female, and capable of "marrying" a man! The results would be nothing if not bizarre.' (One wonders what the writer Jan Morris, assigned male at birth — married, a parent, and at the time making arrangements for her own surgery — thought of Ormrod's logic.)

Ormrod acknowledged that because April was treated as a woman by society, it would seem logical to consider her as such for the purpose of marriage. However, marriage was between a man and a woman and depended on sex, not gender. He accepted Arthur Corbett's evidence that Ashley evaded the issue of sexual relations after they married, but said he had not at first been able to decide whether this should be considered wilful refusal or psychological repugnance. He had decided that the evidence supported wilful refusal and added his own belief that, because of the 'artificial vaginal cavity constructed during her operation', April was 'physically incapable of ordinary and complete intercourse'. This, of course, comprehensively contradicted April's declaration and some medical evidence that her gender-affirming surgery had never prevented her from having successful vaginal sex.

And so, concluded Mr Justice Ormrod, Arthur Corbett was correct — his marriage to April Ashley was not, and had never been, valid. '[Arthur Corbett] is therefore entitled, in my judgment, to a decree of nullity, declaring that the marriage in fact celebrated on 10 September 1963 between himself and [April Ashley] was void ab initio [i.e., from the beginning].' The judgment also meant that April was not entitled to any compensation as a result of the marriage. As she said later with some bitterness, as far as the villa was concerned, she could whistle for it.

As the headline in *The Times Law Report* put it bluntly: 'Bride was not a woman: Marriage void.'

When Arthur Corbett, in Marbella, regained consciousness a few days later and was told about the decision, he said he was 'very pleased', but nothing more. When April was asked afterwards how she felt about what had happened to Arthur, she replied composedly, 'I'm sorry about it. But I shan't be flying out to see him. That part of my life has ended.' For many years afterwards, she barely mentioned Arthur Corbett's name. April's pride and sense of self had taken a beating from which she never fully recovered. She had been so proud of escaping from the slums of Liverpool — proud of discovering for herself the solution to her problems. And all that had been for nothing.

CHAPTER 16

Aftermath

April's solicitor, Terry Walton, wanted her to appeal against Justice Ormrod's decision. The barrier, however, was the usual one: lack of money. April would have to rely on legal aid again, but legal aid funds did not cover appeals. An American foundation had offered to meet the costs of further litigation, but Dr Dewhurst, professor of obstetrics at Queen Charlotte Hospital London and one of Arthur Corbett's medical team, was on their English committee, and so April's legal team declined the offer. Ashley later said she had little energy for fundraising at this point, though she did wish she had tried harder.

Most of the English press reported the *Corbett v Corbett* decision as a simple news story, with quotes from April herself. Even without overt editorial comment on the rights and wrongs of the decision, there were differing attitudes to the case. The *Daily Mail* went for human interest alone with its headline: 'A man! Sex-change April says: "But I'll still wear my gowns"'. April was quoted as being 'absolutely shattered', adding:

I have been married for seven years and I have been treated during that time like a married woman. This is incredible. After all, you

can only be what you function as, and I can't function as a man ...
Socially I'm still a woman although, according to the judge, I'm a
man. I'm still a woman according to my insurance card. Anyway,
if the police arrested me for a crime, they would be in a bit of a
spot to decide what kind of prison to send me to, wouldn't they?[1]

When asked what she intended to do now, she said: 'Carry on.
What else can one do? It just means I can't get married for the moment,
but I have no plans to anyway.'

The *Daily Mirror* was having none of such fortitude:

April Ashley must learn to live in the tragic halfway world between man and woman. A judge ruled yesterday that she was,
and always will be, a man. The verdict was a shattering blow to
the tall, girlish, graceful Miss Ashley, who seemed to the outside
world to have really become the woman she longed to be. She
now knows that not all the beautiful clothes she wears, the drugs
she took to make her breasts grow, nor the sex-change operation
she had ten years ago, can make her dream of complete femininity come true in the eyes of the law.[2]

Some of the press coverage was equally sympathetic to April. The
Sunday Mirror front-page splash featured a photograph of her, shown
in profile, walking alone by the side of a lake, with a pram behind her
— intended, probably, as an implicit reference to her often-reiterated
hope of adopting children. She was quoted as saying, 'I am completely
unprotected and so are all the others in my position.' It was true. The
knowledge that, because of a piece of paper, her lived reality and legal
status were completely at odds was worse than devastating. April's
confidence in who she was had been comprehensively destroyed, with
that picture of the pram a poignant reminder.

April had trouble sleeping and, when she did sleep, she had

horrible dreams; she was buffeted by panic attacks and palpitations and continually exhausted. She dreaded being alone; she left the television set on all the time for company. And, for the first time in ten years, April thought again of killing herself — and she was terrified that she might attempt to do so impulsively, simply to find relief.

After four weeks in the divorce court, April had lost an enormous amount of weight: 'I'd gone down to six and a half stone and I'm five feet ten and a half tall,' she said. She went to a health farm to recuperate, taking a bottle of brandy with her:

> It was a test I set myself, would I drink the brandy or not? And then I heard a man in the room next to me say to someone, *You'll never guess who's in the next room, it's that monster April Ashley.* And I got angry and that was a very good sign, because I was human again. I did not touch the brandy, and I decided to go back and face these people and say, *I'm here and whether you like it or not I am staying.* It took a bit of courage to say that because I wanted to run away, everything in me wanted to hide.[3]

As so often before, her Scouse resilience came to her aid. One of her most notable appearances was on *The Simon Dee Show* a week after the decision; her fellow guests were actor George Lazenby and John Lennon and Yoko Ono. One reviewer said that April — glamorous, calm, and witty, showing no obvious trace of what she had been through — was the star of the show; John and Yoko, banging on about peace, were boring.[4] And the *Daily Mirror* remained a stalwart supporter: only a month after the decision, it published a piece with the headline 'The year's most talked about personality on a subject near to her heart ... April Ashley on Clothes', complete with photographs of a beaming April in a revealing beaded dress and a trouser suit.[5]

Friends helped, and sometimes total strangers went out of their way to boost April's morale. After the judgment had been made public, she received many encouraging and sympathetic letters. One day, in Sloane Square, she felt a tug on her sleeve and turned to see a smartly dressed woman in her 60s. This woman said April should live her life as she chose, taking no notice of what the law had said. 'I watched you,' she said. 'You are very brave.'

Overwhelmed, April fled. It was a long time, Ashley said, before she had the courage to cry in public.

Consolation of a sort came when she was asked to act as 'hostess' in a new Knightsbridge restaurant, to be called April & Desmond's, with restaurateur Desmond Morgan — later abbreviated to AD8, in reference to the address at 8 Egerton Garden Mews. It opened in April 1970. Short of money, April agreed to an extraordinary arrangement: she would sign over to the restaurant managers all her income from newspaper articles and television appearances, including the £5,000 fee the *Sunday Mirror* had paid for her exclusive story in the wake of the verdict.

She was persuaded to hand over her money to avoid having to repay the funds she had received for legal aid: according to the rules, anyone who came into money up to seven years afterwards had to do so. It was estimated that an appeal would cost £7,000, and a substantial amount of this would have to be placed with the court by 24 August. One of Arthur's barristers immediately suggested that she had deliberately disposed of her assets so as to be unable to pay the costs of an appeal. This, April said, was untrue, because any assets had been swallowed up by previous costs.

In return for relinquishing her appearance fees, then and in the future, April would be paid £60 a month, rising to £200, and live in a studio flat above the restaurant. While the *Daily Mail* reported that this arrangement was little short of slavery, April felt she had hardly any choice but to agree to it.[6] And so — still glamorous and with renewed notoriety, thanks to the court case — she gradually regained her equilibrium, however shakily at first.

The publicity she had received had heartened her, too: if the whole awful experience of *Corbett v Corbett* had confirmed anything about her, it was her ability to show herself to her best advantage.

April was back with all guns blazing.[7]

Three weeks after Mr Justice Ormrod's decision, the *Sunday Mirror* published an interview with Dr Georges Burou.[8] Even though he had declined to give evidence, Burou was quite happy to be the subject of a two-page spread, illustrated with photographs.

Headlined 'The surgeon who changes men into women', the article published after the decision in 1970 was highly complimentary. Dr Burou emphasised that he performed gender-affirming surgery only on people with markedly feminine characteristics and that at least two people per day — candidates from all over the world — asked for the surgery. (His wife, to whom he was not always faithful, contributed a nicely double-edged observation: 'It is because my husband knows so much about women that he can perform this operation on men.')

In the article, Dr Burou said of April:

I don't remember Miss Ashley in particular. It was a long time ago [ten years] and I have done so many similar operations since then. But I know how she must feel as a result of the judge's decision. Every human being has the right to try and find happiness, and if people like Miss Ashley can find happiness by living and working as women, why shouldn't they?

It would have been better, perhaps, if the English judge had not needed to make any judgment on Miss Ashley. The decision will cause so much unhappiness to many, many people like her in Britain whose lives have already been so tragic. The law would be better to leave them alone and allow them to live as they want.

Perhaps, despite his evident sympathy for April's case, Dr Burou might have been reluctant to testify at the hearing because he realised he could complicate matters if he were asked to give a solely medical view. Several years later, he was quoted as saying: 'I don't change men into women. I transform male genitals into genitals that have a female aspect. All the rest is in the patient's mind.'[9]

Dr Burou's comments in the *Sunday Mirror* were more outspoken than many English newspapers were prepared to be. Those that gave the most thoughtful attention to the implications of Mr Justice Ormrod's decision were *The Times* and *The Sunday Times*. *The Times* allowed April some dignity by quoting her as saying only that '[b]asically it does not make any difference. I have a lot of friends and I am very well loved', adding that 'she could not at present remarry, but had not been planning to do so'. Nevertheless, *The Times* also quoted one of her solicitors, Peter Maddock (brother of Edward and a trusted friend who would remain her lifelong adviser), as saying that the ruling 'not only affects her but also many, many other people, a lot of whom are happily married but are in the same situation as April. The problem is a social one. Legally she is a male but socially she is a woman.'[10]

Under the heading 'Why sex change is no change', the *Sunday Times* writer Timothy Leland pointed out that Ormrod's decision had, not surprisingly, been welcomed by British lawyers because it cut right through the Gordian knot of gender-affirming surgery and the status of transgender people. Comments from several sources emphasised that sex had many indicators, some of which might easily be in conflict, since genes and internal and external sex organs might not align with the fourth indicator, which was psychological. *The Sunday Times* defined 'transsexuals' as 'men and women who appear to be physically normal but who in fact have a passionate desire to belong to the opposite sex', and it explained that this was a 'problem' — but a psychological, not a physical, one. And, either way, surgery would not change chromosomal structure or the internal reproductive organs, but only the outward and visible sex characteristics.[11]

However, wrote Leland, although the result of surgery and massive doses of hormones might be 'quite striking', as in April Ashley's case, its success was an illusion: it was impossible to change 'a normal man' into 'a normal woman'. In an echo of lingering societal attitudes to gay men, Dr Dewhurst was quoted: '[Being transsexual] is a disease that is incurable. We can't correct it, we can only make it more tolerable ... Society is not sympathetic, on the whole, to this kind of problem.'

The status of the 'problem' of transgender identities and the decision in *Corbett v Corbett* were strongly challenged by several American doctors — most notably, endocrinologist Harry Benjamin, author of *The Transsexual Phenomenon*, a 1966 medical textbook that became a standard for the care and study of trans men and women (Benjamin is said to have popularised the word 'transsexual' in medical circles). According to Benjamin, a 'transsexual person' was someone who identified in opposition to their assigned gender at birth. He left out such emotive terms as 'passionate desire to belong' to another sex and thus provided a more neutral definition than the one accepted by many British doctors at the time.

In his book, which was the culmination of years of research, Benjamin identified seven categories of sex: as well as the medical terminologies, he added that sex could be hormonal, psychological, and social. In his terms, a 'transsexual' was someone whose psychological sex was in opposition to the other sexual categories he defined. In *The Sunday Times*, however, his view was more simply expressed: 'In practical life, the definition of a man is a person who has male sex organs. April Ashley has a vagina, so she is a woman.'

Benjamin then commented on the central issue of Ormrod's decision. Legally, the judge's conclusion — which he described as 'cruel and illogical' — had been that no amount of hormonal treatment or surgery on someone assigned male at birth would produce someone 'naturally capable of performing the essential role of a woman in marriage'. But, demanded Benjamin, what was that?

> Is the essential role to have children? If so, what about women with a hysterectomy? These women can't have children. That doesn't mean they're not female. Is the essential role to be able to satisfy a man sexually? What about frigid women? Just because a woman is frigid doesn't mean she isn't female.

He concluded that April Ashley was 'able to fulfil her role as a female and a wife in every particular except reproduction'.

The Sunday Times also made the point that Ormrod's ruling had profound implications not only for April Ashley and others like her — 'perhaps the most tortured of sexual minorities' — but also for the future of 'that increasingly battered institution known as marriage': 'For however "flexible" marriage has become today, whether it implies the extended family idea or the *ménage à trois* or the lifelong homosexual association, this week's court decision appears to have put a large sign on the legal door that says "Freaks Keep Out!"'

And there was another — perhaps surprising — supporter of trans rights, according to a memoir by Australian human rights lawyer Geoffrey Robertson:

> At lunch I was seated next to Princess Anne, and we discussed LGBT rights. Seriously, forty years before that acronym came into being. Our topic was a recent court decision in the case of April Ashley ... [The case] caused a lot of controversy and Anne was on the side of reforming the law to uphold trans rights. I suggested she might undergo a transgender operation herself so that she could inherit the throne (she was last in line below her wimpish younger brothers, Andrew and Edward). She quite liked this idea.[12]

Outside the United Kingdom, the law was often more flexible, as seen in the southern French town of Grasse less than a year after Ormrod's ruling. Hélène Hauterive had undergone gender-affirming surgery with Dr Burou. She was ruled female for legal purposes in the local court and able to marry, because 'she possesses external genitals of a feminine type and because her psychological behaviour is without doubt that of a woman'.

Likewise, in the case of *M.T. v J.T.*, heard in the Superior Court of New Jersey in the late 1970s, a husband contested his wife's claim for maintenance on the same grounds as *Corbett v Corbett*: that his wife, who had been assigned male at birth and had undergone successful surgery, could never have been validly married to him. In this case, Judge Handler, while accepting that marriage did have to be between a man and a woman, rejected Ormrod's reasoning and upheld the wife's claim. His reasoning was that if a person's physical features conformed with their 'gender, psyche or psychological sex, then identity by sex must be governed by the congruence of those standards'.[13]

It is undeniable that the narrowness of Ormrod's decision in *Corbett v Corbett* set back the cause of trans rights in the United Kingdom, and elsewhere, for more than 30 years.

As April put on her glamorous gowns and went to work at April & Desmond's, leading patrons to their tables with a warm smile, great charm, and dignity, she must have felt that, for her, vindication would never come.

PART FOUR

The Unsinkable April Ashley

CHAPTER 17

Life at AD8

April had signed a five-year contract with Freshrise Ltd, the company that ran April & Desmond's. The restaurant's principal backer was Eagle Star Insurance, but several individuals also put money in. The most celebrated was probably Kit Lambert. The short, dark-haired, and ebullient Oxford-educated son of the composer and conductor Constant Lambert, Kit was famous in rock music circles, but he had started as a film cameraman before linking up with Christopher Stamp, younger brother of actor Terence. The pair came from different worlds, though they shared a wild streak and a sense of possibility: Terence described his brother as a 'rough, tough fighting spiv', while Kit was a cultivated man with a wide-ranging mind. Stamp told an interviewer, 'We were both marginalised, [Lambert] in gayness and me in my [working] class. It was a powerful bond.'[1]

They decided to work together to make a film about the offstage life of a pop group, and they chose the Who. This band had originally been formed as the High Numbers in 1964, with lead vocalist Roger Daltrey, guitarist Pete Townshend, bassist John Entwistle, and drummer Keith Moon — 'four complicated, difficult guys', as Stamp recalled. When Lambert and Stamp came to know them, the Who were well on their way to establishing their reputation as one of the most innovative and important rock bands around. Lambert and Stamp filmed several of their concerts, and soon became thoroughly involved in the band's lives and music. They ditched the documentary in favour of becoming the Who's managers.

Lambert had big plans for the band, wanting them to show how sexually adventurous they were. 'They have to have a direct sexual impact,' he said. 'They ask a question, do you want to or don't you? And they don't give their public a chance of saying no.' It was Lambert, with his flair for publicity, who saw the shock value of having the band trash their equipment on stage — something for which they became notorious. This was, however, an expensive way to run concert tours, so the group turned to recording. It was Lambert who encouraged Pete Townshend to extend his range as the band's resident composer and who gave him the confidence to write the pioneering rock operas *Tommy* and *Quadrophenia*. The Who were always chaotic to manage: they were, said one colleague, an extension of Kit Lambert's manic attitude to life. Pete Townshend always acknowledged him as the group's artistic and cultural mentor.

At the height of his fame, Kit Lambert came to AD8 for dinner almost every night: he said he wanted to eat his £2,000 investment in the restaurant. April said that, though he had a wild reputation as a drug user, he was usually quiet and ate his meals by himself — occasionally joined by Keith Moon and others. April was very fond of Lambert, describing him as thoughtful, intelligent, witty and generous of spirit, though she added that she doubted whether he was tough and ruthless enough for the cut-throat world of rock music.*

*

---

*   Lambert's life gradually spiralled out of control. By the mid-1970s, the band had sidelined him
       as manager and his life disintegrated as drugs took over. He was made a ward of court to escape a
       potential prison sentence for drug offences, and he died in 1981.

AD8 was a smashing success from the start. On its opening night, 2 March 1970 — only a month after Mr Justice Ormrod's judgment — Ashley said that five or six hundred people streamed into a smallish cellar. It continued to be the place to be seen, booked out weeks ahead, and famous names clamoured to be part of it. They included John Osborne, whose play *Look Back in Anger* had already become a classic of British theatre, as well as the tenor Plácido Domingo, who sang Neapolitan love songs until 1.00 am, and Hollywood stars such as Ingrid Bergman and Ava Gardner.

At the AD8 launch party with Desmond Morgan

AD8 sometimes featured cabaret shows. One of the most popular was comedy duo George Logan and Patrick Fyffe, who performed in drag as Hinge and Bracket, two genteel and eccentric old ladies who had spent their lives performing duets from classical opera and musical comedy. In between numbers, they reminisced about their heyday performing with Ivor Novello and Noël Coward. Fyffe and Logan had started their routines in gay clubs, but they had become one of the first drag acts to enter the mainstream — probably because they didn't trade on sex appeal. Dr Evadne Hinge and Dame Hilda Bracket were rounded characters whose comedy often depended on their strenuous efforts to outdo each other. Logan and Fyffe never appeared as themselves on television, radio or on tour; like their contemporary Barry Humphries, best known for playing Dame Edna Everage, they remained firmly in character.*

An almost-guest at AD8 was Princess Margaret, whom Ashley considered a sexy, emotional woman stranded between being royal and wanting to mix in a more creative world. Margaret was torn between insisting on being called 'Your Royal Highness' or 'Maggie', depending on context. April asked her whether she would do the restaurant the honour of dining there. Princess Margaret said, 'I'll send someone along to look at it.' 'Do you mean you'll have someone case the joint first?' April replied. This jocular vulgarity was not well received, and the princess never came, not even under her dining alias 'Maggie Jones'. Ashley thought Princess Margaret could have emulated some of her arty friends by developing a sense of humour.[2]

Gastronomically, AD8 was less successful, with the food writer Quentin Crewe bluntly describing the pâté as 'soap' and the cuisine more generally as indifferent. (This was probably accurate: one of AD8's signature dishes was champagne and Camembert soup.) Despite his status as the most influential restaurant critic in London, Crewe's opinion had absolutely no effect on AD8's popularity, because its patrons did not come for the food. April was shrewdly aware that diners wanted to be seen and to be impressed. Even if they thought the cuisine downright bad, they would not say so for fear of being marked down as not 'with it'.

April was on duty as hostess for seven nights a week: for a long time, she was the restaurant's chief attraction. Almost all the money

---

* Hinge and Bracket — who, in many respects, were heirs to 1930s comedy artist Douglas Byng — also appeared in a West End adaptation of Oscar Wilde's *The Importance of Being Earnest* and released several albums, including a parody of the Beatles' *Abbey Road*.

she made went back into the business via cosmetics, hair styling, clothes, and shoes. The grand, sophisticated image she projected as an 'older woman', as she described herself aged almost 40, meant dressing to the nines in the style of at least one generation before that of the early 1970s. Becoming the 'April Ashley' people expected was not the work of a moment, and she took her job very seriously. Achieving her trademark glamour involved not only diligent attention to her clothes and carefully applied makeup but also such things as hair colour: most patrons were smokers, and the white streaks in her dark hair would turn yellow if she was not careful to dye them back. Once — only once — she rebelled and wore jeans to work, and many of the patrons, who had turned up to see the April Ashley they expected, were very disappointed.

April smilingly greeted guests by name whenever possible, knowing the priceless value of remembering who people were. But though she enjoyed her role most of the time, she had surprisingly little to do with the running of the place. Her habit of giving free meals to people who represented what she considered worthy causes infuriated her partners. The waiting staff, none of whom stayed long, did not take her seriously, and she occasionally had to stage a tantrum to remind everyone that she was not to be ignored. She did manage to negotiate the use of a much bigger flat in Eaton Square for herself. This was one of the most prestigious addresses in London and the home of regular AD8 visitor Ava Gardner, who had taught April how to drink tequila.

Wealthy friends occasionally invited April on holidays, including to the south of France and to Tokyo — where she observed people whose gender was indeterminate and concluded that the Japanese were much more casual about these things than Westerners.*

April also took up her friendship with Sarah Churchill and was

---

* *Funeral Parade of Roses*, an acclaimed Japanese New Wave film about queer nightlife in Tokyo, had been released in 1969. It would be interesting to know whether Ashley met Shinnosuke Ikehata, who played a trans woman in the film.

invited to parties with celebrated figures from yesteryear, including Noël Coward (whom she found warm, charming and, contrary to some reports, not at all brittle) and Cecil Beaton (whom she described as having a mean face and a cold, unpleasant manner). And she renewed her acquaintance with Francis Bacon, whom she had first met in her days with Lord Timothy Willoughby. Francis, Ashley said, always drank too much and had to be helped up the stairs at closing time.

One evening, late in 1972, two uniformed policemen came to see April at work. They asked her whether she had known Edward Maddock, the young man with whom she had lived a couple of years before. When she said yes, they told her that he had been driving back from Saint-Tropez on a wet night to begin his second term at the Webber-Douglas Academy, where he was training to be an actor. He had been killed in a head-on collision outside Paris. When April asked why they had come to tell her the news, they said that hers had been the only address they found on him.

Edward's parents invited April to the funeral: despite their disapproval of her relationship with Edward, they obviously knew how much she had meant to him. After the service, she went up to Edward's bedroom in his parents' house, where, she said, seeing gifts she had given him made her even sadder. In later years, she described Edward as the love of her life. Remembering him years later, she told a journalist, 'Whenever I need advice or get lonely I talk to Edward. Sometimes I'll yell at him: *Edward, you leave those angels alone and help me here!* I always seem to sort things out when I talk to Edward.'[3]

The reverberations of *Corbett v Corbett* continued, and for a long time.

In May 1970 the courts ruled that Arthur Corbett should not be liable for Ashley's legal costs because she had been able to obtain legal aid — even though she had dropped her appeal because legal aid did not cover such proceedings, and she was unable to raise the funds. At the time, the Divorce Reform Bill, allowing divorce by mutual consent after two years of separation, was slowly making its way through Parliament. April might well have realised, as did commentators with 20/20 hindsight, that if Arthur Corbett had waited only another year, the whole sorry saga of *Corbett v Corbett* could have been avoided.

In 1971, the UK Parliament passed the Nullity of Marriage Act. For the first time in British law, marriage was defined as being between a man and a woman, a definition that had previously been assumed. During debate on the bill in the House of Commons, Labour MP Alexander Lyon had argued that the law needed to be clarified because otherwise a gay union would count as marriage, which was 'clearly ridiculous'. Surgery to 'change the sex' of one partner would not solve the problem: Mr Justice Ormrod's decision had become case law in the United Kingdom and Australia, and it remained so for many years.[4] The occasional practice whereby trans people might have their birth certificates altered to conform with their gender identity was also made illegal. These changes codified what trans people already knew: the price of their greater visibility was increased social resistance.

In an immediate illustration of the new climate, in March 1971, Patricia White married Reg Gibbons without disclosing that she had formerly been known as merchant seaman Patrick Read. She had undergone gender-affirming surgery thanks to the National Health Service 11 years before. The General Register Office at Somerset House demanded an investigation of the marriage because White's past as a male had not been disclosed. It's clear that the Somerset House staff were not readers of *The People*, where the whole story had been splashed all over the front page. White declared that nobody at the local registry office had asked about her past, and the registrar in charge asserted that he hadn't known until after the ceremony that White had undergone surgery. The marriage was quietly dissolved and Patricia White disappeared from the record.

April summed up her feelings about *Corbett v Corbett* and

other legal developments affecting trans people in an interview with journalist and author Tina Brown some years later:

> [In *Corbett v Corbett*,] my lawyer was wiped off the floor by Arthur's. My golly, Tina, if you ever want a divorce, Joe Jackson is your man. He'll get you pots of money and make you out a *virgin*. But no, I'm not bitter for myself so much as for all those other poor transsexuals who can never be legally married. Just because Arthur and I made such a farcical mess of things it doesn't mean it couldn't have worked between two other people. Of course there are hundreds of transsexuals living quietly as wives ... but now because of my legal precedent they have to live in terror that one day the men who pardoned them will turn. That seems terribly unfair.[5]

April's life at AD8 continued through the early 1970s and so, apparently, did her assumption that the way she lived would go on as long as she wanted. She seems to have given very little, if any, thought to her future — and why should she? She thought she had found her niche. With her as hostess, AD8 had remained *the* place to be for almost four years, long enough for any restaurant to be regarded as an institution. And when April ran short of money or a place to live, or both, she had been able to depend on her better-off friends and acquaintances to keep her in good food and wine, as well as lovely clothes. She reasoned that if the situation were to change, she would find work somehow. Her rule of life, apart from not allowing herself to stay down for long, was *carpe diem* — seize what opportunities arise: just keep going, don't plan and the future will look after itself.

But cracks were beginning to show. April felt that many employees, especially waiting staff, didn't know their jobs; at one stage, she said, there was a new member of staff virtually every month. Her shouting matches with incompetent staff became common. With increasing frustration, April was using all her energy trying to make the place work, relying on alcohol and pills to keep her going. When she burned her leg on a leaky hot-water bottle at home, she did not take time off but limped to work as usual. Not long afterwards, she fell downstairs and broke her wrist, failed to get it set properly, and it was never right again. And then she slipped and broke her other wrist. Because April did not have consistent hormone therapy after her surgery in 1960, it's very likely that her bones were brittle and that she had osteoporosis. All of these accidents increased her dependence on drugs: she was, she said later, 'swallowing Valium like Smarties'.

April needed a holiday and fortunately she was invited to Barbados with friends. Here, she met Oliver Messel, mentor of her friend James Bailey and still regarded as one of the most sophisticated and inventive designers in 20th-century British theatre. Messel worked on ballets, operas, and musicals as well as plays, and he had been an interior designer for some of Ashley's friends. She enjoyed his company, and the holiday, if only for a couple of weeks, was a refreshing break.

She came back to AD8 to find that things had not improved. Now, she was having constant battles with her partners, not only about the management of the place but also about her own role. Patrons and staff were noticing that her consumption of alcohol was affecting her work. She said that, one evening, she drank 32 martinis, hardly aware of the quantity because she was moving around and chatting, but that she did notice problems with her liver. Early in 1975, her five-year contract had only six months left to run, and she wanted to break it early. Her partners consented, offering her a fee of £3,000. She refused, pointing out her critical role in making the restaurant successful, as well as the money she had provided. When they refused to budge, she didn't have the energy to fight them and so she agreed.

And so April found herself facing another crisis and another change of direction.

She went first to California, a place that proved to be full of pleasant distractions: she met Lenny Plugge again, renewed her acquaintance with other friends (including the actor Roddy McDowell), and travelled south to Mexico. But eventually she had to return to London and — once again — face some unwelcome facts. Her health was not good, she had lost a great deal of weight, she had no work and very little money. Notoriety was all very well, but she was also beginning to weary of being occasional fodder for the tabloid press. She was conscious of getting older in a society that worshipped youth above all, and the last thing she wanted was to be embalmed as a glamorous oddity.

A few days' work as a stage actor provided little respite. She played a glamorous vampire named Countess Josephine in a production of *Dracula* at the Collegiate Theatre in Bloomsbury in September 1974 — the theatre was evidently cashing in on the contemporary fad for the horror movies made by Hammer Film Productions. Publicity stills show April sporting an impressive set of fangs — although her performance appears to have passed without comment.

It was time, yet again, to get out of London. The city was too big, too challenging, too expensive, too indifferent. April liked the idea of distancing herself from the persona she had spent so much time and trouble cultivating, living instead among people who might not see her as some kind of celebrity — somewhere she could live a quiet life for a while.

Impulsively she decided on Hay-on-Wye, close to the border of Wales and England. She had been there in the 1960s with her friend Viva King, and knew it as a quiet market town, close to the Brecon Beacons in the tranquil valley of the River Wye and not far from Hereford.

She had made friends with Viva's nephew Richard Booth, a wealthy entrepreneur who owned and ran several bookshops — and who was looking to open a restaurant in the local castle he had inherited from an uncle.

Perhaps, thought April, she could find work with him.

CHAPTER 18

Making Hay

In a 1973 television interview with Russell Harty, April said, 'I long to get away from that April Ashley image. I long not to see any more press … I long for the little house in the country.'

'And the thatched roof?' asked Harty.

'Oh no,' she said. 'Think of all the lice running around! I'd like something solid, in stone.'[1]

April arrived in Hay-on-Wye — commonly known as Hay — early in 1975. Richard Booth offered her as accommodation not a stone cottage but a small flat above one of the bookshops he owned and ran. The address of her new home in the middle of town was 1 The Pavement, and it had pitched ceilings and small gable windows facing lush moorlands. Hay was green and rather staid, and its quiet was a relief after rackety London.

This was a part of the country April had never known well, and she soon set about exploring. Among the places she visited was the neighbouring village of Clyro, where she went to the local pub, the Baskerville Arms. The name intrigued her, and she asked the owner about it. The owner told her that Sherlock Holmes's creator, Arthur Conan Doyle, had occasionally stayed there as a friend of the family.

During one of his visits, said the owner, Conan Doyle heard about a gigantic hound that haunted the Baskerville family and, when he returned to London, he used this legend in the most popular Sherlock Holmes novel, *The Hound of the Baskervilles*. It is a good story and Ashley, ever on the lookout for a romantic yarn, told it often. But Conan Doyle set his story in Devon, not in Wales. Legends of hellhounds, it seems, were not uncommon.

April's hopes, or wishes, to be anonymous when she came to Hay were quickly dashed. She was far too noticeable. 'Put me down in the middle of the jungle and I'd find some way of painting my eyes even if I had to burn a stick to make eyeshadow,' she once told a journalist.

At first, the people of Hay viewed her with suspicion, staring at her in the street, nudging each other, and making loud comments about her makeup and her London clothes. The children were the worst, Ashley thought — especially pre-adolescent boys. While she shopped in her elegant high-heeled boots and trousers or floaty Laura Ashley dresses, they would follow her: 'Look at her! Hey, are your tits real?' Another time she overheard two boys saying knowingly to each other, 'She's a lesbian, you know.'[2] Torn between amusement and disdain, April assumed that their knowledge about sex came from watching animals on the local farms: how on earth, she wondered, would their parents explain her own identity to them?

One time, when she was suffering from a hangover and hurrying to catch a bus, she was followed by a jeering crowd of young teenagers, and she decided she had had enough. She rounded on the ringleader: 'Who are you to jeer at people? If you want to know something about me, behave like a man and ask me to my face!'

A far more serious problem soon surfaced after her arrival, however. On her way home with a friend one night, April started feeling very shaky, with pain under her ribs. She went to bed, but the pain grew steadily worse until, she said, she felt as if she had been kicked by a horse. Her friend called a doctor, who diagnosed a heart attack, and she was rushed to a private hospital in Hereford.

April stayed in hospital for two weeks. She was extremely worried all the time, not about having another heart attack — she was receiving the best possible care and was assured she was improving — but about the size of her medical bills. To her great relief, her medical insurance proved enough to cover them. When she emerged, she was told to avoid alcohol, sugar, and red meat. She hastily agreed, but soon started drinking again.

A few weeks later, she had another, minor, heart attack — and this time she decided to be sensible. She stopped drinking alcohol and hardly left her flat for five months, and she lived on cabbage and baked beans, with the occasional wine gum for dessert. She was bored out of her mind, of course, but cheered up when a friend invited her to join his yacht at Saint-Tropez.

She also visited the island of Ibiza, where she renewed an acquaintance with the actor Denholm Elliott and his family. For about 30 years, Elliott was one of Britain's most successful character actors, featured in films, plays, and television series. (He was famous for upstaging his scene partners, and it was said: 'Never appear on stage or film with children — or Denholm Elliott.') He asked April to babysit his children for two weeks while he and his wife went to mainland Spain for the filming of *Robin and Marian*, starring Sean Connery and Audrey Hepburn. This was one of the few times in her life that Ashley had looked after children, and she was pleased and relieved to find that the experience, though occasionally stressful, was not unpleasant. She was helped by Jeremy Brett — not yet television's most durable Sherlock Holmes — who offered his services as chauffeur. Elliott — who, like Brett, was bisexual — visited April in Hay several times with his wife, Susie, and insisted on having his own room. Ashley said that he and Susie had an open marriage, and that they were devoted to each other, as well as being loving parents.

When April returned to Wales, she did something she had sworn she would never do: she applied for unemployment benefits. Coming from a proudly working-class family, she had been brought up to pay her own way and hated the idea of taking any form of handout from the state. But now she was poor and ill, and so she swallowed her pride and visited the social security office in Brecon, where she was registered for National Assistance as a disabled person. Though she could not work, she did not want to be idle, and she decided to enrol in a short cookery course in the market town of Shrewsbury, nearly 60 miles away — perhaps with the aim of opening her own café. She found temporary accommodation in the town, although she maintained her flat in Hay.

While April was not the best in the class, she might have been the fastest: after all those years of slicing bacon for the Lundys, she at least knew her way around a boning knife. At first, the others on the course — all in a financial position similar to hers — were suspicious of April's patrician accent and general air of worldly sophistication, but they warmed to her; at the end of the course, several lined up to say goodbye. While the cooking course had been set up to provide marketable skills, and April rarely used anything she had learned, she had found it valuable for another reason: after her shaky start in Hay, she had enjoyed talking to some of the people she had met there.

In November 1978, while April was away from Hay, her stalwart friend and supporter Viva King died. Her death wasn't unexpected: she was 85 years old and had been in poor health for some time. April had made a point of visiting her in London whenever possible — and always on New Year's Eve. Viva had written her autobiography, *The Weeping and the Laughter*, in 1976, dedicated to the openly gay novelist and critic Angus Wilson (whose novels were said to feature characters based on members of Viva's social circle). Although it was well received, sales had been disappointing: evidently the reading public was not particularly interested in 1920s bohemian London. Viva had been forced to sell some valuables because, as she wrote to April, 'I am like Oscar Wilde, dying beyond my means.' April had been very fond of this gallant throwback to an elegant, cultivated older generation and grateful for Viva's friendship. She was very sad to lose her.

Back in Hay, she met Charles Simpson, in his late 70s and twice a widower. He lived in the town's biggest house, having retired from his garage business, and he was very lonely. Here, April thought, was a good cause — someone she could help. (The fact that they liked each other didn't hurt.) She took it upon herself to look after Charles, mowing his lawn, practising her newly acquired cooking skills on his behalf, doing his shopping, and telling him the local gossip. She also supervised his medication and steered him away from drinking too much. She cheered him up by refusing to indulge him or treat him as a two-year-old. April, in short, behaved like a loving but exasperated daughter — even though Charles Simpson had a daughter who lived elsewhere. 'Charlie' was a sweetheart, Ashley said, and she felt responsible for him. At the same time, she was disconcerted to discover how much he depended on her. When she once told him she was thinking of returning to London, he said that if she did so, he would die.

When Charles's physical condition gradually deteriorated, April finally moved into his house to look after him. It was not easy: he was increasingly frail and forgetful, constantly falling out of bed, and she had to watch him whenever he was near the electric fire. He wanted to leave her £10,000 but she refused, saying that the money should go to his daughter. And there things rested until Simpson died in 1980, when April was astonished to learn that he had left her his house. In the first of her two autobiographies, April reports that she accepted the gift straightforwardly, as her due; in the second, she is more defensive, arguing that it was not inappropriate for her to have inherited it, because the house had belonged to Charles's second wife, who had died years earlier. At around the same time, she learned that Viva King had left her a small sum of money, as well as some paintings and sculptures. April, no sentimentalist, gleefully and gratefully sold most of them at Sotheby's. (She retained one, at least for a time: Augustus John's portrait, *Young Viva King naked and masturbating.*)

With the bequests from Charles Simpson and Viva, April now had a sizable house of her own and, if carefully handled, enough money to support herself without needing to depend on social security. Ashley later observed that Charles Simpson and Viva King had adopted the role of parents by looking after her financially, and that, as children often do, she had looked after them. She celebrated her new good fortune by acquiring a small whippet named Flora Bella to keep her company — the kind of elegant, leggy dog often seen crouched at the feet of aristocrats in portraits.

With Flora Bella in the garden at Hay

Although April spent a decade of her life in Hay-on-Wye, it cannot be said that she ever embraced rural life. It is impossible to imagine her discussing the finer points of raising cattle with local farmers or glorying in the production of Welsh cakes or scones at local fairs. In a 1980 documentary, she observed rather ruefully that Hay was a 'very male place', where she had to wait at the pub until all the men — horse dealers, farmers, fishermen — had been served.[3]

But if she thought she was making a clean start, she was mistaken. On a visit to London in August 1980, April was arrested and charged with being 'drunk and disorderly' after being ejected from Morton's Club in Berkeley Square. She referred to the arresting police officers as 'peasants'. When asked why she had refused to leave the club when requested (she was apparently not a member), she said, 'I resented being told that, "We don't like your kind in here." I wanted to know what my kind was.' And then she announced, 'Nobody tells me, April Ashley, what to do' — making her identity clear, if the police had been in any doubt.

According to April's account, one of the policemen twisted her arm behind her back as they took her down to the West End police station. When one of the officers took her statement, he left the charge sheet column marked 'Sex' blank, and he referred to April as 'he' or 'that person'. Incandescent with rage, she lunged across the desk and hit him in the face with her shoulder bag. 'After twenty-one years of being a woman I should be treated as one,' she said — adding that, for all that time, her passport had been in the name of 'Miss April Ashley', and if that confirmed she was a woman, 'I don't see why a police constable shouldn't'.

April was promptly charged with assault — as 'Mr Ashley' — and placed in a cell for men. The station sergeant said that they had put April in there because she had become violent and the cell was closest to the charge room. While they promised they would move her to a women's cell, they did not, and April stayed in the men's cell overnight.

April admitted to being drunk and disorderly. 'I was abusive at the police station,' April later agreed. 'I felt as if I was being baited and it was all rather good fun for the policemen.'

During the hearing at Marlborough Street Magistrates' Court in November, when the policeman gave his evidence about the defendant, referring to April as 'he', the woman magistrate said, 'We have in our register "April Ashley, actress". I think it will be better for all of us if you refer to her as just April Ashley and not he or she.'

April was convicted of assaulting a police officer and fined £10.

In press accounts of the incident, April was usually referred to as 'sex-change model'. The headline in the *Daily Telegraph* was 'Handbag attack by sex-change actress over PC's "he" jibe'. And at least one report reminded readers that April had been 'merchant seaman George Jamieson before a 1960 operation'.[4] All further proof — if any was needed — that April Ashley would be respected as a woman provided she remained quiet and well behaved, but not otherwise.

Echoes of the incident probably reached Hay-on-Wye, but April was happy to retreat there. The town remained a bastion of rural life, but it was changing, thanks mainly to April's friend Richard Booth. He was no mere dilettante bookshop owner but a dedicated bibliophile — and, importantly for April, a fearless eccentric who was determined to change the face of what had been a very sleepy little town.

Booth said that he had probably been destined to love books: 'My father was an army officer in Qatar and he probably spent one per cent of his time on military duties, three per cent playing polo and ninety-five per cent reading books.'[5] Born in Plymouth, Devon, in 1938 and educated at Rugby and Merton College, Oxford, Richard Booth decided not to follow his father's example by joining the British Army but to find a way of leading an interesting life while boosting the British rural economy. A charming, gregarious man, with owlish glasses and messy black hair, Booth followed a well-established British model: he was able to indulge his eccentricity because he belonged to a wealthy and aristocratic family. He later said ruefully that, during his life, he had inherited one fortune, made two, and lost four.

Booth had been in Hay-on-Wye since 1962, after inheriting the local castle from an uncle. He opened the town's first second-hand bookshop and speedily acquired several others, which he stocked by buying up huge quantities of cheap books from various sources, including universities and colleges in the United Kingdom and United States, bankrupt distributors, monasteries, and the libraries of crumbling country houses and deceased estates.[6] Booth worked out the nexus between second-hand books and Hay's economy. His view was that books, which he called 'the major intellectual dynamic of Western civilisation', should be associated with a major industry such as tourism. A customer who had collected 14,000 books on anaesthetics, for example, might wish to add eight more when he came to Hay — so he would spend £5 on books and £500 on meals and accommodation.

Word spread. Other booksellers moved to Hay-on-Wye and opened shops of their own, and by the late 1970s the town was well known as a centre of the second-hand book trade. 'Every publisher in the world is working for Hay-on-Wye,' said Booth, 'because every book in the world becomes second-hand.'*

It is easy to see why Richard Booth appealed to April: she was always delighted to discover and befriend odd people, and Booth — the 'Barnum of books' in the words of *The Guardian*[7] — nicely combined erudition with a shrewd understanding of publicity and its power.

Two years after April arrived in Hay-on-Wye, on 1 April 1977, Richard Booth declared Hay an independent kingdom – the smallest in the world — with himself as 'King of Hay'. 'It is at this point a question of the Divine Right of Kings against the Divine Right of Officials,' he declared. 'This really means "fuck off, officials throughout the world." ... Total chaos and anarchy is the only answer.'

April was part of this new venture: Booth, King of Hay, bestowed royal honours upon her and she became the First Lady of Hay-on-Wye and Duchess of Offa's Dyke.

At last, April Ashley had joined the ranks of the peerage in her own right.

---

* Booth's work in making the village a book town created the ideal conditions for a literary festival. Founded by Peter Florence, the Hay Festival of Literature and Arts began in 1988 and is now one of the most eagerly attended literary festivals in Britain. Its name confused at least one guest, however — playwright Arthur Miller. 'Hay on Wye?' he is said to have asked. 'Isn't that some kind of sandwich?'

CHAPTER 19

Literary lady

Because April was so taken up with books, even at one remove (selling them occasionally for Richard Booth), it's perhaps not surprising that she thought she might venture into the world of literature herself. Several journalists had offered to write her life story or to help her write it, and she had always refused, perhaps unsure whether the money she made would justify the exposure. But now she felt the timing was right — and she thought she had found the perfect author: Duncan Fallowell, the young journalist whom she had known since he was a student.

After Fallowell left Oxford with a degree in modern history, he had headed for London and journalism. He started out, improbably, as the conservative magazine *The Spectator*'s first columnist about pop culture, becoming a significant commentator on rock music.[1]

April and Fallowell had seen a lot of each other during the traumas of *Corbett v Corbett* and afterwards. They had mutual friends: Fallowell described himself as 'formerly bisexual' and later 'pretty much gay'. They were alike in being highly gregarious, yet essentially living alone. And Fallowell had no illusions about April's behaviour. She was fun to be with, he said, but also quite expensive. 'She's one of life's enhancers, but sometimes at great cost to herself and those around her. She's a bizarre and magnificent romantic.'[2]

April had already suggested to Fallowell that he should write about her, but he had been too busy. However, in 1979, he successfully published his first book: an anthology of stories about drugs and drug use titled *Drug Tales*. He decided that his second book should be April Ashley's life story. April agreed. In 1980, he moved to Hay-on-Wye, and they set to work.

Fallowell would have known about earlier attempts to tell April's story in book form. At the beginning of 1973, April's friend and solicitor Peter Maddock had approached author and journalist Peter Burton, widely known as 'the godfather of gay journalism' and the scourge of conservative activist Mary Whitehouse. Burton knew that Robin Maugham, the author for whom he had been a literary assistant, had already abandoned the project, largely because April considered some of his questions impertinent. After some preliminary work, including a series of interviews with April, Burton had also decided not to go ahead — mostly because he and April had clashed about the tone of the book. April thought her life story should be bright and glamorous, while Burton saw it as 'a tragedy enlightened by moments of high comedy'.[3]

Most trans autobiographies had been heartfelt accounts of transition by non-professional writers, except for one. Jan Morris's *Conundrum*, which appeared in 1974, was the work of a well-known, widely admired, and stylish author and journalist. Then known as James, Morris had come to prominence as the only journalist to accompany Edmund Hillary's 1953 Everest expedition. Morris went on to write and publish many books across a wide range of genres, including a three-volume history of the British Empire from the formation of the East India Company to 1960s post-colonialism.

Conundrum — now the book for which Morris is best known — was immensely significant because it was the first book by a literary writer to chart her progress from globe-trotting journalist, parent, and husband to becoming the woman she had always felt herself to be.

Like much of Morris's other work, the writing has a certain guarded, even wry, elegance — possibly even overly detached, considering the searing nature of the story being told. *Conundrum* caused quite a stir, mainly in literary circles, and it offered confirmation and encouragement to those uncertain of their own gender identity. Morris herself, perhaps disingenuously, declared, 'I never dreamt when I wrote it what love and bitterness, hope and sorrow it would unlock in the minds of its readers.' Morris was widely praised for her courage in telling her story.

The book received mixed reviews. Some commentators expressed admiration for the author's elegant writing style; others, unwilling to confront the controversial subject matter, simply described the events of Morris's life. Yet others declared that the writing was twee, almost trivialising the 'personal tragedy' the book described. Some of the criticism engaged not with the book but with the author: Jan Morris was not a 'real woman'. It's worth noting that the majority of these reviewers were men. One of the few exceptions was Rebecca West, who invoked gender stereotyping: 'She sounds not like a woman but like a man's idea of a woman, and curiously enough, a man not nearly so intelligent as James Morris used to be.'[4]

Duncan Fallowell might well have taken note of some of the criticism when he came to work on April's story. His approach from the beginning was straightforward — much less overtly literary in tone and focus than *Conundrum* had been. The difference in the titles of the two books is illuminating: *Conundrum* examines the puzzling nature of gender through the prism of one person's experience; *April Ashley's Odyssey* describes the course of an epic journey to become another person.

For the sake of immediacy — and following the example of other trans stories — Fallowell chose to present April's story as told in her

own words. 'I told April I could never be a ghost writer and I only
agreed to do it if my name came first as author,' he said. 'She agreed
... She was already well into her exiled duchess manner, so I took that
and added an educated underpinning.'[5] April, he said, was not alone
in presenting a glamorous front: in his experience, few trans women,
including April, harboured dreams of being 'normal' women; rather,
he said, 'They aspire to this sort of glamourised idea of womanhood.'
(This certainly did not apply to Jan Morris, who spent her life after
transition living quietly in a Welsh rural cottage with her former wife.)

Fallowell said that it took him two years to interview April and pull
her story together, though he had been thinking about it for longer than
that. While not always light-hearted in tone, *April Ashley's Odyssey* has
the air of a transcribed conversation between two gossipy chums who
know each other well — who share pasts as rebels and obviously enjoy
each other's eccentricity. It's a bit of a romp in places; in others, Ashley
describes her physical ordeals in detail — her attempts to kill herself,
her time in a psychiatric ward, and above all the gruelling surgery in
Casablanca. The details are clearly given and their impact is sobering.

This also applies to the account of *Corbett v Corbett*. Because
no transcript was made in the closed court, it is the most detailed
description of the proceedings, all the more poignant for being seen
through April's eyes.

But, at its most basic, *Odyssey* is a cheerfully brisk tale of
determination: of overcoming daunting obstacles, starting from birth
into a family enduring poverty and misery, going through the horrors
of adolescence and shipboard life, and culminating in some sort of
contentment — or at least relative calm — in Hay-on-Wye.

April also shows herself to be a shameless name-dropper — no
more so than when describing her life in London during the 1960s.

Fallowell showed the manuscript to several of the people
mentioned in April's story. Omar Sharif and Peter O'Toole were
reasonably happy with their role in her life as described, merely asking

for signed copies when the book was published. Others were less accommodating, threatening litigation if their names were included. As April said later: 'In the end we just decided to cut these little people if they started hassling ... It's been a boring 12 months going over all the legal points. It was never intended as a kiss-and-tell biography and I don't understand the pettiness. But life's too short to bother.'[6]

April Ashley's Odyssey, published by Jonathan Cape in 1982, was the signal for another burst of tabloid publicity for April, as well as interviews on radio and television. Despite Fallowell's insistence that his name should appear on the title page as author, he seems to have been given very little press or other attention, and April rarely referred to him in her own publicity. In obvious contrast to the reaction after Jan Morris's book, *April Ashley's Odyssey* was seen as a celebrity autobiography, with greater emphasis on April Ashley as an icon of the 1960s than the fact that she had had her gender-affirming surgery a decade before Jan Morris and was therefore a trans pioneer.

At her most imperious during an interview in May 1982

There was some snobbish commentary about the book's lack of literary style — and reviewers rehashed the details of her life, already much ventilated in the tabloids over the years. One highly critical — even hostile — review was written by Irish psychiatrist Anthony Clare in the *Sunday Telegraph*. In common with some critics of Jan Morris's book, he made a direct and personal attack on the subject herself, declaring that the book revealed April's 'durability and remorseless egotism' — in stark contrast to photographs depicting her as a 'sloe-eyed creation' with an air of 'fragility'. All in all, he wrote, the book 'read like a Hollywood biography' or 'the tale of trans-sexualism's Barbara Cartland':

> Here and there one detects a profound melancholy at the base of the frenetic energy, but very quickly we are back to salons and suitors, and the odyssey ends with our heroine off to a hunt ball ... positively radiating pep.'[7]

Robin Maugham's literary assistant, Peter Burton, who had considered writing April's story a decade earlier, commented that *April Ashley's Odyssey* was very much the book that April wanted: a glossy Hollywood fairy tale. However, 'scandal and disaster have dogged her life – and the reason for this has always to be traced back to Casablanca'. For Burton, the book was a blown opportunity: 'Readers looking for insights into anything will be sadly disappointed ... this is a frivolous and in many ways distasteful book [about a woman] whose notoriety is her only claim to fame.'[8]

Andrew Motion, in *The Times Literary Supplement*, agreed. Of *Odyssey*'s writing style, he observed that:

> [B]etween them she and Duncan Fallowell have more or less exactly captured the diction that certain actors have evolved as their own unmistakable language. It is camp, precious, hyperbolic,

and punctuated with shrieks and giggles ... This sort of thing is an achievement of a kind, but it is hard to take for long.

He added, astutely: 'Although the flashy superficialities cannot help inviting criticism, they also offer a protective covering. They obscure the outline of what April Ashley understandably feels to be a distinctive – and therefore exposed and vulnerable – personality, and lose her in a glittering mass of types.'[9]

Motion put his finger on something that links *Conundrum* and *Odyssey*, apart from their subject matter: the role of language in keeping at arm's length the real anguish of the central character's journey. Like Jan Morris, April Ashley is never fully visible through her own words.

It is illuminating in this context to look at two other autobiographies that appeared at roughly the same time as *Odyssey*. American professional tennis player Renée Richards published *Second Serve* in 1983. Richards, assigned male at birth and named Richard Raskind, became known as one of the best college tennis players in the United States, while becoming qualified as an ophthalmologist. Richards married and had a son, but struggled with gender identity, and began taking hormone injections with a view to transitioning. He finally did so in 1975, adopting the name Renée, meaning 'reborn'.

Richards continued to play tennis but, a year after her surgery, she was outed — she had refused to take a test to verify her sex — and was barred from competition in the US Open and Wimbledon. She sued the US Tennis Association, alleging discrimination by gender, and won. *Second Serve*, however, devotes surprisingly little space to Renée's tennis career or successful court case, concentrating instead on her struggles first to accept, and then to change, her gender identity.*

In 1978, American newspaper journalist Nancy Hunt published *Mirror Image*, her own story of the struggle to acknowledge her

---

* *Second Serve* was subsequently made into a television movie starring Vanessa Redgrave. Renée Richards wrote two other autobiographies and starred in a 2011 documentary film.

transition. This received less publicity than the other autobiographies mentioned here, perhaps because the story bore striking similarities to Morris's: Hunt had been a husband and father and a well-known journalist before transitioning. More fully than Morris or Ashley, Hunt detailed the searing personal consequences of her transition. According to *Kirkus Reviews*, her family 'recoiled' from such candour:

> [N]ot just siblings and already-alienated children but also a much-loved second wife who had at first, somewhat innocently, aided and abetted the conversion process by sharing clothes and makeup techniques ... [Hunt] claims to steer clear of stereotypical transsexual behaviour – unreliability and frills – except for promiscuity, the last an apparent source of pride.[10]

At this distance, it is impossible to say how many copies *April Ashley's Odyssey* sold on first publication in 1982, but it clearly did well enough to arouse interest in being translated to film. One of the first to approach April was film-maker, actor, and author Mark Ezra. He recalled: 'I was introduced to April Ashley at the Chelsea Arts Club in the spring of 1982, at the time of the launch of her biography. April invited me to visit her in Hay-on-Wye to discuss and research a film of her life.' The film would concentrate on the 1960s, though it would follow April's career up to the resolution of *Corbett v Corbett*. Ezra's view was that the court case 'set back the cause of transgender rights as well as depriving April of a reasonable divorce settlement'. He found April surprisingly 'shy and insecure', with a very low tolerance of alcohol (perhaps affected by her health issues): 'Just a couple of glasses would send her head spinning.' He added that she was 'funny, witty and occasionally sarcastic, but never cruel'.

April — or perhaps Ezra himself — was apprehensive about Arthur Corbett's reaction to a film about his relationship with April, and so they both flew to Marbella, where Ezra had an apartment, to ask Arthur to sign a waiver agreeing not to object or seek to influence the proposed film. Arthur was now technically Lord Rowallan, his father having died in 1977, though he had inherited nothing other than the title.

'We arrived,' said Ezra, 'bearing two bottles of champagne which April, somewhat nervously, hoped might lubricate his signing arm.' Rowallan, said Ezra, seemed to be living in reduced circumstances. He had only two cracked glasses for the champagne and directed Ezra to an old bathroom tooth mug covered with green mould; Ezra and April chose to share the same glass. Ezra then left April and Arthur to 'discuss old times', while he walked along the beachfront. Forty minutes later, he returned to find a triumphant April flat on her back in the middle of the road, waving the agreement.[11]

April did not see Arthur Corbett for another ten years — and this particular film was never made.

CHAPTER 20

Securing the legacy

One striking aspect of the publicity April did before and after the publication of *Odyssey* is her increased frankness, both about her life and her beliefs. Another — which may well be related — is that, for the first time, she was being widely interviewed by women, and so presumably she felt more relaxed than she had in the past. When April was interviewed at tea in the Savoy by the *Daily Mirror* journalist and columnist Marje Proops, she picked up the teapot and asked archly, 'Shall I be mother?'[1]

Proops gave a detailed description of April Ashley in her late 40s:

April Ashley is in fact a splendid figure of a woman. She is very tall, five feet ten and a half inches, and sort of stately in her movements. Her hair is thick and greyish blonde ... She wears size 6½ shoes and her hands are comparatively small for such a tall woman. Smaller actually than mine. She said, 'People always look at your hands and feet. I suppose they hope spitefully they'll be huge and manly.' She's used to it all. She can take it – now ... There's humour and good nature and a bit of bitchiness and there really is a touch of motherliness she insists she feels. She loves children. She told me a touching story of how she once went to the park with an ex-lover and his little boy and they sat on the grass and she played with the child and pretended he was hers.[2]

April had recently been to the United States to stay with friends, and was looking forward to a trip to Australia to promote *April Ashley's Odyssey*. As she talked with Proops, she radiated enthusiasm: 'I'm forty-seven but I still feel sixteen. Okay, sometimes I look in the mirror in the morning and say, Darling, you look great, and other mornings I look like an old dog and count the chins.' She also claimed to be about six kilos overweight — something she said she would not normally admit, but 'when you've been medically examined from head to toe and the evidence given in open court, you learn not to be embarrassed'.[3]

April went further than describing her physical condition. 'Like homosexuals, transsexuals are not created or influenced by other people,' she said. 'It is a response and feeling that comes from within. If I hadn't been able to have that operation twenty-two years ago, I would not have been here talking to you today. I would have killed myself.' She admitted to a few sexual encounters with men during her 20s, but she declared that sex wasn't important to her. 'It never has been,' she said.

Speaking of her experiences across class boundaries, she added, 'It's always the middle class I've had most trouble with. It's hardly ever the aristocracy or the working class' — an interesting comment, considering her not entirely satisfactory experiences of both. 'Perhaps that's because the middle class are the most insecure and screwed up,' she added.

When asked about her future, she replied, rather wistfully, 'I'll probably just grow into a glamorous old bird.'

Another interview, this time in the *Newcastle Journal*, was accompanied by a photograph of April and Duncan Fallowell: she looks her usual tailored self, while he projects a certain casual loucheness. Journalist Maureen Fairley commented on April's 'sharp, gutsy sense of humour' and her courage.[4]

April's Australian trip to promote *April Ashley's Odyssey* took
place later in 1982. She was interviewed by Michael Parkinson as
a guest on his television series *Parkinson in Australia*. (Parkinson
presented his interview series on Australian television from 1979 to
1983: he was a frequent visitor to the country, which he described
as his 'second home'.) The programme on which April appeared was
especially notable because the other guest was Grahame Bond, a local
actor and comedian well known for his character Aunty Jack. This
monstrous creature — tall, with pince-nez, a voluminous dress, boots,
and hair in plaits — was a parody of the 'aunties' in children's television
programmes, and he would bellow the catchphrase 'If you don't behave,
I'll jump through your TV set and rip yer bloody arms off!' Bond was
not interviewed as Aunty Jack, but it was intriguing that the producers
chose to have a male actor well known for playing a pantomime dame
— the travesty of a woman — on the same programme as glamorous
trans woman April Ashley. This juxtaposition of guests can hardly have
been a coincidence, but Parkinson made no comment about it, and
neither did local reviewers.

Parkinson was markedly more relaxed in talking to Bond than
to April, asking little about Bond's choice of alter ego. With April he
displayed surprisingly little of his trademark bonhomie, concentrating
instead on serious, searching questions. In the 20-minute interview, he
went through the events of her life from the beginning — particularly
before her surgery. Judging by the hardening of April's eyes behind
her coquettish eyelashes, this was a line of enquiry that did not please
her. However, she patiently talked about her family, being bullied
at school, her childhood ambitions, whether she shaved in the years
before her transition, and whether she had come across gay men in the
merchant navy. (She said she had not.) At one point, Parkinson asked
whether she had ever been tempted to behave in 'a masculine way'
when annoyed, and she said no. It was a crass question, but he might
have been referring to her assault of a London police officer two years

earlier. In measured tones and presumably acknowledging the presence of Grahame Bond, April took it upon herself to explain to Parkinson the difference between a drag artist and a transvestite: 'What I did [as a cabaret artist in Paris] I did for a living. A transvestite is someone who gets a sexual kick out of dressing as the opposite sex. I never got a kick out of it at all.'[5]

When Parkinson reminded April that she was 47 years old and asked how she would sum up her life to date, as well as how she felt about growing old, she said, 'I've almost become an institution in England, and now that Granada are thinking of making a film about my life, who knows what the future will hold? It could be very bright.'

And when Parkinson asked, 'When you look back on your life, do you feel you have been cheated? Do you feel you have been dealt a bad hand of cards?', April responded firmly: 'Yes, but life has also dealt me good cards. I've always been able to pick out the good things of life.'[6]

April was clearly not about to let down her guard for the sake of an Australian television audience.

One of those good things of April's life was her meeting in Sydney with Michael Hutchence, lead singer and songwriter of Australian rock group INXS — soon to become internationally famous. 'I met him in a hotel in Sydney,' she later said:

> He came in with about fifteen people. He was very young ... the most incredibly handsome man I had ever seen. He came over and said, 'Would you like a drink?' I said, 'Yes.' I hadn't the foggiest idea who he was. It was rather nice because he then said, 'Would you like to come up to my room and have a bottle of champagne?' So I did, and we made love, and very nice it was too.

She added, 'When I came downstairs in the morning, swinging my knickers around my finger, a friend of mine said, "Do you know who you've just been to bed with?" I didn't. I'd never heard of his band.'

The story of April's one-night stand with Michael Hutchence was told again and again in the media — almost every one of her newspaper obituaries mentioned it — and she never gave any further details, except for an approving comment about his 'manhood'.[7]

April Ashley's Odyssey was highly successful in attracting even more publicity for April, attention of the kind she most enjoyed. There was talk not only of movies but also of television documentaries: clearly, issues of sexuality and gender were beginning to come to popular attention and to be treated more seriously.

As Britain's best-known trans woman, April felt a responsibility to others. 'I think it is too sad that because of my divorce case, transsexuals cannot marry and, if they do, their marriages can be annulled,' she told a journalist in 1980. 'The fact is that in this country the law has failed to keep up with medical science. It really is about time that something was done about it.'

Supported by the National Council for Civil Liberties, she decided to try to get the judgment in *Corbett v Corbett* overthrown by taking Britain before the European Commission for Human Rights, a body set up to try to reach conciliation when member states' own legal remedies had been exhausted. If mediation did not succeed, the Commission could formulate a legal opinion and refer the case to the European Court of Human Rights, whose decision was binding.

There was a precedent in April's case: a Belgian trans man seeking the right to marry had recently taken his case before the commission. No finding had been made because the commission had decided that the man had not explored all possible domestic legal solutions — but the commission did observe that insufficient respect had been shown for the applicant's private and family life (to which he was entitled under Article 8 of the European Convention on Human Rights). In April's case, the right to privacy was bound up with her inability to amend her birth certificate; in the United Kingdom, the right to marry had been defined in narrow biological terms.[8]

April's nemesis Mr Justice Ormrod, who had since been elevated as Lord Justice Ormrod of the Court of Appeal of England and Wales, left the law in 1982 at the age of 71 — four years before the statutory age for judges' retirement. The announcement giving notice of his departure from the bench alluded to *Corbett v Corbett*, now his best-known case, but he had lost none of his sardonic approach in his later career, ruling that a wife who complained she had sex only once a week was not entitled to a divorce. April's comment, when told of his retirement, was that, because he had ruled her a man, 'I won't get a state pension at the women's age of sixty, I'll have to wait, like a man, until I'm sixty-five.'[9]

The 1980s was a decade of seismic change in the United Kingdom — with the rise of Margaret Thatcher, the waning of the Labour Party, the return of military confidence as a consequence of the Falklands War, the miners' strikes, and the decimation of the trade unions. The decade was also distinguished by increased wealth in certain well-defined areas of British society; indeed, many shared the view that the nation was being swept along on a glittering tide of money. The decade's central figure — and the chief target of those unable to take part in this prosperity — was Margaret Thatcher herself, who, according to journalist Andy Beckett, was 'so myth-encrusted, so stylised and armoured in her personal presentation from the mid-80s onwards, so much written about that the historian's gaze often just bounces straight off [her]'.[10]

It was against this background that the part-drama, part-documentary *Ligmalion: a musical for the 80s* came into being in 1985. Broadcast as an episode of BBC television's *Arena*, its subtitle was 'Or How to Help Yourself in Self-Help Britain' — a reference to Margaret Thatcher's often-expressed belief that people should lift themselves up by the bootstraps, with very little help from the state. The satire, which was an hour and a half long, took its punning title from the verb 'to lig', meaning to get something for nothing by wit and ingenuity: Thatcher's Britain, the title implied, was a nation of freeloaders. Critics praised it for exposing the ugly values at the core of Thatcherism, epitomised by Thatcher herself — that is, an insistence on climbing the social ladder in search of wealth and prosperity, whatever the cost.

Offering the main character, Gordon Shilling (played by Jason Carter), a 'lig-up' were assorted celebrities, as well as fictional and historical characters including Tim Curry as chief mentor Eden Rothwell Esq., Alexei Sayle as John Bull, Sting as Niccolo Machiavelli, and Ken Campbell as Victorian self-help expert Samuel Smiles. April had a significant role, though she was on screen for little more than three minutes. A voiceover, with stills, reprises the events of *Corbett v Corbett* with the 'Flower Duet' from Delibes's opera *Lakme* on the soundtrack. Then April, majestically beautiful in a flowing black gown and full makeup, sweeps down the staircase of a stately home and invites the main character into a salon. She introduces herself as the Duchess of Hay and Offa's Dyke — 'but you can call me April' — before mentioning *My Fair Lady* and describing its source: the Greek myth of Pygmalion, a sculptor who carved the perfect woman, Galatea, out of ivory and fell in love with her. When Gordon Shilling asks whether she identifies with the story, she says, 'Oh, absolutely,' and recalls 12 May 1960 as the day when she became 'a self-made Galatea'. She tells Shilling, 'If you're going to impress somebody, impress them with your own self. Be truthful to yourself, young man, and you will be magnificent.'

This is all delivered in April's measured, aristocratic tones, and with impressive authority and aplomb. The last two sentences, though presumably written by the film's scriptwriters, carried the message that April repeated in innumerable public appearances for the rest of her life.

CHAPTER 21

Milestones

April's 50th birthday in 1985 heralded a new round of interviews in the press and on television. She carried them out with her usual lofty graciousness and continued to look younger than she in fact was, made up and coiffed with increasing care as the years passed. But, in a self-deprecating moment, she said she had attracted this attention because 'they wanted to see what I looked like'. She still thought that most people considered her a freak.

At about this time, April learned — years after the fact — that her mother had died. She did not say how she had found out. Ada's passing was hardly a source of regret to her, or even a surprise; in 1973, April had told television interviewer Russell Harty, with a shrug, that she had no idea whether her mother was alive or dead. And as usual, on that occasion, she hadn't missed the opportunity for a joke at Ada's expense. (Harty: 'What was your mother's reaction to your decision to have the operation?' Ashley: 'She thought I had had a nose job.' The studio audience laughed, and Ashley joined them.) In her second as-told-to autobiography, *The First Lady*, published in 2006, she said Ada had died of cancer.[1] Ada's work in the munitions factory during World War II, plus her lifelong consumption of Woodbine cigarettes, were very probable causes of her death. April gave the wrong date in her book, writing that Ada had died in 1974, when in fact she had lived until 27 November 1978.

Ada's estate was valued at just over £12,000 — a large sum for a woman whose life had been a litany of poverty and hard graft. Bernie Cartmell had probably inherited money from somewhere: a 1964 advertisement in the *Liverpool Daily Post* requested 'Bernard Hodgson Cartmell, a Merchant Navy Seaman who was last heard of in Liverpool and Manchester' to contact a firm of Lancashire solicitors[2] — a form of words generally used when money is in prospect. Perhaps a legacy had enabled Ada and Bernie Cartmell to buy Ada's treasured bungalow and set up the grocery shop in Manchester. We do not know what happened to the money, but nothing suggests that April was given any share of it.

Knowing Ada was dead did not soften Ashley's view of her mother in any way. For the rest of her life, she continued to describe Ada's cruelty. As late as 2015, when April was 80, she told the *Daily Express*, 'My mother hated me. She used to whack me and I would say, "Mother, why did you do that?" And she replied, "In case you did anything." She was threatened with prison by a doctor because of the injuries on me.'[3] And yet she also told another journalist that 'I spent my whole life trying to win the love of my mother, but there was never any reconciliation.'[4]

It's difficult to judge how true this was. On the one hand, it is well known that some children spend their lives trying to please difficult parents. Perhaps Ashley's continued public condemnation of her mother was her response to what she saw as withheld love. (It was also part of Ashley's carefully curated story: *See what horrors I have overcome!*) At the same time, when it suited her, Ashley made use of her mother and Ada cooperated, for instance when she played the part of admiring mother in the *News of the World* serialisation (for which Ashley was paid a handsome fee). And it is interesting that among

Ashley's effects after her death was an expensive card festooned with red roses and inscribed, 'To a dear daughter on her birthday'.

In late 1985, a friend suggested to April that she might consider living in the United States. She had loved the country ever since her first visit in the early 1950s, and it was an idea she found immediately attractive. Hay was becoming expensive: the house she had inherited — which she described to one journalist as a Gothic, slightly sinister redbrick — needed repairs she could not afford. The idea of returning to California in particular was an attractive one; she had made friends there, and she thought she would be able to find work. And so, yet again, she decided to leave England — this time, in 1986.

First, she went to New York, where she contacted and struck up a friendship with the writer and theatrical performer Quentin Crisp, who had emigrated to the United States in 1981 and lived on the Lower East Side of Manhattan. Although they hadn't met before, they must at least have known of each other. Crisp — nearly 80 when April finally encountered him — was still enjoying the afterglow of his 1968 memoir *The Naked Civil Servant*, made into a television documentary and a very successful television play starring John Hurt. Crisp — with his lipstick, eyeshadow, carefully arranged hair, tilted hat, and rhinestone jewellery — had made a career out of being emphatically himself. (When asked by the American Embassy before his departure from England whether he was 'a practising homosexual', he replied, 'I don't practise, I am already perfect.')

Extremely popular socially, Crisp once declared that he was invited to enough parties to enable him to live on peanuts and champagne.[5] Certainly, he made his living for many years by writing and presenting monologues based on his own life and work, showing consummate skill, style, and humour. Displaying the epigrammatic wit of Oscar Wilde (but with much better judgement), he once said that 'The fair name of vice is now being dragged through the mud by the English newspapers.'

Crisp said that he had thought of himself as a woman when he was young but had later realised that it was necessary to live in the 'real world'. He had believed then that he was not a woman but only, in some sense, feminine and that he had to live in a society where, statistically, he was a man. The interviewer asked him, 'If you did not want to become a woman, what did you want to become?' His response: 'All I wanted was that the world should understand what kind of person I was so there would be no misunderstanding.'

At the end of his life, Crisp offered another perspective: 'At the age of ninety,' he said, 'it has finally been explained to me that I am not really homosexual, I'm transgender. I now accept that. All my life I have wanted to be part of society without having to alter my daydream, my own reality.'[6]

Like April, Crisp had had a tough time in his youth, being beaten up regularly. He described one encounter: 'Covering my ... ornate façade with my hands to prevent rivers of mascara from running down my cheeks, I said, "I seem to have annoyed you gentlemen in some way."' His attackers were so taken aback by his sangfroid, Crisp said, that they let him go.

After leaving New York, April travelled to Los Angeles. Here, friends introduced her to a tall, dark-haired Texan named Jeffrey West. Details of West's life are sparse, but he was an occasional screenwriter who ran the Pink in Santa Monica: a nightclub that attracted a celebrity clientele, including David Bowie. West and April quickly decided they liked each other, and April moved into his house in Santa Monica. She refused to live on West's income; she intended to make her own way. But to work in the United States, she needed to become a permanent resident, which meant getting a Green Card, and the easiest way of doing that was to marry an American citizen. This casts some doubt on Ashley's later assertion that her decision to marry Jeffrey West was a romantic impulse.

Fleet Street gossip writer Nigel Dempster certainly thought April's decision to marry was wholly pragmatic, and he lost no time in telling Arthur Corbett about it — all for the sake of a column:

> No-one was more surprised to learn that April Ashley, the former seaman who underwent a sex change operation, had remarried than Lord Rowallan, 66 ... 'I don't suppose she'd be allowed to do it in Britain, but American law must be different. I haven't been in touch with her since the great debacle,' croaked Lord R when I rang his Costa del Sol flat with the news.[7]

Corbett assured Dempster that he had no intention of marrying again.

April Ashley and Jeffrey West were married on board the *Queen Mary* in Long Beach, California, on 13 July 1986. The venue was probably April's idea, with her memories of Liverpool's Cunard connection and what it had meant to young George — as well as movie-fed fantasies about the glamorous 1930s.

The massive liner had been transformed into a hotel by the Wrather Corporation in 1980. It advertised a 'Royal Wedding Chapel' on board:

> When you say 'I do' you become part of the *Queen*'s official wedding record. And when you sign the *Queen*'s log for the first time as 'Mr and Mrs' you will become a part of the *Queen*'s romantic history. We will also offer the bride & groom the elegant *Queen*'s bridal suite for five days, a beautiful wedding cake in her choice of decoration design and color and to top it off a silk wedding cake ornament with mini lights.[8]

Every ship — even a docked former ocean liner — must have a captain. The *Queen Mary* needed someone who would wear gold braid and look purposeful at afternoon tea and other elegancies of the 1930s in what was effectively a floating theme park.

Enter John Gregory, a former officer in Britain's Royal Air Force and hotel manager, and a close friend of the president of Wrather Hotels.

The original operators of the *Queen Mary* allowed Gregory to wear the official braid and badges of a Cunard Line captain. 'I am not playing a role,' he said with pride. 'I am fulfilling the role. On this ship I do everything that previous captains did when the ship was in port. I have become the titular head of this ship.'

Gregory, always addressed as 'captain', took to his role with great enthusiasm; he had four changes of uniform, as well as tropical whites. He became a qualified ship's chaplain, estimating that he performed 2,000 weddings (but no burials at sea because the *Queen Mary* was not in open water). *The Los Angeles Times* approved of him: 'By the salute, the authoritative courtesy, the Hampstead accent, the walk ready to lean into a roll, and the veterans who swear Gregory was on the bridge when they sailed aboard the troopship *Queen Mary* during World War II, the transformation of Gregory has been total.'[9]

Pictures of April and her new husband look very much like posed movie studio shots, reinforcing the fantasy aspects of their union. April said very little about this second wedding in press interviews, if she mentioned it at all, further suggesting that it had been a marriage of convenience. Even so, she and West were together for about four years, and they were apparently great pals. Ashley said that, eventually, West decided he wanted to live alone, and they quietly divorced. She kept her Green Card in the name of 'April Ashley West'.

After a disappointing time in San Francisco, a city she had never liked, April moved to San Diego, where she worked in art galleries, as a tourist guide, and as an occasional fundraiser for Greenpeace, which was then ramping up its campaign against the oil company Exxon. Journalist Jessica Berens gave a vivid account of April's new life, describing San Diego as a neat, palm-lined 'country-club kind of place with trolley tours and whale watching and affordable handicrafts'.[10] Entertainment consisted of clean-cut chanteuses singing folk-pop with a positive Christian message.

April, said Berens, worked in a gallery specialising in artfully constructed animals, including wolves, poison toads, and swans. April's rather stressful job was to sell $1,000 worth of wolves or swans a day, but she enjoyed telling children interesting things about the animals — especially the cheetahs. And, as she told Berens:

> The other day a man came into the gallery and said to me, 'What is it like to be extraordinarily beautiful?' Things like that blow you away because all you're thinking is, 'I've got another four hours to go, my feet are killing me, shall I take another pill to stop the cramps in my legs ...?'

Friends in the mall did not know she was trans, she said, although she would tell them if they should ask her. As Berens reported, 'She makes no effort to hide herself. "I'm always in the directory. I think if the Queen can be in the telephone book, so can I."'

The Greenpeace job proved equally challenging. April wasn't used to knocking on people's doors and asking for money, but she discovered she was quite good at it — even though it had a few horrific moments, including being threatened by a man wielding a crossbow.[11] She also did some television advertising for a racetrack. According to the *Daily Express*:

> She is known as a rather eccentric, perfectly mannered English gentlewoman and relishes her anonymity ... 'In the USA I'm just April. I don't hide what I've been but I don't volunteer it either and my bosses don't know. Being anonymous is awfully nice, but it's never going to happen to me.'[12]

In 1993, April heard that Arthur Corbett was very ill — he had had one leg amputated and developed gangrene in the other — and was not expected to live. She flew to his hospital bed in Marbella. According to Ashley later, he burst into tears when he saw her: she was the only woman he had ever loved, he said. He admitted having cheated her out of the villa and in the divorce; he knew he had hurt her and asked her to forgive him. Ashley described their meeting as very difficult because it brought back the miserable time surrounding their divorce — but, she said, she did what was required.

On 24 June 1993, Arthur Corbett died of a stroke, aged 73. His death rated only a brief announcement in *The Times*, as well as a longer story in the *Aberdeen Press and Journal* under the headline 'Baron in sex change scandal dies'.[13] The story — which emphasised Corbett's marriage to April and Ormrod's ruling, saying little about Arthur's early life and nothing about his own sexual history — continued:

> Lord Rowallan, who became distanced from most of his family, spent his latter years in Marbella, Spain. His flamboyant character won the hearts of locals there and he was known affectionately as 'Lord Arthur'. His funeral, in contrast to his life, was a very private affair, attended by his son the Hon. John Corbett.

Three years later, April told a *Daily Mail* journalist: 'When I saw him I knew he didn't really give a damn about anyone.'[14] It was a dismal epitaph.

It is interesting that April chose never to speak about the HIV/AIDS crisis — a defining issue of the 1980s that affected many of her friends in the United Kingdom and the United States, including her actor friend Denholm Elliott, who died in Ibiza from AIDS-related tuberculosis in 1992. Neither did she discuss the Thatcher government's notorious

1988 amendment of the Local Government Act 1986.

At the 1987 Conservative Party conference, Prime Minister Margaret Thatcher had said: 'Children who need to be taught to respect traditional moral values are being taught that they have an inalienable right to be gay ... All of those children are being cheated of a sound start in life.' The new Section 28 banned local authorities and schools from even mentioning same-sex relationships. Councils were prohibited from funding books, plays, leaflets, films or other materials showing gay relationships, while teachers were forbidden to teach that they existed.[15]

Television actor Michael Cashman, who appeared in *EastEnders* as one of the first gay characters in a national soap opera, said years later:

> What was so incredible was the political opportunism. Section 28 had been brought in on the back of the stigmatisation and dis- crimination suffered by gay men, in particular those dealing with AIDS and HIV. Some people were facing the most appalling deaths, and this was designed to kick us firmly underground.[16]

The bill prohibited the promotion or 'acceptability of homosexuality as a pretended family relationship'. Michael Dance, a trainee teacher at the time, added:

> A lot of teachers didn't want to deal with the subject out of fear. Bigoted teachers were emboldened. A lot of schools pretended that homosexuality did not exist and it allowed a lot of misinfor- mation, prejudice and abuse to go unchallenged. And of course it had a terrible effect on young people. Students suffered ho- mophobic abuse in silence and teachers and schools did nothing about it.[17]

So much for the 1967 law that had liberalised some gay relationships.

The reaction to Section 28 was immediate. A group of lesbian women stormed the BBC television news studio; others abseiled into the House of Lords. About 20,000 people in Manchester took to the city streets in protest. And during a radio debate on Section 28, well-known actor Ian McKellen made headlines when he came out as gay. But the government remained unmoved. Section 28 was an easy populist win for them, capitalising on the increasingly widespread suspicion of gay men at the time of AIDS.

For trans people, there was a small glimmer of hope. In 1996, a trans woman referred to as 'P' in court proceedings had been dismissed from her job when she told her employers that she was in the process of transitioning. She took her employer — the Cornwall County Council — to an employment tribunal, which agreed that she had been dismissed because of her 'gender reassignment' but could not rule that P had been discriminated against on the basis of sex because the Sex Discrimination Act 1975 did not protect trans people. As a member of the European Community, however, the United Kingdom was bound by the Equal Treatment Directive. The tribunal referred the case to the European Court of Justice, which ruled that, according to the Directive, no employee could be sacked for any reason related to 'gender reassignment'. The tribunal was then able to rule in favour of P, who received compensation. According to the law professor and trans rights campaigner Stephen Whittle, this was the first time anywhere in the world that discrimination in employment or vocational education because of transgender identity had been prohibited by law.[18]

The decision was welcomed by many, but trans people remained unable to change their birth certificates. In 1996, April was hard up again and increasingly bitter about her inability to claim the pension a woman was entitled to at the age of 60. The pension age remained a live issue for others, too, and two trans women applied to the High

Court for a review of the Registrar-General's refusal to alter their birth certificates. The court dashed their hopes: it upheld the decision in *Corbett v Corbett* and the women were refused permission.[19]

April could not let that decision pass without comment. In an interview for the *Daily Mail*, she said:

My rights have been violated for years. Britain is the most civilised country on Earth, but so backward about sex. I still love my country – I grew up in Liverpool during the war when it was being bombed flat – and my heart will always be British, but the government has condemned me to being a freak who lives in exile.[20]

April was still living in San Diego, alone apart from her cat: a fluffy creature she had named — with typically camp humour — Lily Ashley John Wayne Bobbit Tonya Harding.* April said she had spent all her savings during the three years it had taken her to get a Green Card, and she continued to scrape a living by doing part-time jobs. She told one newspaper that if she had stayed in England and remained on 'the dole', she could have had a full pension, housing, and benefits. But, she added, depending on the state was not 'the Liverpool way', and so she continued to earn what income she could in San Diego.

April celebrated her 60th birthday by working her passage across the Pacific on a 42-foot yacht, with a German man she had met on a blind date. Because she had always dreamed of cruising the Pacific, she characteristically ignored her friends' objections that being alone on a yacht for weeks with someone she hardly knew was a recipe for disaster.

She regretted her insouciance on their first day at sea when the

---

* John Wayne Bobbitt made international news when his wife, Lorena, whom he had violently abused for years, cut off his penis with a kitchen knife while he was asleep. (It was surgically reattached.) Tonya Harding was an American Olympic figure-skating champion who had authorised a physical attack on her rival, Nancy Kerrigan.

German proudly showed her a photograph of himself as a member of the Hitler Youth. Her growing suspicion that this was not likely to be a comfortable voyage was confirmed when he tried to rape her. She managed to fight him off, but they later quarrelled, and he punched her in the face.

April fell overboard. With bruised ribs and a swollen face, she managed to climb back onto the yacht. When they made landfall in Tahiti, 220 nautical miles away, she declared their association at an end. The German paid for her to fly to Los Angeles.

At home, remembering that she had also met Arthur Corbett on a blind date, April commented ruefully: 'This was only the second rendezvous of that kind I've had and both were utter disasters. Do you think I've learned my lesson?'[21]

CHAPTER 22

'You cannot leave us in limbo'

After 19 years in the United States, mostly in California, April moved to the south of France in January 2005. The last few years in San Diego had been difficult — and not only financially: she had contracted chronic fatigue syndrome, which meant constant muscle and joint pain, exacerbated by arthritis. She had to be careful about exerting herself because of her previous heart attacks, and the lack of hormone therapy after her original surgery had made her bones fragile. Not surprisingly, she did not wish to compromise her glamorous image by broadcasting these issues. 'I've been very ill, but although I'm not out of the woods I'm feeling much better,' she told a sympathetic journalist.[1]

April was now 70 and feeling her age. Even though she had previously announced that she was looking forward to growing old, she now admitted to finding it 'a bloody bore':

I miss being strong. I miss being able to run. There is nothing more lovely than being able to run and leap in the air. I used to waltz around the room to *Der Rosenkavalier*, now I have to shuffle round. I always think of myself at twenty-five. If I could afford a facelift, I'd have one tomorrow. Everything has gone south. When I take my bra off now, I say, God, that floor is cold.[2]

April was living in the misty hills above Nice, the tenant of a small apartment belonging to a graphic designer friend. With its small swimming pool in need of a clean and with fairy lights hanging from the awnings, luxurious it was not. 'It's not a typical Riviera scene,' she said. 'I call this place Withering [*sic*] Heights. It's a twenty-five-mile round trip to the supermarket, and I don't have that many friends around here. But I've been to the United States and Britain three times this year, so I'm not exactly sitting around.'

But describing her as a faded beauty living alone with her cat and her memories, as a couple of journalists did, is hardly accurate. April Ashley was no Miss Havisham: she had far too robust a sense of humour and grasp of realities. ('I like that falling mist,' she said of the weather. 'I need all the soft lighting I can get.') She had busily embraced technology, setting up her own website to showcase extracts from her life story and photographs, and communicating mostly by email. Her correspondents did not include her family: she had discovered over the years that, apart from her elder brother, all her siblings had died, and she was not in regular contact with any of their children, even though one of her nephews was also in France.[3]

April's hair was now white — or lavender-streaked, depending on the journalist and perhaps on the day — and she walked with a cane, but she remained regally tall and glamorous. Her voice was still 'unmistakably British, languidly upper-class with an old-fashioned huskiness that implies a life well lived,' according to one admiring report. And, importantly, she was still newsworthy.

The latest burst of publicity had surrounded publication of her second autobiography, *The First Lady*, written with Douglas Thompson. Like Fallowell's book, *The First Lady* purported to describe Ashley's life in her own words, with Thompson as writer. And like

April Ashley's Odyssey, this new version was well received — with added buzz when it was announced that a Hollywood producer had optioned the movie rights and had lined up Catherine Zeta-Jones to star. April was delighted: 'I like to think that she epitomises everything I stood for when I was young – which was sheer old-fashioned Hollywood glamour. And she's very like me physically when I was that age. When you look at my old photographs you can see the resemblance.'[4]

Her first biographer, Duncan Fallowell, said he first heard about the rival book in 2005 when April told him that someone else was writing her story. On its publication, Fallowell was struck by how similar Thompson's book was to *April Ashley's Odyssey* — and one unnamed publishing insider agreed: 'It's been shortened, tweaked, and a tiny amount of new stuff has been added but that's it. It's self-evident to anyone who has seen both books.'

Fallowell brought a case alleging copyright infringement against *The First Lady*'s publisher, John Blake. The judgment went against the company; by November 2006, John Blake had pulped the run and paid Fallowell undisclosed damages. To add insult to injury, the Zeta-Jones movie never went ahead. April had been depending on royalties and the movie to be her pension well into her old age. However, she and Thompson eventually made up and remained friends.

April continued to use her celebrity to draw attention to transgender issues. She had spoken for many when she said in a 1970 interview for the *Sunday Mirror*:

> I thought I was the only person in the world tormented by my particular physical and mental problem. I thought that nobody would ever understand, and that there was nothing that could be done for me.
>
> In fact there are many people living the awful life that I lived ... I am not a monster. I am flesh and blood, a human being with all the human, feminine feelings of a woman ... I was not created

by medicine or science but I am part of the advances of both. I am medicine's stepchild and its child. Medicine and science simply completed what nature had started ... The operation did not transform me, it completed me. There are a great many people like me. We exist, and society has got to acknowledge us and accept that we are human beings. You cannot leave us in limbo.

In the years since 1970, many had attempted to circumvent, and even overturn, the ruling in *Corbett v Corbett*, using case law, legislation, and social justice. Two activists in particular stand out.

Stephen Whittle, assigned female at birth, came out as a trans man in 1974, beginning hormone therapy the following year. He joined the Manchester Gay Alliance — the first group set up for trans people in the United Kingdom — in 1975, and he continues to be active on behalf of trans people.

Stephen and his partner, Sarah Rutherford, unable to marry legally, had four children. He had taken his case all the way to the European Court of Human Rights, seeking legal recognition as the father of his children — but his birth certificate stood in the way. 'I face an inadequate legal framework in which to exist,' he wrote. 'We [do not exist] within a world that only permits two sexes, only allows two forms of gender role, gender identity or expression. Always falling outside the "norm", our lives become less, our humanity is questioned, and our oppression is legitimised.'

In common with other transgender people, Whittle, a teacher, was unable to work as soon as his trans status was publicised, this time on the BBC, when he was the subject of a radio documentary, *Make Me a Man*, that described his life after his surgeries.

Whittle decided to fight. With Mark Rees, actor Myka Scott, and airline pilot Krystyna Sheffield, he founded Press for Change in 1989 as a lobbying and legal support organisation for trans people in the United Kingdom. It became one of the nation's most prominent trans organisations, working to change the laws and attitudes that affect transgender people.

The second activist — someone whose life paralleled Ashley's experience to a startling degree — was Caroline Cossey. She was assigned male at birth, in 1954, and diagnosed with Klinefelter syndrome: a genetic condition whereby an individual develops both masculine and feminine characteristics. Raised as a boy, an adolescent Caroline realised that she was 'psychologically female'. At 17, she left home and found work as a dancer: she was one of the Bluebell Girls — tall and beautiful cabaret artists who were famous in Europe, especially Paris. She used the name Tula and saved the money she made to fund gender-affirming surgery. Under her new name, Caroline, she then embarked on a career as a model.

In 1978, after she had scored a part in a British game show, a tabloid journalist told Caroline he was planning to expose her as trans, and she had to leave the programme. Three years later, she was cast as an extra in the Bond movie *For Your Eyes Only* — and this time she was publicly outed in the *News of the World* under the headline 'James Bond's girl was a boy'. Her career in the entertainment industry was over, but she decided to fight, telling *Cosmopolitan* magazine, 'I just got sick of being ashamed of something I'd never had any control over, which was my assigned gender.'[5] In 1982 — the same year as Duncan Fallowell's *April Ashley's Odyssey* — she published her first autobiography, *I Am a Woman*.

In 1989, Caroline married a Jewish millionaire businessman named Elias Fattai. However, immediately after the honeymoon, his Orthodox family saw the tabloid headline 'Sex change page three girl weds' and the marriage was annulled. Cossey spent almost a decade lobbying the European Court of Human Rights to have the law changed in the United Kingdom, not just to change her own birth certificate but on behalf of others in the same position.

As Ashley had done, Caroline later moved to North America,

where she married a Canadian: 'A 90s odd couple: Montreal man to
marry transsexual' was the not-especially-sensitive response of the
Canadian press. She nevertheless continued to lobby the European
Court and wrote several books about her life to increase awareness of
trans issues.*

In 1990s Britain, there were other signs that trans awareness was
on the rise. Gender-affirming surgery had been performed under the
National Health Service since Roberta Cowell's surgery in 1948, on
the basis that gender dysphoria could be explained as a physiological
disorder and alleviated by means of surgery. Press for Change was
increasingly vocal and visible — particularly after a 1996 private
members' bill unsuccessfully attempted to change the legal status of
trans people. Trans visibility was boosted in 1998 when the actor Julie
Hesmondhaugh joined long-running soap opera *Coronation Street* as
trans character Hayley Cropper. (Hesmondhaugh played the role for
16 years, winning several awards.) Commentary in the press became
strikingly more sympathetic. And even the Church of England —
hardly a radical institution — was beginning to accept the view that a
person's God-given biological sex might not be the whole story, after
a number of trans Christians left the Church in distress about their
treatment.

When a Labour government came to office in 1997, with Tony
Blair as prime minister, many hoped that the divisive sexual politics of
the previous government would be laid to rest. In his party's manifesto,
Blair had assured the nation:

> I want a society in which ambition and compassion are seen as
> partners not opposites – where we value public service as well
> as material wealth ... where we hold many aims in common and
> work together to achieve them. How we ... tackle the division

---

* An interview with American TV host Phil Donahue, in which Caroline Cossey is very frank, can
be found on youtube.com/watch?v=CXvrtBsyCbc.

and inequality in our society; how we care for and enhance our environment and quality of life; how we develop modern education and health services; how we create communities that are safe, where mutual respect and tolerance are the order of the day.[6]

Ashley wrote to Blair, asking for a new birth certificate, pointing out that her passport and tax returns described her as female — but he did not reply. However, in 1999, the government did respond to the judgment of the European Court of Human Rights about rights for trans people in the workplace. The Sex Discrimination (Gender Reassignment) Regulations amended the 1975 Sex Discrimination Act to extend legal protection for unfair dismissal to anyone planning, undergoing, or having had 'gender reassignment surgery'. This was the first legislative success for Press for Change, who combined with other transgender groups to urge further reform. Following the time-honoured process of any executive when confronted by difficult issues, the Blair Labour government set up an interdepartmental committee to review its legislative options, including the question of amending birth certificates.

April hadn't persisted in making her own approach to the then European Commission for Human Rights, citing lack of money and time. However, several trans people besides Caroline Cossey and Stephen Whittle had brought the British government before the European Court of Human Rights, citing its breach of Articles 8 and 12 of the European Convention, in force since 1990. Article 8 guaranteed every individual's right to privacy in their home and family life, and its terms spanned sexual orientation, correspondence, dress, and appearance. (This right had clearly been violated when transgender people were outed, and it applied to the question of amending birth certificates.) Article 12 stated that 'Men and women of marriageable age have the right to marry and found a family, according to the national laws governing the exercise of this right.' At the time, the United Kingdom was one of only four countries in the Council of Europe that failed to recognise gender reassignment as legally valid. (The others were Ireland, Andorra, and Albania.)

But things were about to change. In 2002, Christine Goodwin claimed before the ECHR that the United Kingdom had violated the articles in terms of 'the legal status of transsexuals in the United Kingdom, and particularly their treatment in the sphere of employment, social security, pensions and marriage'.[7] Goodwin, assigned male at birth in 1937, had undergone gender-affirming surgery at an NHS hospital in 1990. She claimed that between 1990 and 1992 she had been sexually harassed at work and that the employment tribunal before which she had taken her case had dismissed it on the basis, she said, that she was considered in law to be a man. Goodwin had subsequently lost her job, and she argued that this was because of her status as a trans woman.

When Goodwin started work with a new employer, she tried unsuccessfully to change her National Insurance number on the grounds that, otherwise, her new boss might find out about the situation with her previous employer. She claimed that the new employer had traced her identity and that she then started having problems at work, including ostracism.*

Like April Ashley, Goodwin was told that she would be ineligible to claim a state pension when she turned 60 and would have to wait until she was 65, continuing to pay National Insurance contributions until then. At the time she made application to the court, Goodwin was not quite 65 years old. Though she had not had surgery until she was 53, she had lived most of her life as a woman, but one unable to take advantage of certain kinds of assistance, such as a loan conditional on life insurance, a remortgage offer, and entitlement to a winter fuel

---

* National Insurance contributions in the United Kingdom are a portion of income paid by employees, employers, and the self-employed, alongside income tax, to fund the NHS and to build an individual's entitlement to certain benefits such as the state pension. Information provided on a person's birth certificate was used during registration.

allowance, because her birth certificate identified her as male. She also had to pay higher motor insurance premiums.

Having heard similar stories from transgender British nationals for almost 16 years, the European Court of Human Rights had had enough. It decided unanimously that the British government had violated Articles 8 and 12 of the European Convention on Human Rights; the fact that the state authorities still considered Christine Goodwin to be a man had adversely affected her right to a pension and to an earlier retirement age. The decision, the Court said, acknowledged that '[t]here have been major social changes in the institution of marriage since the adoption of the Convention, as well as dramatic changes brought about by developments in medicine and science in the field of transsexuality'. They added that the court 'was not convinced that the inability of the transsexual to acquire all the biological characteristics took on decisive importance'.[8]

Goodwin's solicitor, Robin Lewis, said that the ECHR decision would mean that the British government would eventually have to change its laws. It was encouraging that, after 15 years, the hated Section 28 of the Local Government Act had been stripped from the statute books of England and Wales — three years after it had been wiped in Scotland. But Ashley was gloomy about the prospects, largely because of Prime Minister Tony Blair's lack of response to her. 'People say things have changed, but they haven't changed at all,' she told a journalist. 'I'm still treated as a joke and I can't escape that. I'm stuck with it for the rest of my life.'[9]

While appetite for reform was by no means universal, on 27 November 2003, the Gender Recognition Bill was introduced into the House of Lords. It was passed in the House of Commons on 25 May the following year and became law on 1 July 2004. Described as 'ground-breaking legislation', the Act granted transgender people legal recognition, allowing them to change the sex recorded on their birth certificate. Transgender adults were able to apply for a Gender

Recognition Certificate (GRC), though under strict conditions. They had to provide medical evidence of gender dysphoria and give details of their treatment; they had to live in their 'acquired gender' for a minimum of two years; and they were required to sign a statutory declaration that they would continue to do so.

There was a further sting in the tail. During the debate, David Lammy, the Parliamentary Under-Secretary of State for Constitutional Affairs, had acknowledged that the bill 'must account for the situation of the relatively small number of transsexual people who are in existing marriages':

> After recognition in the acquired gender such couples will become same-sex couples, and marriage is of course an insti-tution for opposite-sex couples. It has always been so and the Government intend it to remain that way. That means that existing marriages will have to end. We acknowledge that this will have emotional and practical repercussions.
>
> The decision to require existing marriages to end was not taken lightly. Ultimately we believe that these same-sex couples should be treated in the same way as other same-sex couples and should therefore have access to the civil partnerships that the Government propose to make available for same-sex couples, but marriage should remain an institution for opposite-sex couples.[10]

Trans rights advocate Christine Burns said: 'I cannot think of an issue that challenges marriage more. This law is absolutely indefensible. The law considers relationships for trans people and those who love them to be disposable.'[11]

The Act was problematic in other ways. As it turned out, trans men and women in England and Wales often had to wait more than five years to acquire a Gender Recognition Certificate, largely because the NHS was chronically underfunded and the Act failed to acknowledge people who identified outside of the gender binary. Feminist groups argued that opportunistic men might abuse the Act to access women's spaces and rights, actually putting women in danger.

April was among the first to apply for a GRC. Ever the consummate networker, she contacted for help someone she had last seen as a dashing young man when they were both working at a hotel in St Asaph in the Channel Islands: John Prescott — now deputy prime minister. 'He was so helpful to me,' she said. 'With Tony Blair I got nowhere. But when I got in touch with my old friend John, things happened very fast. He pointed me in exactly the right direction, made sure I got all the forms to the right people. He was ever so supportive.'[12]

When the time came, it was John Prescott who presented his old friend April Ashley with her entirely new birth certificate: 'Name: April. Sex: Girl.' The very last trace of George Jamieson had disappeared.

It should have been a joyous moment, but April had mixed feelings. Interviewed on BBC radio programme *Woman's Hour* in 2013, she was asked, 'When the status of transgender people was fully recognised with the Gender Recognition Act — that moment in 2004 when you were legally recognised as female and issued with a new birth certificate, what was that moment like?'

'I was awfully happy for the people who came after me,' replied April:

I thought it was the most marvellous thing. But for me it was too late.

I was living in the south of France and [in August 2005] this brown envelope arrived announcing that I had a reissued, new birth certificate. People said, 'Oh April, we'll celebrate,' and I said, 'No, we'll just have a nice bottle of champagne, which we do anyhow.'

'Was it not a moment you'd dreamed of?' the interviewer asked.

'No. I was too old by then. I was seventy-odd and it didn't mean a thing.'[13]

But although she did not yet know it, April Ashley was about to undergo another renaissance.

CHAPTER 23

Grande dame

When April was asked whether she would ever return to England to live, she always said that was her intention. Typically, she added a sardonic twist. In 2005 she told the *Liverpool Echo* — the newspaper that had always kept tabs on her changing fortunes — 'I'll definitely move back to die. They can drape me in a Union Jack and throw me in the sea.'[1]

In fact, April left the south of France and returned to London in 2008, settling in a modest flat in Fulham. This wasn't her favourite neighbourhood — that was Chelsea — but at least Fulham had the requisite SW address. And the area was reassuringly upmarket and familiar, even though London wasn't quite the place she had known 40 years before. Before too long, the area — particularly the Brown Cow pub on the corner of April's street — was to become the epicentre of Prince Harry's London bachelordom. Ashley said that, whenever they were in the pub at the same time, he — one of the most gossiped-about people on the planet — always avoided catching her eye. She believed that this was because she was still considered 'a freak' — a reputation she felt she would never escape.[2]

The Equality Act — passed in 2010, shortly before the New Labour government lost office — undoubtedly raised general awareness of transgender issues. This wide-ranging legislation was intended to protect people from public 'discrimination, harassment and victimisation' on the basis of one (or more) of nine categories, including 'gender reassignment'.

The Act was not perfect: its failure to legislate for same-sex marriage was quickly noted. And, as April and so many others were fully aware, discrimination and harassment come in many forms, and the law has always been a blunt instrument.

However, one of the first beneficiaries of respect for the transgender community was April herself. In June 2012, she was appointed Member of the Order of the British Empire (MBE) in the Queen's Birthday Honours, for 'services to transgender equality'. She was not the first transgender person to have been so honoured: Stephen Whittle had been awarded Officer of the Order of the British Empire (OBE) in 2005 for 'services to gender issues'; and Jan Morris had accepted — 'out of polite respect', she said — her appointment as Commander of the British Empire (CBE) in 1999 for 'services to literature'.

April, now aged 77, was delighted and 'stunned' by the honour. 'I kept rereading the letter with the news. I wanted to scream out loud with excitement and tell everyone,' she told the *Daily Mail*. She added, 'I never thought I was doing anything special, quite frankly. So to be suddenly awarded was astonishing and hugely gratifying.'[3]

It was all the sweeter because some felt she had done little for the transgender cause; she said herself that she had fought more strongly for her own rights than for the good of Britain's trans community. But she had never ignored others, either: 'You know, when you get letters and emails from people who are desperately unhappy, you respond to them. Not just trans people, but gay men and lesbians and women who are unhappily married. You can't just sit there and ignore them or delete them, so I responded' — usually by letter.[4] April believed her own experience was the best form of advocacy.

The media met the announcement of April's MBE with general

approval. 'To have queen and country calmly, unshowily recognise Ashley's long, bruising fight for transsexual rights is inspiring,' wrote Libby Purves in *The Times*. And Patrick Barkham of *The Guardian* commented: 'Trans people deserve rights and respect. And now the elderly and frail Miss April Ashley, MBE, stands as an elegant, honoured, living proof of the fact that Britain has moved on. Out of an age of prurient fear, bullying, insult and mockery into a better one.'[5]

These were fine sentiments — but they were not universal. One 'old friend' said acidly that the award had been given for 'services to champagne, more like'.[6]

On 13 December 2012, wearing a broad-brimmed black hat, a silver-grey brushed velvet suit, a shocking pink pashmina, and pearls, April advanced carefully — with the aid of a cane — towards Prince Charles in Buckingham Palace and stood as he pinned the medal to her lapel. She might have reflected upon a comment she had made in a BBC interview some years earlier: 'Once you become an institution, you become respectable again. What happens in between is another story.' '[Prince Charles] was awfully nice,' she said. 'He's better-looking in real life. And he was very sweet. As I walked up to him, he said to me, "April, this has been a long time coming, hasn't it."'

The proudest day of April Ashley's life: 13 December 2012

In 2013, it was the turn of April's birthplace to honour her. The Museum of Liverpool hosted an exhibition devoted to her life, *April Ashley: portrait of a lady*, curated by the arts and social justice organisation Homotopia, with many exhibits drawn from April's own archive. Present at the ceremony were Liverpool's new Lord Mayor Gary Millar and his civil partner, Steve MacFarlane — underlining how much the city had changed since Ashley lived there.

April was self-deprecating as usual — 'I suppose this exhibition will be a bit like an obituary' was her response — but, as well as showcasing April's extraordinary life, the exhibition had a wider purpose: to acknowledge and recognise the lives of transgender people, to tell hidden stories, and to promote diversity. During the 17 months of its run, an estimated 930,000 people saw the exhibition. One visitor commented: 'It allowed other strands of trans to be seen as well — transvestites, queer, gender non-conforming, no gender — everybody was included and that's what it's all about, inclusion.' April cherished the friendships she forged during this time with new, younger people, many of whom remained her supporters for the rest of her life.[7]

In June 2014, three months after legislation permitting same-sex marriage took effect in Britain, Homotopia combined with National Museums Liverpool to hold an international conference under the rubric of the Un-Straight Museum, aiming to explore the role of cultural institutions, curators, and archivists in representing marginalised communities.[8] As a spokesman said: 'The impact April's life has had on law and legal definitions of gender and identity has been enormous, and her strength and determination [are] admired by many.'

In 2014, April was given a lifetime achievement honour at the European Diversity Awards. And to celebrate her 80th birthday in 2015, she became an honorary citizen of Liverpool. The woman who as George Jamieson had hardly been the star student at St Teresa of Lisieux school was also awarded two honorary degrees: by the University of

Liverpool in 2016, and by the University of London three years later. April calmly and graciously accepted all these honours.

She also felt, in return, a responsibility to explain her own trans experience to younger people and for as large an audience as possible. Her appearance on the ITV lunchtime programme *Loose Women* — a panel discussion hosted by a cross-section of friendly women presenters — is typical.[9]

Wearing a soft pink suit, with immaculate lavender hair and a statement necklace, April spoke about her decision to undergo gender-affirming surgery. 'It was rather terrifying,' she said. 'But I was never frightened because if it didn't work, I didn't want to live anyhow.' This provoked a sympathetic intake of breath from the audience — women in their 30s and older, many of whom were unfamiliar with April's story. And when she admitted, 'My mother detested me ... my father was the only person who ever loved me,' she was met with expressions of sympathy and sorrow.[10]

As might perhaps be expected, April was asked what she thought about American media personality and former Olympian Caitlyn Jenner — perhaps the most visible transgender person in the world at the time. While she said she wished Jenner well, she couldn't resist a dig: 'Caitlyn? Terrible name.'[11]

But when she was asked, 'What advice would you give to people who may be feeling they are trapped in the wrong body?', April's heartfelt reply was greeted with warm applause:

> I write to people all the time. I think that's why I got an MBE from Her Majesty the Queen. It's a terrible thing to go through any kind of deformity, feeling so isolated and they don't know who to turn to or what to turn to. And so the advice I always give is, I cannot help you, I'm not a professional, but I would be very kind to myself and to other people, be beautiful inside and that makes you beautiful outside, and be *bloody* brave.[12]

April amplified these comments in a filmed interview at about the same time. 'It's the inside that matters,' she said. 'I think if you don't make it physically, it's awfully sad, but if you need to go through the change and it makes you happy, who cares what the world thinks? That's my philosophy.'[13]

When asked whether she ever cared about what the world thought about her, she was very firm: 'Nope. Not at all. Never cared. I had such a terrible childhood, I gave up [caring about people's opinions] long ago. When you have a mother who beat you every day of your life and wouldn't hold your hand, who wouldn't touch you, you have to get used to rejection.'[14]

According to *Time* magazine, 2014 was a pivotal moment for trans rights. Captioned 'The transgender tipping point', the magazine cover featured the Black television actress Laverne Cox, its first trans cover star.

> Almost one year after the Supreme Court ruled that Americans were free to marry the person they loved, no matter their sex, another civil rights movement is poised to challenge long-held cultural norms and beliefs ... This new transparency is improving the lives of a long-misunderstood minority and beginning to yield new policies, as trans activists and their supporters push for changes in schools, hospitals, workplaces, prisons and the military. 'We are in a place now,' Cox tells *Time*, 'where more and more trans people want to come forward and say, "This is who I am."'[15]

Journalist Katie Steinmets did point out later in the article that a 2011 survey of transgender people in the United States — 0.5 per cent of the population — found that they were disproportionately likely to be poor, unemployed, and wishing to kill themselves. But, said Cox, it was also true that more trans people were 'living visibly and pursuing our dreams.'

O, brave new world.

Greater visibility does not always mean acceptance. In January 2013, freelance journalist Julie Burchill caused a stir with her comments on a *Guardian*-owned website, describing trans women as 'screaming mimis', 'bedwetters in bad wigs', and 'dicks in chicks' clothing'. Her column was taken down by the editor; it was republished in *The Telegraph*.

In 2015, well-known feminist writer and academic Germaine Greer took a similar stance. When discussing the stereotyping of women in her groundbreaking 1970 study *The Female Eunuch*, Greer had declared Ashley a perfect example of the female stereotype: 'As long as the feminine stereotype remains the definition of the female sex, April Ashley is a woman, regardless of the legal decision ensuing from her divorce. She is as much a casualty of the polarity of the sexes as we all are.'[16]

On BBC programme *Newsnight* in October 2015, Greer said that, while she was not questioning the wish to have surgery, she did not think that 'transgender men, i.e. M to F', were women: 'I think a great many women don't think that post-operative, or even non-post-operative transsexual M to F transsexual people look like, sound like or think like women, but they daren't say so.'[17] She added that she would be prepared to use female pronouns in referring to someone, if that was their preference, as 'a courtesy'.

How awkward, polarising, and fractured this debate could be was shown by the afterlife of Lili Elbe.

In 1930, Lili Elbe — born in Denmark and assigned male at birth — underwent gender-affirming surgery: one of the very first people to do so. She died in 1931 — three months after her fourth operation. A fictionalised account of her life by American writer David Ebershoff was published in 2000 under the title *The Danish Girl*; 15 years later, the book was adapted for a movie starring Eddie Redmayne.

April worked with Redmayne to help him prepare for the role, and he was subsequently nominated for an Academy Award. 'I told him not to be coy, not to be camp, just to be himself vocally,' she told the

Liverpool Echo. 'You can always lighten up your voice without making it artificial. And he kept looking at all my gestures as we spoke, taking everything in.'

When April saw the finished movie, she did not believe Redmayne had followed all of her instructions: 'I didn't think he should be dropping his eyelashes every two minutes, but then he most probably got direction to do that.'[18]

By 2021, Redmayne felt compelled to say that if asked to play the role again, he would have refused. 'I made that film with the best intentions, but I think it was a mistake,' he said. 'There must be a levelling, otherwise we are going to carry on having these debates', that the entertainment industry had enjoyed 'years of cisgender success on the back of trans stories', and that he hoped trans actors could play trans parts in future (which raises the question whether April would have had greater success finding work as an actor these days). He added that any actor should be able to play any part if they did so with a sense of 'integrity and responsibility'.

Journalist and trans commentator Debbie Hayton took issue with some of Redmayne's comments, pointing out that he had played the physicist Stephen Hawking in another biographical drama. 'Was it OK for a physicist to be portrayed by someone who is not a physicist?' Hayton asked:

> As a trans physicist I fail to see the distinction between these two films, unless an assumption is being made that trans people are somehow distinct from the rest of humanity ... Redmayne should not worry about upsetting the trans lobby; they will never be satisfied. [He] should be proud rather than ashamed of playing Lili Elbe.[19]

Near the end of her life, April expressed 'very strong thoughts' about gender issues — especially on trans self-identification, the idea that trans people should be able to determine their gender without a medical diagnosis. She echoed the possibility raised by 'gender-critical' commentators that a man convicted of rape could 'throw on a wig' and insist he was a woman, be sent to a women's prison, and commit the same crime.

It was ironic that she should reject self-identification, since she herself had followed — if not actually forged — that path. After all, when she was first hospitalised and had undergone conversion therapy, she had rejected the psychiatrists' advice that she should go away and live as a gay man. She had also sought out and paid for her own gender-affirming surgery, without any medical imprimatur.

What really annoyed her — always — was 'political correctness' and what she saw as the shutting-down and demonisation of unpopular opinions. Her lament for the absence of eccentrics was an appreciation of those who insisted on going their own way: she had always valued people who were prepared to do and live as they liked, who embraced non-conformity and refused to follow the herd. By early 2020, she was expressing the opinion that the current political climate — with its fear of challenging or offending people — was 'ridiculous' and 'so stupid'. She argued that activist voices were becoming 'too powerful' — that 'it's stopping free speech and can be dangerous'. Boy George, who idolised her and who had become a friend, is an example of someone who felt the full force of an online backlash after calling the focus on and proliferation of personal pronouns 'a modern form of attention-seeking'. April's defence of him was blunt and to the point: 'You can say what you like!'[20]

She also had strong views about what it meant to be transgender. 'I think what people don't realise is that changing sex really has nothing to do with your looks or your body,' she told researcher and writer Tom Roberts. 'It's your *brain*. Because I remember from the moment I could think that I was the wrong sex, and I didn't even know what the word "sex" meant.'[21]

An interview she gave in Australia in August 1982, while she was promoting *April Ashley's Odyssey*, casts fascinating light on April's views. She spoke to John Lawson, a journalist with Sydney's *Oxford Weekender News*. This was a newspaper for Sydney's gay community, its title a reference to Oxford Street in east Sydney, the centre of the city's gay quarter at the time. Presumably because April was a long way from home — and because of the nature of the newspaper — she was franker than usual. 'Of course I call myself a woman,' she said:

> And I'm as close to being a natural woman as I can be. But the fact remains that I'm not a natural female and that will always be. I can never change the fact that my body started its life with male attributes ... [Within] myself I am a woman, as I've always believed, but I'm not exactly the same as other women in that I was never a little girl and I've had to accept that.

As for her role within the trans community, she said:

> I never advise other transsexuals. If they need to ask me if they should have the operation, then they shouldn't have it. I can't make that decision for them ... I suppose that I am a transsexual pioneer, but I rarely have any dealings with transsexual groups ... I didn't go through all I endured to just constantly run around playing Margaret Mead.

She continued to be in demand for personal appearances on television and in newspaper interviews, often expected to appear without pay. Her motto was 'no fee, no me', and at one point she turned down a magazine cover shoot with Kate Moss.[22]

In April's last years, her health issues became increasingly intrusive and debilitating: not just her damaged heart and fragile bones, but the possibility of breast cancer. Still, she carried on: seeing friends and exploring new opportunities to tell her story.

April Ashley's flat in Rostrevor Road, Fulham, was in a pale terrace of three-storey houses, still elegant, with wrought-iron balustrades, steep mansard roofs, and dormer windows: the south-west London version of a Parisian street scene, but with a fringe of sickly poplars and cars aggressively parked at the kerb, all of them oversized and expensive.

April's place wasn't difficult to find. On the sash bar of a ground-floor bay window that faced the street, she had balanced the model of an ocean cutter in full sail — an echo of her early career and a fitting emblem of this, her last port of call. For privacy, the curtains behind were drawn day and night, the window never opened.

The flat itself was small — clearly converted from a much bigger house — with high ceilings and abruptly truncated cornicing. It consisted of a bedroom, bathroom, and kitchenette/sitting room overlooking other people's back gardens. Like most slice-and-dice conversions, the building was poorly insulated, with noise coming from residents upstairs — an annoying contrast to the space and peace April had enjoyed in the south of France. She kept her flat very warm: she couldn't stand being cold, she said, and she insisted on heating, despite the cost.

Facing visitors in the narrow hallway was a framed headshot of April wearing a polka-dot headscarf, taken during her heyday as a model. Every wall in the place, it seemed, was covered with photographs — some happy snaps, others professional shots from her glory days: April meeting Winston Churchill; with the AD8 kitchen crew; with Alan Jay Lerner, the librettist of *My Fair Lady*, featuring four bottles of champagne on a restaurant table; April with David Hemmings, and Princess Anne, and John Prescott, and Peter Maddock. There was also an old promotional shot of trans man Mickey Mercer, the compère of Le Carrousel, who had always fascinated April. Other framed photographs and awards were stacked against the walls of the sitting room. There was a coloured print of Polperro in Cornwall and another of the Pacific Ocean, two places April often wished to visit again. And in the sitting room was a small television set on which April loved watching reruns of classic Hollywood movies.

The bedroom was crammed with dresses and coats and gowns from the 1960s and later — clothes spread across the bed, in boxes and piles and dust covers, pushing against the curtains that faced the street and endangering the precariously balanced sailing ship. There were so many clothes that there was no room for April: she slept in the armchair in the sitting room. Some of the key documents and items from her life were already on loan to the exhibition in Liverpool. Everything else — a lifetime of press cuttings and records of interview appearances — was carefully stored in boxes and stacked.

There were few books: the printed word did not play a great role in April's life. But she kept up an extensive correspondence — mostly using her smartphone — with photos and messages from friends all over the world. She wrote all her responses in capital letters: 'She lives her life in block capitals,' observed her friend Simon Callow, in tribute to her flamboyance. It's a nice line — and it expresses a poignant truth: April, dyslexic since childhood, found typing in block capitals much easier than upper- and lower-case lettering.

She kept up many friendships via her computer and smartphone, and she occasionally made new friends. One of the more noteworthy was Norman Scott, the former model who had become a key figure in one of the major British political scandals of the 1970s. His ex-lover, Liberal Party leader Jeremy Thorpe, had allegedly planned to murder Scott after the latter threatened to reveal their relationship to the media. Scott and April had a certain amount in common: both had become notorious, both were brought down by the forces of class and the establishment, and both remained resilient to the end. April claimed that it was she who suggested Scott should write his memoir; it was published under the title *An Accidental Icon*. But she said she never asked him about his sexual past: 'I could never ask him ... I think he's been through enough.'

April dressed for comfort in her own style. She wore trainers covered with twists of bright colour, loose-fitting drawstring trousers, and shawls and pashminas — layers of soft, rich fabrics, including wool, mohair, and brushed cotton. She never left the flat without full makeup — foundation, concealer, powder, and lipstick. Age and infirmity made applying all this an even longer and more exacting process than it had always been. Her eyelashes were sparse and her eyebrows were drawn on, her own long lost to the plucking of an overenthusiastic hairdresser. She often added a dab of Mitsouko (a scent that its creator, Jacques Guerlain, called — rather appropriately, in April's case — 'subtly androgynous yet wildly feminine').

With a fleecy hat crammed over her white hair, she was ready to go out — although not before checking the deep pockets of her quilted coat for dog biscuits in preparation for her regular welcome by some of the local dogs. Animals had always been important to her — from the time she had fed the local Liverpool pigeons and especially when her brother brought home Prince, the dog who became George's champion.

April never walked very far from her flat. She shopped at the local Tesco Express at the end of the road, and its staff carried her shopping back to the flat for her — a kindness for which she was enduringly grateful. She might sometimes ask a visitor to go to Tesco to get her a carton of sweet iced coffee and a packet of wine gums — treats for someone who had craved sugar during wartime rationing, and her favoured way of keeping her energy up when she had been too ill or poor for proper meals. She usually took six teaspoons of sugar in her coffee, though none in her tea.

At the other end of April's street, in a flat-faced brick building at the intersection of the bustling high street and Rostrevor Road, was her local pub, the Brown Cow. A battered aluminium milk churn by its entrance recalled her very first job delivering milk as a young child, and the pub's name had another ironic resonance for April, 'how now, brown cow' being an often-parodied example of the rounded vowels that elocution teachers in her era had considered necessary for 'correct' speech. The pub also had a large glass jar by the front door, from which she replenished her supply of dog biscuits.

A visit to the shabby-chic Brown Cow was something not to be undertaken lightly, given April's mobility issues. Old age was not something she enjoyed. 'All my old friends are dead,' she told a television interviewer. 'It's very strange when all your friends are dead, because as you get older, people don't really notice you. Once you've got white hair you seem to disappear off the face of the planet.'[23]

When she turned 80, she gave a description of her health to a journalist at *The Times*. 'Fragile,' she said:

> Chronic kidney disease, I only have one kidney, and it's on the blink. I have liver disease. I've had three heart attacks. I have terrible osteoporosis in the legs and I've had three blood clots in the same leg. And my leg is totally deformed, almost black, and will never be the same again. And diverticulitis ... The list is endless. I'm a walking bloody miracle.[24]

Nevertheless, April sometimes lunched at the Brown Cow, often treated by an interviewer or a friend. She rarely finished her meal, requesting a box for the food that remained: this, she said, would keep her going for a couple of days. But she could seldom resist 'an April Ashley-sized glass of wine'. The Brown Cow's clientele — typically, for that part of London — were largely young mothers with toddlers and dogs in the morning, local office workers at lunchtime, and the affluent young professionals of Fulham later in the day. April was welcome there at any time, her elegant presence marking her as a celebrity even though some were unsure exactly why she was famous. She would regale those paying court to her with tales of her past — including an encounter with Michael Hutchence's 'magnificent manhood'. All described by this elegant old woman with the voice and demeanour of a duchess.

April Ashley died in her flat in Fulham on 27 December 2021. She was given a simple Catholic funeral and buried at the Ford cemetery in Liverpool. She had requested that, instead of flowers, donations in her name should be given to the Alder Hey Children's Hospital, which had looked after George as a child.

There was a small group at the graveside. In deference to April's former life, the pallbearers — carrying a coffin draped with the red ensign — were all uniformed naval personnel, and the service was led by Father John Williams, a naval chaplain, who described April as 'a lady of great determination and great courage'.

The graveside eulogy was written by April's longtime friend and adviser Peter Maddock and read by Bev Ayre, a friend she had made in Liverpool during her later years and one of her executors.

'April was a princess in bare feet her whole life,' wrote Maddock, who had known her since 1965. 'She walked as if she was on the runway at a Paris fashion show. There was a part of her that lived in a fairytale, and another part firmly planted in the north of England. She loved ballet and opera ... her humour was essentially northern.'

A young woman trumpeter played the 'Last Post', and April's coffin was lowered into the grave while the sailors saluted. Appropriately, a bottle of champagne retrieved from her flat was uncorked. April was buried beside her adored father.

April Ashley's death made headlines around the world and tributes flowed. *The New York Times* summed her up succinctly: 'She modelled for *Vogue*, partied with John Lennon and Mick Jagger, and married into minor nobility, all while fighting for legal recognition of her gender.'

There were heartfelt comments, too, from Ashley's admirers.

Boy George wrote: 'RIP April Ashley! A force of nature and transgender high priestess!' (A keen photographer, he had in his home a huge portrait photograph of Ashley he had taken in 2013.)

And Hannah Graf, a former captain in the Royal Electrical and Mechanical Engineers and the highest-ranking transgender officer in the British Army, described Ashley as 'a true pioneer for the trans and wider LGBTQ community': 'April Ashley MBE will be remembered for being unapologetically herself in a world that was stacked against her. I and many others owe her a great debt. May she rest in power.'

For April, the political and the personal had always been intertwined. A friend of April's named Glyn told the *Liverpool Echo* that 'April was a very proud woman ... one of the things she was most proud of was being embraced by the same city that had treated her badly as a kid. She died happy, knowing her city accepted her as a woman in every sense of the word.'[25]

Like Hans Andersen's mermaid, Ashley had never flinched from the physical and emotional pain that her decision to change her body had caused her. But, unlike the mermaid, she never regretted what she had done. When, in her 70s, she met the son of her surgeon Georges Burou, she told him, 'I still retain a little bit of that joy that I had the day after your father operated on me. I have never lost that. It is always, always with me.'[26]

Trans activist Christine Burns has observed of the woman she described as 'a wonderful person': 'She was just trying to live her life to the full at a time when society wasn't ready for the idea. She took the rap for all of us — and she paid the price through a life of exile. The knocks she suffered in the sixties put an extra shine on her defences.'

When April was in her 80s, she often acknowledged that the social climate of the early 2000s was very different from the one she had known when young. 'I'm very happy for the young people who came after me as transsexuals who are leading decent, interesting, wonderful lives as surgeons and doctors and computer specialists,' she said. But there was sadness, too: 'I couldn't, of course, because of the way my name became known. While I'm very happy for them, they have no idea what it was like for me.'[27]

As one perspicacious *Liverpool Echo* journalist — the paper's shipping correspondent, suitably enough — wrote towards the end of Ashley's life:

> It wasn't enough. This could have been the mantra of April Ashley, the Liverpool boy who went from ship's dockhand to transgender grande dame via one of the world's first sex-change operations. It wasn't enough to accept being effeminate. Instead, the then George Jamieson became a sailor to toughen up as a real man. It wasn't enough to accept this had failed. Instead the 15-year-old George attempted suicide by jumping overboard into the Mersey.

Why, the journalist continued, did Ashley undergo 'life-threatening' surgery instead of simply leading 'a gay life in a seaport used to such characters'? Ashley's own words answered the question: 'Because it wasn't enough. It wasn't satisfying. I wanted proper fulfilment. If I wasn't a woman by the age of 25 I didn't want to live.'[28]

And despite all the pain, the setbacks, the humiliations, the implication was that April Ashley had achieved what she wanted, that she had found fulfilment.

Was it enough?

Anyone who saw her on television or read her story, the anecdotes polished through the years to a smooth gloss, was in no doubt. This woman, admired for her realism, caustic wit, and toughness, had triumphantly overcome everything the world could throw at her. She looked assured and contented — at peace with herself and the person she had become.

But there was also something April never forgot. Treasured among her memories of her life she had so fully lived and the celebrities she had known was a painting she had seen in the Getty Museum in Los Angeles. This was *Irises* by Vincent Van Gogh. She had loved its rich colour and profusion, but her attention had been caught by the lone iris at the edge of the canvas, stark white against its blue and purple neighbours. Why Van Gogh had put it there she did not know, but to her it represented solitude and loneliness. April Ashley had gazed at that painting for a long, long time.

Acknowledgements

We wish to thank the following for their help in preparing this book:

April Ashley herself, posthumously, for having been so forthright and generous with detail in her many interviews over the years

Staff at the Bishopsgate Institute, the London School of Economics, the University of Victoria, the Digital Transgender Archive and the British Library

Vicki Oglikowski-Broad at the National Archives, Kew

Sian Wilks at the Special Collections and Archives, University of Liverpool Library

Dr Dian Jordan from the Harold Stevenson Estate

Sir Roy Strong

Patricia Clough

Suzanne Falkiner

Rose Storkey

Andrew Gordon and David Evans of David Higham & Associates

The team at Scribe Publications — especially Simon Wright, Laura Ali, and Adam Howard

Last, but certainly not least, we thank our partners, Tim and John.

Select bibliography

Books

Arnold, Ken, Mick Gordon and Chris Wilkinson (eds), *Identity & Identification*, Black Dog, 2009

Brown, Geoff, *I Want What I Want*, Weidenfeld & Nicolson, 1966

Brown, Tina, *Life as a Party*, David & Charles, 1983

Burns, Christine, *Trans Britain: our journey from the shadows*, Unbound, 2018

Churchill, Sarah, *Keep on Dancing*, Coward, McCann & Geoghegan, 1981

Clements, Paul, *Jan Morris: life from both sides*, Scribe, 2022

Cowell, Roberta, *An Autobiography: Roberta Cowell's story*, British Book Centre, 1954

Debrett's Peerage

Doggett, Peter, *Growing Up: sex in the sixties*, Vintage, 2021

Fallowell, Duncan, *April Ashley's Odyssey*, Jonathan Cape, 1982

Feaver, William, *The Lives of Lucian Freud, Vol. 1: the restless years*, Bloomsbury, 2015

Flannery, Mike, with Mike Brocken, *Standing in the Wings: the Beatles, Brian Epstein and me*, The History Press, 2013

Freedland, Michael, *Peter O'Toole: a biography*, W.H. Allen, 1983

Greer, Germaine, *The Female Eunuch*, MacGibbon & Kee, 1970

Hall, Lesley A., *Sex, Gender and Social Change in Britain since 1880*, HarperCollins, 2000

Haslam, Nicholas, *Redeeming Features: a memoir*, Edge, 2009

Hogarth, Tim, *The Dazzling Lady Docker*, Scratching Shed, 2018

Hutton, Christopher, *The Tyranny of Ordinary Meaning:* Corbett v Corbett *and the invention of legal sex*, Palgrave Macmillan, 2019

Miles, Barry, *Paul McCartney: many years from now*, Secker & Warburg, 1997

Playdon, Zoe, *The Hidden Case of Ewan Forbes*, Scribner, 2021

Prescott, John, with Hunter Davies, *Prezza*: *pulling no punches*, Headline Review, 2007

Pruvot, Marie-Pierre, *Le Carrousel*, Editions ex Aequo, 2013

Rowallan, Thomas Godfrey Polson Corbett, *The Autobiography of Lord Rowallan*, Harris, 1976

Thompson, Douglas, *The First Lady*, John Blake, 2006

Newspapers and periodicals

Aberdeen Evening Express, *Aberdeen Press and Journal*, *Birmingham Mail*, *Bristol Evening Post*, *Canberra Times*, *Country Life*, *Daily Express*, *Daily Mail*, *Daily Mirror*, *Daily Telegraph*, *Evening Standard*, *Female Mimics*, *Gay News Literary Supplement*, *The Guardian*, *The Independent*, *Kensington Post*, *The Lancet*, *The Listener*, *Liverpool Daily Post*, *Liverpool Echo*, *Newcastle Journal*, *News of the World*, *The Observer*, *The Oldie*, *The People*, *Prospect*, *Reynolds's Newspaper*, *The Spectator*, *The Stage*, *Sunday Mirror*, *Sunday Pictorial*, *The Sunday Times*, *Tatler*, *Time*, *The Times*, *The Times Literary Supplement*, *Vanity Fair*, *Who's Who*, *Woman's World*

Television, radio, and film

Bambi, dir. Sébastien Lifshitz, Epicentre Films, 2013

Good Afternoon, Thames TV, 1977

I Am a Woman Now, dir. Michiel van Erp, 2012

Ligmalion: or how to help yourself in self-help Britain, dir. Nigel Finch,
   Arena, BBC2, 1985

Loose Women, ITV, June 2015

Mr Lucas's Diaries, BBC Radio 4, August 2022

Parkinson in Australia, Channel 10, 1982

Russell Harty Plus, LWT, October 1973

Time of Their Lives, ITV, March 2001

What Am I?, ATV, 1980

Woman's Hour, BBC Radio 4, October 2013

Notes

Introduction: 'I was my own Pygmalion'

1   *Good Afternoon*, Thames TV, 1977.
2   youtube.com/watch?v=wX-NhWb47sc.

Chapter 1: 'Please let me wake up as a girl'

1   iwm.org.uk/history/the-liverpool-blitz.
2   youtube.com/watch?v=wX-NhWb47sc.
3   April interviewed by Mavis Nicolson, *Good Afternoon*, Thames Television, 1977.
4   *Daily Express*, 28 July 2000.
5   *Parkinson in Australia*, Channel 10, Sydney, 1982.

Chapter 2: Ways of escape

1   Interview, *Good Afternoon*, Thames TV, 1977.
2   John Follain, 'You can't imagine the joy of becoming a girl', *The Sunday Times*, 11 June, 2006.
3   April Ashley accepting an Honorary Degree of Laws, University of Liverpool, 7 December 2016, youtube.com/watch?v=SAJDAuq7iSg.
4   *Liverpool Echo*, 7 June 1940.
5   *Parkinson in Australia*, Channel 10, Sydney, 1982.

6   *Good Afternoon*, Thames TV, 1977.

Chapter 3: All at sea

1   'My story' (serialisation), *News of the World*, 13 May 1962.
2   gloucesterdocks.me.uk/sharpness/vindicatrix.htm.
3   'My story' (serialisation), *News of the World*, 13 May 1962.
4   *Ibid*.

Chapter 4: 'Shouldn't they have seen what was wrong?'

1   Joe Flannery, with Mike Brocken, *Standing in the Wings: The Beatles, Brian Epstein and Me*, The History Press, 2013, p. 101.
2   *Liverpool Echo*, 15 November 1953.
3   youtube.com/watch?v=HRjSSaqpUn4.
4   *Ibid*.
5   history.rcplondon.ac.uk/inspiring-physicians/charles-mathurin-vaillant.
6   'I have absolutely no regrets', *Daily Post*, 15 February 2006.
7   *Ibid*.
8   'A pal with a difference', *The Independent*, 17 June 2012.
9   'Britain's first transsexual reveals', *Daily Mirror*, 28 September 2013.

Chapter 5: Bona coves and zhooshy dishes

1   'My strange life', *News of the World*, 8 May 1962.
2   Douglas Thompson, *The First Lady*, John Blake, 2006, p. 59.
3   'My story' (serialisation), *News of the World*, 20 May 1962.
4   Graham Stewart, 'The accidental legacy of a homophobic humanitarian', *The Times*, 2 October 2000.
5   *Mr Lucas's Diaries*, BBC Radio 4, August 2022.
6   See, for example, *Sunday Pictorial*, 2 February 1953. The Jorgensen story was serialised in the *Sunday Pictorial* during February and March 1953.

7   *Yorkshire Evening Post*, 28 December 1935; english.radio.cz/zdena-
     zdenek-interwar-czech-champion-who-changed-genders-8720071.

8   Roberta Cowell, *An Autobiography: Roberta Cowell's story*, British
     Book Centre, 1954, p. 96.

9   ericlindsay.wordpress.com/heaven-and-hell-coffee-lounge-in-soho-w-i/.

10   'My strange life', *News of the World*, 27 May 1962.

Chapter 6: 'I felt completely at ease for the first time in my life'

1   Interview, Tom Roberts, 20 February 2020.

2   *Female Mimics*, undated.

3   Nicholas Haslam, *Redeeming Features: a memoir*, Edge, 2009, p. 69.

4   Mario A. Costa, *Reverse Sex*, Challenge, 1965, p.55.

5   *Bambi*, dir. Sébastien Lifshitz, Epicentre Films, 2013.

6   'At the court of Queen Lear', *The Observer*, 24 December 2000;
     'Amanda Lear: the androgynous muse to Dalí who made disco
     intellectual', Angelica Frey, *The Guardian*, 1 June 2022.

7   *News of the World*, 27 May 1962.

8   'Obituaries: Coccinelle', *The Independent*, 16 October 2006.

Chapter 7: 'Au revoir, monsieur ... Bonjour, mademoiselle'

1   youtube.com/watch?v=ImZgPALy_NY.

2   Paul Clements, *Jan Morris: life from both sides*, Scribe, 2022, p.
     282.

3   *Ibid*.

4   *Parkinson in Australia*, Channel 10, Sydney, 1982.

5   *Ibid*.

6   *Ibid*.

Chapter 8: 'I always carried a spare pair of eyelashes'

1   winstonchurchill.org/publications/finest-hour/finest-hour-183/
     sarah-churchill-winstons-right-hand-man/.

2   tiktok.com/@..dollhistory/video/7247963573719272747.

3   William Feaver, *The Lives of Lucian Freud, Vol. 1: the restless years*, Bloomsbury, 2015, p. 502.
4   Haslam, *Redeeming Features*, p. 140.
5   haroldstevenson.com/the-new-adam.

Chapter 9: '"Her" secret is out'

1   *The People*, 27 August 1961.
2   *The People*, 19 November 1961.
3   *The People*, 11 April 1954.
4   See gender.org.uk/conf/1990/90king.htm.
5   See Zoe Playdon, *The Hidden Case of Ewan Forbes*, Scribner, 2021.
6   *The Time of Their Lives*, ITV, 26 March 2001.
7   Thomas Godfrey Polson Corbett Rowallan, *The Autobiography of Lord Rowallan*, Harris, 1976, p . 29.
8   *Hansard*, Sexual Offences Bill, HL Deb., 10 May and 16 June 1966.
9   Letter, *Daily Mail*, 21 October 1999.

Chapter 10: Bombshells

1   *News of the World*, 10 June 1962.
2   Interview, Tom Roberts, 7 November 2022.
3   *Reuters*, 1 May 1962.
4   *Daily Mirror*, 30 April 1962.
5   *News of the World*, 20 May 1962.
6   *News of the World*, 6 May 1962.
7   Email to Tom Roberts, 7 November 2022.
8   *News of the World*, 6 May 1962.
9   *News of the World*, 13 May 1962.

Chapter 11: Spanish fantasy

1   *The Time of Their Lives*, ITV, 26 March 2001.
2   Michael Freedland, *Peter O'Toole: a biography*, W.H. Allen, 1983, p. 80.
3   *Parkinson in Australia*, Channel 10, Sydney, 1982.

4   *Ibid.*

5   Freedland, *Peter O'Toole*, pp. 80 *et seq.*

6   *Ibid.*

7   *The Time of Their Lives*, ITV, 26 March 2001.

8   Bobby Corbett, obituary, *The Times*, 3 April 1999.

Chapter 12: *La dolce vita matrimoniale*

1   Per Ormrod J in *Corbett v Corbett* [1970] 2 All ER 33, available at
     pfc.org.uk/caselaw/Corbett%20v%20Corbett.pdf.

2   'It's a mad, mad world when the sun comes out', *Daily Mail*, 28 April
     1964.

3   Barry Miles, *Paul McCartney: many years from now*, Secker &
     Warburg, 1997, p.133.

4   Interview, Nigel Farndale, *Daily Express*, 21 April 2015.

5   beatlesinterviews.org/dbbtspb.int2.html.

6   Peter Doggett, *Growing Up: Sex in the Sixties*, Vintage UK, 2021.

7   *The People*, 28 September 1962, pp. 203–205.

8   *The Sunday Times*, 17 April 1966.

Chapter 13: Youthquake

1   'Roz Kaveney meets the unsinkable April Ashley', *Gay News
     Literary Supplement*, no. 240, date unknown.

2   Home Office, *Report of the Departmental Committee on Homosexual
     Offences and Prostitution* (Wolfenden Report), HM Stationery
     Office, 1957.

3   *Ibid.*, paras 13 and 14.

4   'Sex-change April and the tycoon she lost', *Sunday People*, 14 January
     1973.

5   *Ibid.*

6   *Sunday Mirror*, 3 March 1972.

7   'Why I think the judge was wrong over April', Robin Maugham, *The
     People*, 8 February 1970.

8   Charles Duff, *Charley's Woods: sex, sorrow, and a spiritual question in Snowdonia*, Zuleika, 2019, p. 10.

9   See 'Viva King, Queen of Bohemia', bonhams.com/auction/23577/lot/221/.

10   Interview with April Ashley, *Oxford Weekender News*, Sydney, 5–18 August 1982.

11   'The first lady', *The Independent*, 7 February 2006.

12   Quoted in 'Biographer reveals intimate knowledge of transsexual April', *Daily Express*, 9 January 2007.

Chapter 14: *Corbett v Corbett:* the trial

1   *The Times*, 1 August 1969.

2   theoldie.co.uk/blog/april-ashley-in-new-documentary-duncan-fallowell.

Chapter 15: *Corbett v Corbett:* the verdict

1   *Daily Mirror*, 3 February 1970.

2   Ormrod J in *Corbett v Corbett* [1970] 2 All ER 33, available online at pfc.org.uk/caselaw/Corbett%20v%20Corbett.pdf. See also blog.nationalarchives.gov.uk/april-ashley-the-legal-battle/.

Chapter 16: Aftermath

1   *Daily Mail*, 3 February 1970.

2   *Daily Mirror*, 3 February 1970.

3   *Parkinson in Australia*, Channel 10, Sydney, 1982.

4   *Simon Dee Show*, 8 February 1970, missingepisodes.proboards.com/thread/12653/time-simon-show-missing-guests.

5   *Daily Mirror*, 4 March 1970.

6   'April Ashley signed slavery contract', *Daily Mail*, 28 July 1970.

7   *Daily Mirror*, 4 March 1970.

8   *Sunday Mirror*, 22 February 1970.

9   'The sexes: prisoners of sex', *Time*, 21 January 1974.

10   *The Times*, 3 February 1970.

11   'Why sex change is no change', Timothy Leland, *The Sunday Times*, 8 February 1970.

12   Geoffrey Robertson, *Rather His Own Man: in court with tyrants, tarts and troublemakers*, Biteback, 2018, quoted in *Mail on Sunday*, 10 June 2018.

13   Quoted in 'The definition of marriage in English law', Sebastian Poulter, *The Modern Law Review*, 1979.

Chapter 17: Life at AD8

1   'The aristo and the spiv: the true story of the men behind The Who', Edward Helmore, *The Observer*, 22 February 2015.

2   'Notoriety and then the quiet life', *Liverpool Echo*, 22 April 1982.

3   'Interview with April Ashley', John Lawson, *Oxford Weekender News*, Sydney, 5–18 August 1982.

4   *Birmingham Daily Post*, 3 April 1971.

5   Tina Brown, *Life as a Party*, David & Charles, 1983, p. 142.

Chapter 18: Making Hay

1   *Russell Harty Plus*, LWT, 19 October 1973.

2   'Judy Hughes talks to April Ashley', *Western Mail*, 2 December 1980.

3   *What Am I?*, ATV, 1980.

4   *Belfast News Letter*, 4 November 1980; *Daily Telegraph*, 4 November 1980; *Liverpool Daily Post*, 4 November 1980.

5   youtube.com/watch?v=F1FIQvmLRc82001.

6   'Obituary: Richard Booth', Oliver Balch, *The Guardian*, 22 August 2019.

7   *Ibid.*

Chapter 19: Literary Lady

1   'David Bowie, Bryan Ferry and me: a day in the life', Duncan Fallowell, *Independent on Sunday*, 18 May 2003.

2   'The first lady', *The Independent*, 7 February 2006.

3   'The star who never was', Peter Burton, *Gay News Literary Supplement*, May 1982.

4   '*Conundrum*', Rebecca West, *New York Times Book Review*, 14 April 1974.

5   'Writer Duncan Fallowell on the New Journalism Movement and upcoming projects', *AM FM Magazine*, 17 March 2021.

6   'Andrew Morgan talks to April Ashley', *Liverpool Daily Post*, 26 April 1982.

7   'Duckling into swan', *Sunday Telegraph*, 2 May 1982.

8   'The star who never was', Peter Burton, *Gay News Literary Supplement*, May 1982.

9   'The blossoming of the ultimate weed', Andrew Motion, *The Times Literary Supplement*, 14 May 1982.

10   kirkusreviews.com/book-reviews/a/nancy-hunt/mirror-image-4. See also chrome- glbtqarchive.com/literature/autobio_transsexual_L. pdf for a summary list of other biographies of trans individuals.

11   'Lives remembered: April Ashley', *The Times*, 11 January 2022.

Chapter 20: Securing the legacy

1   Marjorie Proops, *Daily Mirror*, 13 May 1982.

2   *Ibid.*

3   *Ibid.*

4   *Newcastle Journal*, 29 April 1982.

5   *Parkinson in Australia*, Channel 10, Sydney, 1982.

6   *Ibid.*

7   *Daily Mail*, 17 June 2012.

8   'Judy Hughes talks to April Ashley', *Western Mail*, 2 December 1980.

9   *Ibid.*

10 'Bang! A History of the 1980s by Graham Stewart: review', Andy Beckett, The Guardian, 17 January 2013.

Chapter 21: Milestones

1   Thompson, The First Lady, p. 152.
2   Liverpool Daily Post, 24 January 1964.
3   Interview, Nigel Farndale, Daily Express, 21 April 2015.
4   Daily Express, 29 July 2000.
5   'Obituary: Quentin Crisp', Clive Fisher, The Independent, 22 November 1999.
6   huffpost.com/entry/the-last-word-by-quentin-crisp-us-exclusive-serialization_b_5a14217ae4b05ec0ae844579
7   Nigel Dempster, Daily Mail, 18 July 1986.
8   'Queen Mary: bigger than life', advertising brochure.
9   'The skipper whose ship has come in', Paul Dean, The Los Angeles Times, 4 October 1986.
10 'Altered ego', Jessica Berens, The Observer, 25 March 2001.
11 Thompson, The First Lady, p. 348.
12 Daily Express, 28 July 2000.
13 Aberdeen Press and Journal, 3 July 1973.
14 Daily Mail, 21 February 1996.
15 legislation.gov.uk/ukpga/1988/9/section/28/enacted.
16 'Section 28 protesters 30 years on', The Guardian, 27 March 2018.
17 Ibid.
18 gires.org.uk/wp-content/uploads/2014/09/employment-dis-full-paper.pdf.
19 R v Registrar General for England and Wales, ex parte P & G, 1996, unreported, judgment available at pfc.org.uk/caselaw/R%20v%20Registrar%20General%20for%20England%20and%20Wales,%20Ex%20parte%20P%20&%20G.pdf.
20 Daily Mail, 19 February 1996.
21 Ibid.

Chapter 22: 'You cannot leave us in limbo'

1   Nigel Farndale, *Daily Express*, 21 April 2005.

2   *Ibid.*

3   John Prescott, *The Independent*, 2 February 2006.

4   *Ibid.*

5   *Pink News*, 1 May 2021.

6   labour-party.org.uk/manifestos/1997/1997-labour-manifesto. shtml.

7   *Christine Goodwin v United Kingdom*, App. no. 28957/95 (2002) 35 EHRR 18.

8   hudoc.echr.coe.int/fre#%7B%22itemid%22:[%22001-60596%22]%7D.

9   *Daily Express*, 28 July 2000.

10 api.parliament.uk/historic-hansard/commons/2004/feb/23/gender-recognition-bill-lords-programme.

11 Patrick Barkham, *The Guardian*, 22 January 2013.

12 *Ibid.*

13 *Woman's Hour*, BBC Radio 4, 4 October 2013.

Chapter 23: Grande dame

1   Janet Tansley, *Liverpool Echo*, 4 May 2005.

2   'April Ashley: transgender pioneer', David Jenkins, *The Times*, 13 June 2015.

3   'A day at the Palace for April Ashley', Rebecca English, *Daily Mail*, 14 December 2012.

4   Interview, Tom Roberts, 20 February 2020.

5   'Voices from the trans community: "There will always be prejudice"', Patrick Barkham, *The Guardian*, 22 January 2013.

6   'April Ashley: transgender pioneer', David Jenkins, *The Times*, 13 June 2015.

7   liverpoolmuseums.org.uk/whatson/museum-of-liverpool/exhibition/april-ashley-portrait-of-lady.

8 youtube.com/watch?v=2qc93DknMb8.

9 *Loose Women*, ITV, 15 June 2015.

10 youtube.com/watch?v=ImZgPALy_NY.

11 youtube.com/watch?v=BOtOsw7oJfw.

12 *Ibid.*

13 *I Am a Woman Now*, dir. Michiel van Erp, 2011.

14 *Ibid.*

15 *Time*, 29 May 2014.

16 'The stereotype', in Germaine Greer, *The Female Eunuch*, MacGibben & Kee, 1970, p. 63.

17 *Newsnight*, BBC1, 23 October 2015.

18 'How Liverpool transgender icon April Ashley coached Eddie Redmayne for The Danish Girl', Dawn Collinson, *Liverpool Echo*, 12 February 2016.

19 'Not all transsexuals think "trans women are women"', Debbie Hayton, *The Spectator*, 22 November 2021.

20 Interview, Tom Roberts, 7 February 2020.

21 Interview, Tom Roberts, 20 February 2020.

22 David Jenkins, 'To leave it to your sixties like Caitlin Jenner must be hell', *The Times*, 13 June 2013.

23 youtube.com/watch?v=PQSVREQ8TLw.

24 'April Ashley: transgender pioneer', David Jenkins, *The Times*, 13 June 2015.

25 '"Icon, trailblazer and legendary activist": April Ashley remembered in special service', Paul McAuley, *Liverpool Echo*, 16 June 2022.

26 youtube.com/watch?v=pHCXO-Htjps.

27 *The Independent*, 2 February 2006.

28 'April Ashley's remarkable journey from terraced house to pioneer transsexual', Peter Elson, *Liverpool Post*, 2 August 2012.

Index

Maugham, W. Somerset, 156
Maxwell Fyfe, Sir David, 53
Mercer, Mickey, 69, 267
Messel, Oliver, 161, 203
Millar, Gary, 260
Miller, Arthur, 213n
Mills, Ivor, 174
Mirabelle restaurant, 92, 94
Mr Blue (dog), 109, 135
Mistinguett, 63
Mitchum, Robert, 25, 27
Mitford, Nancy, 153
mods and rockers, 56
Monroe, Marilyn, 146
Montagu of Beaulieu, Lord, 53, 151
Montgomery of Alamein, Viscount, 152
Moon, Keith, 195–6
Moore, Dudley, 160
Morgan, Desmond, 186
Morris, Jan, 77–8, 181, 216–22, 258
Morton's Club, 211
Moss, Kate, 266
Motion, Andrew, 220–1
Moustique, Kiki, 69, 73–4, 98
My Fair Lady, 68, 231, 267
Myra Breckenridge, 147–8

National Council for Civil Liberties, 229
National Health Service (NHS), 44, 201, 250, 252, 254
New York Daily News, 58
New York Times, 271
Newcastle Journal, 226

News Chronicle, 59
News of the World, 49, 61, 104, 111–12, 114–16, 133, 149, 154, 234, 249
Newsnight, 263
Newton, Helmut, 152
Nicholson, Mavis, 1–2
nose jobs, 67
Novello, Ivor, 197
Noyes, Alfred, 149
Nullity of Marriage Act (1971), 201

oestrogen, 58–9, 69, 73, 80
Oliver, Vic, 85
Onassis, Alexander, 91
Ono, Yoko, 185
opera, 161–2
Ormrod, Mr Justice, 167–72, 174–83, 187–91, 197, 201, 230, 240
Orwell, George, 52
Osborne, John, 145, 197
O'Sullivan, Maureen, 25
O'Toole, Peter, 125–8, 134, 218
Oxford Weekender News, 266

Paget, Lady Caroline, 157
pantomime dames, 63, 227
Paper, Doris, 16
Parker, Colonel Tom, 72
Parkinson, Michael, 227–8
Paterson, Vincent, 20–1
Paul, Sandra, 91
Peki (Amanda Lear), 73
Penny, James, 9
pension age, 230, 242–3, 252–3